Cognitive Behavioural Therapy

Teach Yourself®

Cognitive Behavioural Therapy

Christine Wilding and Aileen Milne

For UK order enquiries: please contact Bookpoint Ltd,
130 Milton Park, Abingdon, Oxon OX14 4SB.
Telephone: +44 (0) 1235 827720. *Fax:* +44 (0) 1235 400454.
Lines are open 09.00–17.00, Monday to Saturday, with a 24-hour message answering service. Details about our titles and how to order are available at www.teachyourself.com

For USA order enquiries: please contact McGraw-Hill Customer Services,
PO Box 545, Blacklick, OH 43004-0545, USA. *Telephone:* 1-800-722-4726.
Fax: 1-614-755-5645.

For Canada order enquiries: please contact McGraw-Hill Ryerson Ltd,
300 Water St, Whitby, Ontario L1N 9B6, Canada. *Telephone:* 905 430 5000.
Fax: 905 430 5020.

Long renowned as the authoritative source for self-guided learning – with more than 50 million copies sold worldwide – the **Teach Yourself** series includes over 500 titles in the fields of languages, crafts, hobbies, business, computing and education.

British Library Cataloguing in Publication Data: a catalogue record for this title is available from the British Library.

Library of Congress Catalog Card Number: on file.

First published in UK 2008 by Hodder Education,
part of Hachette UK, 338 Euston Road, London, NW1 3BH.v

First published in US 2008 by The McGraw-Hill Companies, Inc.

This edition published 2010.

Previously published as *Teach Yourself Cognitive Behavioural Therapy*.

The **Teach Yourself** name is a registered trade mark of Hodder Headline.

Typeset by Macmillan Publishing Solutions.

Printed in Great Britain for Hodder Education, an Hachette UK Company,
338 Euston Road, London NW1 3BH, by CPI Cox & Wyman Ltd, Reading,
Berkshire RG1 8EX.

Impression number   10 9 8

Year   2014 2013 2012 2011

For Dr Adrian Winbow, MB BS FRCPsych DPM, whose early encouragement and support made such a positive difference to my now established and interesting career as a CBT Therapist. With grateful thanks.
(C. W.)

To my family, friends and colleagues and the questing spirit within us all.
(A. M.)

Contents

Foreword

Cognitive behavioural therapy (CBT) has come of age. Research has demonstrated its effectiveness in dealing with both clinical depression and anxiety-related disorders such as phobias, panic attacks and obsessive compulsive disorder. The approach is grounded in a sound theory that is relatively easy to understand; our thoughts, ideas, perceptions, attitudes and beliefs influence how we feel emotionally.

This is not a new idea. The Stoic philosophers such as Epictetus two millennia ago asserted that people 'are not disturbed by things but by the view they take of them'. Centuries later William Shakespeare in *Hamlet* wrote, 'Why, then, 'tis none to you; for there is nothing either good or bad but thinking makes it so'. What is new is that the academic research now exists to show how and why CBT works.

In the 1960s Dr Aaron Beck developed cognitive therapy. He had become dissatisfied with the lack of scientific basis for psychoanalytical theories based on the work of Sigmund Freud. Beck used a combination of clinical client observation, measurement and self-observation to formulate a new theory of personality.

This remarkable book, *Cognitive Behavioural Therapy*, by Christine Wilding and Aileen Milne, explains in detail the theory and practice of CBT covering all the key aspects of therapy.

I congratulate the authors on writing a concise and easy-to-understand book.

Professor Stephen Palmer
City University
Department of Psychology
London

Meet the authors

Welcome to Cognitive Behavioural Therapy!

I am a cognitive behavioural psychotherapist, author of several self help books and a Chartered HR professional (Chartered MCIPD). The extent of the psychology studies necessary to gain this professional status as well as an innate interest in problem-solving led me to eventually undertake further studies and training as a CBT psychotherapist. I have undertaken work within the NHS, working alongside GPs and been a member of the steering committee set up to develop guidelines for the treatment of depression within the NHS, researched by East Surrey Health Authority. I have worked at the private Cygnet Hospital in Sevenoaks, Kent for several years as a CBT therapist with both day-patients and in-patients as well as for the Crown Prosecution Service, working with staff including barristers and solicitors. I am currently working in a busy private practice in Epsom in Surrey, working with GP and psychiatric referrals and specialising in issues such as low self esteem, stress management, depression and anxiety disorders including OCD, panic, phobias and health and social anxiety.

Christine Wilding

I have a BA Hons, Diploma in Counselling (from a BACP accredited course), MBACP and have worked as a counsellor for 15 years, in private practice and in a variety of other settings. These have included a young people's counselling service, an employment assistance programme service, educational institutions and local authorities. I use an integrative model of therapy, which includes cognitive behavioural therapy. I am the author of several books including *Understand Counselling*.

Aileen Milne

You must be the change you want to see in the world.
Mahatma Gandhi (1869–1948)

Only got a minute?

Cognitive behavioural therapy (widely known as CBT) is a systematic and down-to-earth approach to therapy. It is a problem-solving model that offers skills for daily living. In therapy, the workings of CBT would be made transparent to you. You would be coached so that you understand the main principles and are then encouraged to practise the skills. In this book we use the same basic structure and sequence as you would experience in therapy. We cover a variety of CBT skills which are simple to learn and to use.

CBT is a popular form of psychotherapy that helps people by engaging them in a process of self-awareness and self-responsibility. It is currently favoured by the UK's NHS; doctors frequently refer anxious or depressed patients for CBT. There are many reasons for this, not least that its techniques are suited to short-term work, it is designed to teach people techniques to self apply, it is cost effective and there is strong clinical evidence to support its success.

From the beginning of the book you have the opportunity to test the skills for yourself and see how effectively they work. The ultimate goal in the therapy is to educate you in problem-solving by creating a more balanced way of thinking and behaving. You will learn to recognize and gain control of your negative thinking patterns and modify your moods and behaviour. Controlling your thoughts and behaviour is very different from suppressing them; you can establish self-understanding, and see that negativity breeds more negativity and then construct alternative, more realistic, helpful and balanced ways of approaching life.

Once you have assimilated CBT skills into your understanding, you will have these psychological tools at hand for life.

5 Only got five minutes?

Cognitive behavioural therapy (CBT) is currently the 'buzz word' in therapy, but has been around since the 1960s. Aaron T. Beck and Albert Ellis were the prime innovators of what was then a new system of psychotherapy called *cognitive therapy*. Cognitive theories and techniques developed and were combined with behavioural experimentation methods leading to the birth of CBT. It was the first therapeutic approach to concentrate on thought processes and their connection with emotional, behavioural and physiological states. The concept that people could make choices about how they interpreted events in their lives was exciting and radical. CBT is centred on the idea that a person is capable of changing their cognitions and the effects of their thinking on their emotional well-being.

Its reputation and popularity have grown for a variety of reasons. Not only is it a clinically proven therapy applicable to a range of emotional problems but it also makes a process of change achievable in a short time, usually 6–20 sessions. It does this by breaking down self-defeating thoughts and beliefs, and by forming alternative life enhancing viewpoints. CBT has also proved its efficacy in brief therapy, which is usually completed in 4–6 sessions.

Scientific evidence shows that CBT is effective on its own or alongside medication. The therapist provides coaching in techniques and skills; which can then be practised independently, reducing the need for ongoing treatment which may be lengthy and expensive.

CBT is considered to be a practical, systematic and highly effective method of addressing an array of emotional and psychological problems. It has traditionally been offered by psychologists or psychotherapists, but has more recently become available through trained counsellors.

Strong structure and active participation is crucial to the success of the therapy. The kind of emotional problems helped by CBT, and addressed in this book, include anxiety, depression, panic disorders, phobias, post-traumatic stress disorder, and obsessive compulsive disorder.

How does CBT work?

CBT addresses emotional and behavioural problems by drawing attention to thinking patterns and moods. When you are absorbed in emotional problems, you won't be at your most rational. You are likely to think in ways that further upset you. Negative emotions will escalate and your behaviour may become unhelpful, adding to the problem. As negativity builds, common sense and self-care disappear. You may 'catastrophize' and healthy thoughts may develop into self-defeating thoughts such as 'nobody loves or understands me' or 'I'm useless'. It's easy to see how this type of thinking becomes a vicious cycle of negative thoughts, emotions and behaviour.

CBT skills have been transferred to this book. You are encouraged to engage in your own problem-solving. Techniques and skills will be explained and, where appropriate, are illustrated by simple diagrams. You can then try the techniques for yourself.

A crucial CBT concept is that thought processes – thoughts about yourself, other people and life situations – have a huge effect on your emotional well-being. This is summed up by the statement: 'what we think is how we feel' or 'what we think decides how we feel'.

CBT proposes that when you replace self-denigrating thoughts with more realistic, self-accepting ones, positive changes will happen. The central aims of CBT are:

▶ *to make you aware of your thought processes and their effects*
▶ *to enable you to make positive changes in your thoughts, beliefs and assumptions by enhancing your self-observational powers and self-reflective skills*
▶ *to increase your awareness of the effect of negative behaviours in the maintenance of your problems.*

In this book, on a continuum that matches your growing understanding, you are coached in techniques to assess how your thinking affects your emotions and behaviour, and how your body (physiologically) registers the resulting stress. With the assistance of many tools from the CBT toolbox, we teach you how to use CBT skills and techniques so that you can gradually become your own competent therapist.

We guide you to use practices that will enable you to look at your problems from different perspectives, understand what maintains your problems and, ultimately, gain control over how you think and behave in relation to your problems. CBT techniques and skills encourage you to openly question, with interest, how you function on a day-to-day basis. You learn to influence control over your thinking patterns and feelings as a means of improving your quality of life. CBT aims to help you achieve more *realistic* and *balanced* thinking. Remember that:

▶ *there are many practical techniques to deal with your problems*
▶ *what you think is how you will feel*
▶ *addressing unhealthy, unrealistic thinking is crucial to making positive changes.*

Introduction

Do you feel frustrated with how your life is going? Do you have specific problems or difficulties that you find hard to resolve (or don't believe that you can resolve)? Is your mood often low? Do you wish that you had more confidence, better relationships with others, and didn't worry so much about things? Put simply, would you like to feel happier than you do?

Most people consider that life events and circumstances, either activated or happenstance – the cards we are dealt, if you will – decide how well we enjoy our lives. Many people spend a great deal of time trying to discover how to feel better about themselves, others, and the world around them.

How do you achieve this? Books are written and avidly purchased with titles suggesting that feeling good is out there somewhere if you search hard enough and turn over enough stones. Yet feeling good isn't 'out there' at all. It is actually right here, within you, simply because happiness, confidence and feeling good about yourself are emotions, not life events, not something you can touch, feel, purchase or pursue.

> **Happiness cannot come from without. It must come from within. It is not what we see and touch, but that which we think and feel and do...**
>
> Helen Keller (1880–1968)

Happiness is simply an emotion that you feel, dependent not on external events but on your thoughts about those events. Things often go wrong in people's lives – other people act selfishly towards you, you make mistakes, disappointments occur. If your thoughts about such events are negative – perhaps you blame other people, or the weather, or yourself for things going wrong – then these views will decide how you feel emotionally (angry, frustrated, anxious, resentful, for example) and possibly how you behave as a result.

> **Men are disturbed not by things, but by the view which they take of them.**
>
> Epictetus, philosopher (AD 50–120)

What you think decides how you feel

This is the basic premise of cognitive behavioural therapy (CBT), a therapy model that, if you learn to understand it and apply it, will enable you to get not only from minus nine back to zero on your life scale, but also – if you wish it – from zero to plus ten (or twenty or thirty). CBT will help you to recognize some of your own styles and patterns of thinking that create unhappiness and distress, and to learn how to counteract these so that you can deal with potentially upsetting situations in a more helpful way.

This book will teach you enough about CBT to allow you to deal with any specific difficulties in your life and also to get more out of the life you already have.

In *Cognitive Behavioural Therapy* you will find:

▶ *the basic methods, techniques and applications of CBT*
▶ *ways to help you identify your problems, set goals and move towards a healthier outlook on life*
▶ *guided methodology in how to become adept at identifying and changing your thoughts, attitudes and beliefs for the better*
▶ *ways of testing negative theories and predictions for their accuracy and validity*
▶ *the skills for addressing specific problems such as anxiety and low self-esteem*
▶ *relevant examples and case studies throughout the book*
▶ *worksheets and diagrams that you can replicate and use.*

Who will benefit from reading this book?

▶ **Those who are interested in its self-help aspects.** *You may have heard about CBT through the media or friends and be interested in learning more about it as a self-help skill. Your interest may be general, perhaps the acquisition of new skills and greater self-understanding, or you may have specific problems that you would like to resolve and that could benefit from the structured and focused, skills-based approach of CBT.*

▶ **Those who are considering the possibility of professional therapy.** *Having long been recognized in the US as an effective therapy treatment, CBT has more recently become the psychological treatment of choice in the National Health Service (NHS) in the UK. Organizations and companies that offer their staff counselling as part of a welfare package are increasingly turning to CBT. You may have already embarked on therapy and may be looking for a book like this to support the work you have already undertaken with a therapist.*

▶ **The trainee counsellor.** *You might be looking at this book because you are planning to train in counselling or psychotherapy and you would like to learn more about different approaches before you commit yourself to a particular approach. Reading this book will give you a good overview of the principles and help you to decide if CBT is a method that would appeal to you as a therapist. The book will also be helpful as an adjunct to your learning if you are already in training.*

▶ **Established therapists.** *This is a useful book for counsellors who primarily work with other therapeutic models but are interested in integrating other ideas into their work with clients. Increasingly, an integrative model is used by therapists where two or more schools of therapy are merged to form a cohesive model. CBT is likely to be one of these models.*

▶ **Those considering CBT as their primary model of therapy.** *We hope that this book will be helpful to you in this regard. Where you want to use CBT as your primary therapeutic approach, you will also, of course, require specific CBT training. However, this book serves as a useful guide and reference manual if you proceed with your studies.*

You don't need to be experiencing serious difficulties to feel the benefits of learning CBT techniques and skills. Becoming familiar with its methods can have enormous benefits in the workplace and in personal relationships as well as at an individual level. CBT helps you to develop skills to function more effectively in everyday life situations. The practice of these techniques not only gives insight into yourself and your thinking patterns, it can also help you to understand other people better and how they too can become stuck in their ways of thinking and behaving. Those working in nursing, human resources, teaching and management are examples of people who would benefit from learning CBT skills and techniques.

The book's structure

In principle, this book is to enable you to teach yourself the skills and techniques of CBT. Therefore we will be avoiding jargon wherever we can (or we will explain its meaning clearly when we do use it), and we will be writing in a down-to-earth way that we hope will help you to make substantial life changes yourself, without becoming confused by psycho-babble or feeling that you need professional help to get started. This does not mean that, for serious problems, turning to a professional is not a good idea (it is an excellent idea) and we do look at this aspect in the last chapter. However, this book is not essentially about the sort of serious problems for which professional help is needed – it is simply about a really good way of learning to improve your life and sort out any difficulties you may have.

CBT is often called 'the psychology of common sense'. You are perhaps beginning to understand why already, and will learn more of what this means as you progress through the book. Don't be misled into believing that the skills you start to work with and changes you may decide to make are easy and obvious. They will still require hard work and perseverance. However, one of CBT's great strengths is that it helps you to discover what is preventing you from resolving your problems, and it works with you as a co-detective to find out exactly what is going wrong – and then to discover what is required to put things right.

Using the chapters as therapy sessions

We would like to suggest that you use the core chapters as DIY therapy sessions, and we have written the book in this way. Chapters 2–10 contain a 'building blocks' model of the basic skills of CBT, with each chapter or 'session' covering a self-contained topic or skill that will build on what you have learned in previous chapters. For this reason, we advise you to read these particular chapters in sequence – as individual therapy sessions. As well as the learning, there are practical exercises both throughout and at the end of each chapter, to allow you to consolidate your learning and use it 'outside the session'. CBT therapists call such exercises 'homework' and we have kept that term for clarity.

PART ONE

The first part of the book covers CBT's general skills and will be both educative and helpful to all readers.

PART TWO

Part two is what you might call 'CBT in action'. We focus here on the basic problems that CBT was specifically and originally developed for, so that you can see this therapy 'at work'. If you are a therapist or trainee, this part of the book will help you to develop your own skills in these areas. If you are struggling yourself to overcome one (or more) of these difficulties, we offer you basic guidelines on how to achieve this. However, we do wish to stress that this book is a primer, and can only offer a 'whistle-stop tour' of these problems and their treatments. For this reason, at the end of each chapter in Part two, we refer you to specific further reading on each topic where you might wish to develop your knowledge and skill base further.

PART THREE

In Part three we show you how you can use CBT to develop strengths. If your self-esteem is adequate but not great, if you have a problem standing your ground rather than running away or difficulty negotiating well with others instead of being a doormat, if you find that hot emotions such as anger are hard to manage or that a quest for perfection leaves you feeling inadequate, then in this section you will learn how to develop (or eliminate) some of the common character traits that can hold many people back. As in Part two, we refer you to specific further reading on each topic which will be helpful to you if you wish to investigate further.

PART FOUR

In Part four, we offer a few final thoughts on questions that often remain for those who have used elements of CBT skills through self-help methods and reading. These questions usually focus on what to do when your gains seem to be slipping away from you, and – often linked to this – at what point you should consider professional help. Here, we answer these questions for you.

The 'homework' element: getting ready

One of the features of CBT is that you are asked to write down a lot of things. So, before you start, make sure that you have two hard-covered A4 lined pads, a few working pens, and a safe, quiet personal place in which to use and keep them. Using a hard-covered book has several advantages. If you use a soft-covered pad, you are far more likely to mislay it, find someone else has taken it, or use a different but similar-looking one by mistake, and you will either lose much of your good work or have it stored all over the place in different workbooks, and your momentum may well go.

Ideally, we suggest you use two workbooks – one for practising the exercises we recommend and for jotting down answers to questions, etc.; the other for putting together a book of your own, tailored to yourself, which contains all the best skills and techniques that you have personally found helpful and may like to refer to again in the future. So a 'scribble book' and a 'skills book', in a sense.

WHY IS WRITING EVERYTHING DOWN IMPORTANT FOR COGNITIVE BEHAVIOURAL THERAPY?

Writing things down serves several purposes.

- ▶ *It helps things to 'stick' in your mind.*
- ▶ *It makes sure you actually do give proper time and thought to your learning.*
- ▶ *It serves as a written record for the future, to help you notice changes and improvements, and also to recall how you used the skills of CBT should you need them again.*

CBT is as much a life-skills model as a problem-solving model and, as such, it is a great asset to your life learning. This is because CBT is educational – it teaches you to become your own therapist. Not only do you feel better, you actually know exactly why you feel better, and you can do it again and again (and teach others how to do it) if you need to.

So, if your pencils are sharp and your notebook is at the ready, let's start…

Part one

The basic skills of CBT

In this part of the book you will learn about the cognitive behavioural therapy (CBT) model and a little of its history, and then the basic skills and techniques that will help you to develop your own abilities.

CBT is an educational model and the emphasis in professional CBT therapy is on teaching the client to become 'their own therapist'. The skills you will learn in this section can be applied to any area of your life that is problematic or that you wish to enhance, and they will – if you practise them and maintain them well – last you throughout your life.

Chapters 2–10 follow a particularly structured 'building blocks' approach to the basic skills of CBT, and you have the opportunity to treat these chapters as DIY therapy sessions, bringing to them any personal difficulties you may be having and working through these difficulties.

1

....

CBT: the basics and background

In this chapter you will learn:
* *the basic cognitive behavioural therapy model and the ideas behind it*
* *the history of cognitive behavioural therapy*
* *reasons for cognitive behavioural therapy's modern-day popularity*
* *an evaluation of some of the criticisms of cognitive behavioural therapy.*

At the start of any cognitive behavioural therapy (CBT) session with a professional therapist, you will together construct an 'Agenda' for the session so that the time is used meaningfully and wisely. At the start of each chapter, we set you a similar agenda, as above.

The basic CBT model

We are mindful that many readers will already have a grasp of the basic principles upon which CBT is founded. However, for those who do not, if you can understand the premise of CBT in its simplest form before we go further, you will benefit more from the early chapters of the book when the ideas will be quite new to you.

> **Jargon dictionary: A 'cognition' is simply another word for a thought.** Beck et al. (1979) describe a cognition as 'either a thought or a visual image that you may not be very aware of unless you focus your attention on it'.

You will understand the concept of a 'cognition' better by thinking about it yourself, rather than merely reading a didactic explanation. Try the exercise below. This requires you to write down some thoughts, so have your notebook at the ready.

Exercise

This exercise will help you to understand the basic premise of CBT. Think of the most recent occasion when things went wrong and your thoughts were fairly negative. Perhaps something bad happened, or you felt that you, yourself, acted in a way that disappointed you and that you regret. Write down what this occasion was and then write answers to the following questions.

What thought(s) went through your mind? How did you feel, both physically and emotionally? (Feelings can usually be described with a one-word answer – happy, sad, cheerful, miserable, etc. – but we may feel several emotions at once.) You may also have noticed feeling drained, or that your stomach was churning, possibly you were tense, etc. Note down any physiology of this kind.

What did you do? Did you act in a way that made the situation better or that made it worse?

Now, do exactly the same for a recent *good* event or an occasion when you felt that you acted in a way that made you feel good about yourself and your thoughts were more positive. Write your answers to the following questions.

▶ *What happened?*
▶ *What did you think?*
▶ *How did you feel, both emotionally and physically?*
▶ *What did you do?*

Write down any connections that occur to you.

THOUGHTS, FEELINGS, BEHAVIOURS: HOW THEY LINK TOGETHER

From the above exercise, can you see a connection between what you thought about the events, how you felt, and what you did? You will most certainly have noticed that if you had negative thoughts, your emotions would also have been negative; you may have noticed adverse bodily sensations and you may have reacted behaviourally in a less than positive way. On the other hand, where your thoughts were positive, it would be extraordinary if your emotions were not also quite upbeat; you would have felt physically energized and acted very positively. In other words, how you felt about the event depends on your view of the event – rather than on the event itself.

In simple graphical terms, this can be explained by Figure 1.1. This, in its very simplest form, is the basic CBT model. At this point, it is important to be aware that our thoughts are not the only predictors of outcomes, but they do play a very powerful role in shaping how we feel.

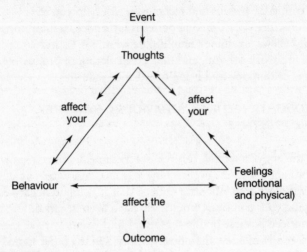

Figure 1.1 The CBT model.

THE POWER OF EMOTIONS

In fact, thoughts on their own have very little effect on people. You can think whatever you like – it is only the **emotions that your thoughts engender** that delight or disturb you. It is the thought-emotion fusion that is all-powerful and shapes your responses and reactions, which may in turn decide outcomes.

The development of CBT

To put CBT's development into context, it is worth appreciating that psychology itself is a young discipline, coming into existence seriously only towards the end of the nineteenth century.

THE MOST FAMOUS PIONEER

Possibly the best-known early pioneer of psychotherapy is Sigmund Freud (1856–1939). His psychoanalytical therapy emphasized the role of unresolved, unconscious conflicts from childhood as determinants of how we feel and behave. Freud believed that the way forward to emotional good health was for people to recall and make sense of their early childhood experiences.

In recent years, various experts have challenged Freud's theories, specifically pointing out that it was very hard to empirically prove their efficacy. However, this should not undermine the fact that one of Freud's great contributions was to develop the idea that you might be able to resolve your emotional problems by talking about them rather than simply turning to medication.

BEHAVIOURAL THEORY...

While many therapists continued to work with ideas developed by Freud, the 1950s saw the development of a psychology called 'behaviourism'. Based initially on work with animals, it purported that psychological problems were caused by faulty learning, and that most problems could be resolved by teaching people to change or modify their behaviours to achieve more positive results. In certain areas, such as anxiety disorders, the therapy (which involved facing up to fearful situations rather than avoiding them) was very successful. However, it was unable to make such a difference with other disorders, for example, depression.

One of behaviourism's most positive contributions was its adherence to empirical testing and reporting of its studies and findings. This has led to testing now being widely used in different psychological treatments in order to verify proposed clinical outcomes.

... AND THE DEVELOPMENT OF COGNITIVE BEHAVIOURAL THEORY

In the 1960s, an eminent American psychiatrist, Aaron (Tim) Beck, was becoming increasingly disillusioned with psychoanalytical therapy and what he considered to be its lack of efficacy. Beck became extremely curious about the emotions his clients exhibited that didn't seem to relate to the stories about their childhoods that they were telling him. While working with a particular client, Beck described his first clear-cut example of a train of thought running parallel to the client's reported history. During the session, this client became quite upset, and on being asked by Beck how he felt, the client said, 'guilty'. However, the patient then volunteered some further information – that the guilt he was feeling was *nothing to do* with his story about his past; it was his present situation that was causing this emotion. Probing the client, Beck found that what was actually worrying the client was that Beck might find what he was saying boring. His guilty thoughts were not about childhood misdemeanours, but about what was going on then and there in the therapy session. For example:

▶ *'I've said the wrong thing...'*
▶ *'I'm wrong to criticize Dr Beck...'*
▶ *'I'm not a nice person...'*
▶ *'Dr Beck won't like me.'*

Beck became fascinated by what he called 'parallel thought processes' (in effect, the client would be saying one thing, but thinking another) and the fact that the emotions they evoked were related to the patient's conscious mind and to the 'here and now', rather than to the mystique of a long-lost childhood. Beck discovered that many of his clients had similar thoughts quite regularly in their interactions with other people. By working with clients' conscious thought processes – as he called it, 'turning on the intercom' – he was able to obtain very precise definitions of the clients' key problems.

Thus the seeds of cognitive therapy were born – the idea that your conscious thought processes affect how you feel. By the early 1960s, Beck was developing cognitive therapy as a theoretical model, particularly, at that time, for the treatment of depression. His book, *Cognitive Therapy of Depression* (1979) is regarded as a classic authority on the subject.

At around the same time, another US psychiatrist, Albert Ellis, was also developing a cognitive model, rational emotive therapy (later to become rational emotive behaviour therapy – REBT). Together with Beck, Ellis became one of the most influential pioneers of cognitive therapy – sharing the view that most disturbances arise from thinking errors and faulty processing, and that the remedy is to challenge and re-evaluate thoughts and make behavioural adjustments. Both Beck's CBT and Ellis' REBT were directed at correcting these faulty thought processes. Both concentrated on current problems and present thinking as opposed to past history that was the cornerstone of other psychotherapies, and both incorporated the use of behavioural experimentation.

Nonetheless, there were also some differences between the two therapies. Ellis' persistent and strong advocacy of his own form of rational therapy failed to attract as much attention as Beck's CBT. This was due in part to Beck's more rigorous clinical approach in presenting his theories. Beck's work also attracted huge interest because he focused initially on CBT as a treatment for depression, a clinical problem that had, up until then, defeated those using a purely behavioural approach. However, the skills of REBT are today widely used as an alternative cognitive model with many similarities to CBT, to the extent that some therapists use a blend of skills from both models in treatment.

A NEW STYLE OF THERAPY

Since its development in the 1960s, cognitive theory has been widely researched – not the least by Beck's own Institute for Cognitive Therapy and Research, which flourishes in Pennsylvania – and treatment protocols have been developed to treat most psychological disorders.

In recent years, other similar therapies have built on these new ideas of working with conscious thought processes. These therapies have placed their emphasis, for the first time, on the idea that present thinking, rather than past experiences, could play a huge role in psychological disturbance. This is not to say that experiences in childhood and earlier life do not have a great influence on how people think and, thus, how they feel. Nevertheless, we know many people with stable childhoods who still develop psychological problems as adults, as well as those with miserable childhoods who have grown up to be well adjusted and resilient.

WHAT MAKES COGNITIVE BEHAVIOURAL THERAPY SO POPULAR NOW?

CBT is now the treatment of choice for a wide range of psychological problems. Its boundaries are being consistently enlarged and developed, while its basic principles remain unchanged. It is widely used within the UK's NHS, and recognized as a fast and effective problem solver and life enhancer. If CBT has been around since the 1960s, why has it only in recent years been seen as such an important mainstream therapy, currently in very high demand?

▶ **The rise in popularity of therapy generally for offering helpful assistance to those in distress.** *Therapy used to be the province of a wealthy elite (psychoanalytical therapy could involve visiting a therapist two or three times a week for several years, so the financial and time investments were great), but as more people came to see therapy as a helpful option, the therapy itself needed to be adapted to offer speedier and cheaper solutions to a broader range of people. The development of 'brief therapy' was required.*

▶ **Past generations may have been brought up with 'keep a stiff upper lip' and 'you simply get on with it' approaches.** *In the present day, things have changed greatly and people are much more open about expressing how they feel and discussing their emotions. They accept the idea of talking things through with a professional when things go wrong emotionally. This has enormously popularized the idea of counselling as helpful and not in the least stigmatic. Indeed, it is now widely regarded as sensible to seek help, rather than weak.*

▶ **The value of measurement.** *CBT can prove its efficacy by its ability to be empirically measured. This has encouraged the NHS in the UK to invest in it as a psychological therapy as* *successful outcomes are accurately audited and the therapy is able to show its value.*

▶ **The mid-1990s onwards have also seen a huge increase in 'positive psychologies'** – *therapy models that are not only interested in how to help people out of specific personal difficulties, but that are also practised to teach people to further enhance lives that already work reasonably. Personal coaching has developed to help people maximize their lifestyle potential, and neurolinguistic programming teaches people to model excellence. Other therapies are similarly developing to ensure that none of us lead lives that are less happy and successful than we wish them to be if we are willing to learn the skills and put in the work.*

CBT has fitted the bill here exactly. Compared to insight-based therapies, such as psychodynamic therapy, CBT is a solution-focused, short-term therapy, and because it involves the client in doing a great deal of work for themselves, CBT is an educational model – results are quick, effective and lasting.

Increased demand from a wider audience has turned CBT into a star performer. People understand it. It makes sense. People have a great deal of control over outcomes. They can take its skills away with them. Relapse is much less common than with other therapies, and even if you do have a hiccup, you can revisit the skills and techniques you learned to get back on track. CBT has also flourished in modern times because it has an empirical (scientifically measurable) base. Research funds are more easily come by where outcomes can be measured and the therapy is proven statistically to work. More money is being spent on developing the discovery of new contributions to well-being – and this is all being done extremely successfully.

CRITICISMS OF COGNITIVE BEHAVIOURAL THERAPY

However, none of this is to deny other therapies and, naturally, CBT has had its fair share of criticisms as well. Here are some of them and some reasons why we believe they don't hold true.

▶ **CBT is only helpful to the articulate and intelligent.**
The argument here is that people have to be able to articulate their thoughts, detect their dysfunctional thinking, carry out and review homework assignments, and consider and evaluate their learning. Surely those with limited intellectual abilities will flounder hopelessly? CBT is a very flexible model, and is able to completely match the pace of thinking and intellectual level of anyone using it. It is not necessary to use jargon and psycho-babble (this book won't) but simply to focus clearly, using as much time as necessary, to help the client's understanding of the process.

▶ **CBT is simply common sense.** *CBT is indeed a logical and understandable therapy – which is one of its great assets. However, its purpose is not just to teach you common-sense solutions, but also to ask a much more important question: 'If the solutions are obvious, what is preventing you from acting on them?' This is the case for many, if not most people. CBT helps you to work out why you are 'stuck' and to rectify this. Even common sense has its limits and, as Beck (1976) says, 'fails to provide plausible and useful explanations for puzzling emotional disorders'. For example, a person may have severe health anxiety: no matter how many medical checks they have, including visits to top specialists, all of which show that there is nothing physically wrong with them, the person still consistently agonizes that they are going to fall ill, that odd twinges might be cancer, etc. In effect, no amount of reassurance or evidence to the contrary will allow them to adopt the common-sense view that they are physically well. CBT will be able to 'play the detective' with this person, to discover what is preventing them from using common sense, and to put that right.*

▶ **CBT does not focus enough on emotions.** *The very name 'cognitive behavioural therapy' does give the idea that the focus is all on thoughts and behaviours and that feelings are excluded from the process. Certainly, there can be a large practical element to treatment, depending on the problem, but this does not mean that a practical solution cannot positively affect a person's emotions. (If you are finally encouraged to* tackle something that has been worrying you, will you not feel emotionally better for it?) As we mentioned earlier, it does not really matter what you think – it is the emotions that those thoughts engender that let you feel either contented or bothered. Nonetheless, the connection between thoughts and emotions and the idea that, in most instances (though not all), it is our thinking that decides our emotions, places high value on working with cognitions in order to manage emotions. If adjusting our thinking failed to alter our emotional reactions, CBT would go straight into the rubbish bin as a therapy process.

▶ **CBT is not interested in important background information about the client's past.** *CBT is interested in a client's past, but only in order to discover how they may have developed certain beliefs and assumptions that are unhelpful to them in the present time. For example, if certain elements of your childhood left you with a belief that you were never good enough, it would be extremely helpful to discover this in order to work out the reason why you never apply for promotions at work, say, or always bail out of emotional relationships. By finding out a client's beliefs about themselves, CBT can help to check the present accuracy of such beliefs and adjust the client's thinking to embrace more helpful and appropriate beliefs for the present and the future, rather than continuing to believe something that may have been learned, probably incorrectly, a long time ago, and that is no longer valid. However, CBT doesn't believe that returning to the past, simply to trawl through it, dwell on it and ruminate over things that happened a long time ago, serves any great purpose towards meaningful change.*

FURTHER APPLICATIONS AND DEVELOPMENTS IN COGNITIVE BEHAVIOURAL THERAPY

The enormous number of applications of CBT extends far beyond those described within the scope of this book. Eating disorders, relationship problems, substance misuse, bipolar disorder, agoraphobia, chronic fatigue syndrome, sexual problems and psychosis, borderline personality disorder, avoidant personality disorder paranoia and schizophrenia – to list a few – are all examples of psychological problems that respond well to CBT. Its applications can be used with a diverse population and in a variety of settings and, at this point, we simply want to alert you to the versatility of CBT – it goes far beyond the foundations of the therapy that we give you here.

CBT protocols are also developing widely, and associated therapies now include (but are not limited to) schema-focused therapy, compassion-based therapy, mindfulness-based cognitive therapy (MBCT), dialectical behaviour therapy, acceptance and commitment therapy, and behavioural activation.

Insight

The majority of people enjoy the challenge of carrying out tasks between sessions as homework – it keeps them linked with the therapy and gives a continuity in the work. It also cements the learning that has taken place in the session and starts the process of working towards 'self therapy'.

HOMEWORK

We would like to introduce a structural idea that is integral to CBT. We call it 'homework'. Were you to find yourself in sessional work with a CBT therapist, at the end of each session you would jointly decide on the elements of your learning that you could practise between sessions. As the general style of CBT is to hand skills over to the individual to use whenever needed, it makes sense for someone learning these skills to have opportunities to practise them in real life. Homework is usually based on the topics covered 'in session' so that practical learning can reflect and cement the theoretical learning. Homework assignments are as good at showing you what doesn't work as they are at showing what does work. Homework is very experimental – in a sense, you are working as a detective, looking to see what might happen if you did this or changed that or thought the other. You don't know in advance, although you will be encouraged to make an educated guess.

For the purposes of this book, and to encourage you to work at your learning, we would like you to consider each chapter as a DIY therapy session and, at the end of each chapter we will devise a homework task (or two!) that will help you to cement your learning. In therapy, the decision is collaborative between therapist and client, so we are not going to be prescriptive but will make suggestions and ask you to pick what you think would be most helpful to you. Let's take a look at some possible homework assignments for this chapter.

▸ *Practising the exercise for developing your understanding of the link between thoughts and feelings would be an excellent choice. Using the format given (see page 4), go through it again and again – writing possibilities down in your workbook – each time identifying what was going on, what you thought and how you felt.*

▸ *If the history of CBT is of interest, you might like to do some internet research on the therapy or even get hold of a copy of Aaron Beck's seminal 1976 book* Cognitive Therapy and the Emotional Disorders. *Here he describes the theory of emotion, and the relationship between emotions and psychological distress.*

▸ *Re-reading the chapter and ensuring that it all makes sense before you go on to Chapter 2 is a beneficial exercise.*

SUMMARY

At this point, you should have a good idea of the thought/feelings/behaviour connection that is the basic principle on which CBT therapy has developed. Some of you will already be very familiar with this, but for those who are not, you now have a basic concept on which to build all the further skills and techniques for positive change that you will be learning as you go through the book.

▸ *Although not part of your practical learning, we hope you will have found the brief overview of the history of the development of CBT helpful in setting the context for its popularity today. See the 'Taking it further' section for one or two recommendations for further reading which you might take up if you want to know more about this aspect of the therapy.*

▶ *Of great interest are the changes made through the twentieth century in relation to the treatment of psychological disorders. Once confined to the seriously ill in mental institutions, psychological therapy started offering help to a limited group of people who still functioned in day-to-day life. This has now gathered such momentum that, together with loss of the stigma attached to attending therapy, it has become a popular choice for many people to deal with problems that relate as much to positive personal development as to adverse circumstances.*

▶ *All therapies have their critics and it is right to consider a few that are levelled at CBT and to consider their accuracy.*

THINGS TO REMEMBER

▶ *The basic premise of CBT is summed up by the phrase: 'What we think decides how we feel'. CBT is a theoretical model that links our thoughts with our emotions and behaviour.*

▶ *As a theoretical model, CBT is a mix of cognitive theories and behavioural experiments. Ideas in psychology – of which psychotherapy, psychoanalysis and counselling are strands – are a continuum and new ideas are frequently incorporated into theory and practice.*

▶ *While psychoanalysis was seen as a branch of medicine, behaviourism brought psychology into science by employing empirical methods of experimentation, testing and collating information.*

▶ *Aaron T. Beck and Albert Ellis are regarded as the main originators of cognitive therapy, which came to prominence in the 1960s. While Beck called his new approach cognitive therapy, Ellis named his approach rational emotive therapy (RET, later to be called REBT to incorporate the behavioural element). Both cognitive approaches focused on negative thinking as the prime cause of psychological disturbance. Modern-day CBT incorporates theories and applications from both approaches along with techniques and applications from behaviourism.*

▶ *CBT is rich in techniques, strategies and applications and clients can experiment with different techniques and see for themselves how they work. Homework tasks are agreed between therapist and client as a way of cementing what is learned in the session.*

2

Clarifying the problem

In this chapter you will learn:
- *how to clarify your problems by using the cognitive behavioural therapy model*
- *how to develop a 'map' to clarify your problems*
- *how to identify patterns in your thoughts and behaviours that maintain, rather than resolve, your difficulties.*

CBT doesn't just say, 'think positively', it says, 'consider as many different angles as possible'.

Christine Padesky, US psychologist

Formulating problems

Stepping into therapy-speak for a moment, we want to introduce you to the idea of working out what your problems are and what is maintaining them by 'formulating' them.

Insight

A formulation is simply a type of diagram you make to help you identify different components that contribute to your problem, which may include what is happening in your life in the present and past events that continue to impact on your life.

In cognitive behavioural therapy (CBT), the case formulation (or map or conceptualization, as it can be called) is the driving force of the therapy process, and you can learn to use this yourself.

DEFINING THE PROBLEM

Before you can tackle your problems, you need to identify what they are. For some, this may be easy and straightforward. However, sometimes, identifying what is wrong in an exact way is extremely difficult. A common problem can be that of not being able to define exactly why you feel as you do. Some problems might be clear-cut, such as financial difficulties or relationship problems that are easily identifiable. Other problems may be harder to define and can be expressed in more general terms, such as feelings of isolation or worries about the future.

HELPING YOU TO UNDERSTAND WHAT IS GOING ON

Formulating your problems is a means of helping you to understand them and understand what maintains them from a cognitive behavioural standpoint. It also helps you to understand what may have caused the problems in the first place. At its simplest, a formulation focuses on negative cycles that link thoughts and emotions. Nonetheless, you will constantly change and add to this 'map' of your difficulties as you work through the book and become more aware of the contribution of various life events to your views and outlook. In Chapter 10, we help you to develop your formulation to include your earlier life experiences and the beliefs and assumptions that emanate from these.

Think of this map as a piece of plasticine where you are able to constantly change its shape and appearance when – as you work through this book – new information comes to light that may cause you to want to adjust your ideas and perceptions.

Jargon dictionary: A 'case formulation' or 'case conceptualization' (they are one and the same thing) is really just a map. It shows you where you are, how you got there, why you have stopped, and what alternative routes onwards there might be.

A good map will answer the questions you might be asking, such as:

► *Why me?*
► *Why now?*
► *Why won't my difficulties go away?*
► *What do I need to do to feel better?*

Formulating your problems will increase your sense of understanding and control over them, which will also help you to avoid them cropping up again in the future. The formulation is tailored specifically for you, rather than leaving you to follow some sort of generalized self-improvement guide that may not take your special and particular circumstances into account. See the example below.

John and Elinor both had difficulties with confined spaces, and they would feel highly anxious and panicky. Travelling on trains or using lifts was difficult for them, and they avoided both of these forms of transport. However, explaining why they were so frightened of the panic and anxiety they felt would ensue in these circumstances, John said that he feared it would lead to a heart attack and that he might die. Elinor, on the other hand, feared that she would lose control, do something stupid and look a complete fool in front of other passengers, which would be extremely embarrassing and was to be avoided at all costs.

Thus, one very common problem had completely different meanings for two separate individuals, and because of this, the approach to overcoming the problem would be at least partially different for each of them.

IDIOSYNCRATIC THINKING

The above is an example of what we call 'idiosyncratic thinking'. Everyone has different ways of interpreting their experiences. Different people give their own interpretation to the same experience. This is why discovering the meaning to you of what has happened or might happen is all-important. Unfortunately, we don't always interpret experiences in ways that help us, and the task of CBT is to consider our interpretations and appraise them to see how well they fit with reality and how well they help us. This chapter is extremely important as a starting point for you.

HOW TO START CREATING YOUR OWN MAP

The vital ingredient of your map is the personal meaning to you of what you think and what you do. Look back at the basic CBT model in Chapter 1 (see Figure 1.1) and review the link we established between a particular event and your thoughts, feelings and behaviours. Now create a model that is personal to you. Remember that CBT relies on you being very specific and doesn't like generalizations. Find a recent, *specific* event that had a negative impact on you and work out what was going through your mind, how you felt, how you behaved – and what the outcome of all this was. The outcome might have been a consequence of your actions and reactions, but it might also be simply the meaning you have placed on the series of events.

First of all, Figure 2.1 is 'one we made earlier' to guide you. This will, almost certainly, bear no relation at all to your own concerns or circumstances, but it will show you how to fill out your own route map.

NB: If you are already familiar with the idea of a case formulation/ conceptualization – or you become familiar with them as you read and study more about CBT – you will notice that they come in several different varieties! Psychologists all tend to have their own favourite way of developing a conceptualization, so you don't need to feel that one is right or wrong. You will probably find one model easier to work with than another, and more easily understandable.

Insight

Since the idea of creating a formulation/conceptualization can be daunting at first, we introduce you to a simple version in this chapter – an extension of the basic CBT model you became familiar with in Chapter 1 – to get you started.

A detailed formulation will take into account information from your past, and what has brought you to where you are now, so that very basic beliefs you may have about yourself and life in general can be identified. We want to keep things a little simpler for you now, but when you reach Chapter 10, on assumptions and beliefs, we will explain this more detailed conceptualization. For the moment, look at the example questions below and Figure 2.1.

Some questions to help you develop your own map
If you are feeling depressed or anxious, ask yourself:

▶ *What am I depressed or anxious about?*
▶ *What situations or life events have led me to feel this way?*
▶ *What are the thoughts that contribute to these feelings that overwhelm me?*

Also think about answers to the following:

▶ *What are my current problems?*
▶ *How did these develop?*
▶ *When did they develop?*
▶ *How are my problems being maintained? (What keeps them going and prevents me from resolving them?)*
▶ *What thoughts, ideas and beliefs do I have that support the problems? (For example, if my relationship is going wrong, do I believe that I am not especially lovable or that I am letting my partner treat me poorly?)*
▶ *What reactions do I have in association with these thoughts – emotionally (how I feel), behaviourally (how I behave) and physiologically (bodily tension, fatigue)?*

Look at the outline in Figure 2.1, and then use the answers to the above questions to fill in your own map.

> **Key point: Take several photocopies of this simple formulation/ conceptualization (you will find a blank version in the Appendix, page 322).** You can then use it for a variety of different situations when you want clarity about what is going on.

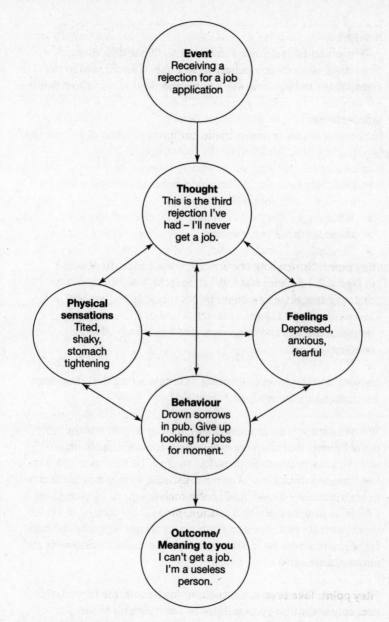

Event
Receiving a rejection for a job application

Thought
This is the third rejection I've had – I'll never get a job.

Physical sensations
Tited, shaky, stomach tightening

Feelings
Depressed, anxious, fearful

Behaviour
Drown sorrows in pub. Give up looking for jobs for moment.

Outcome/ Meaning to you
I can't get a job. I'm a useless person.

Figure 2.1 An example formulation/conceptualization.

Insight

The object of creating a formulation of your difficulties is to draw out a clearer picture of not only what has led to the problems but also what you think and do that maintains them.

Interpretation

In the case of our fictitious friend in Figure 2.1 who didn't get the job they wanted, ask yourself the following questions:

▸ *Did their thoughts, feelings and behaviours resolve their problem or maintain their problem?*
▸ *What might this person's conclusion about themselves suggest about their life experiences?*

Key point: Notice how the arrows in the conceptualization in Figure 2.1 go both ways. What does this tell you? It means that we maintain our problems by our thoughts and actions, and we also make things worse. It is a vicious circle, with negative thoughts, feelings and behaviours feeding off each other constantly.

Looking at the conceptualization, it is easy to see that they were maintaining their problems.

We will explore this in more depth in Chapter 10, but the probability is that this person will have learned that failing to achieve something made them feel useless. This belief might have been learned in childhood or possibly from a life event (or events) in early adulthood, and could have been triggered by something as simple as someone saying, 'you're useless'. This may have caused them to retain this idea as a truth about themselves, and the brain rushes to throw it back out when seemingly similar situations and circumstances arise.

Now apply the above questions and answers to the conceptualization you have filled in for yourself.

- *Can you see the link between thoughts, feelings, behaviour and physical sensations?*
- *Can you see what is maintaining the problem for you?*
- *Are you able to identify a personal meaning for yourself?*
- *Can you work out where this personal meaning might have come from?*

Case study

Lucy was at a company dance with her boyfriend, Dan. They hadn't been going out for long and Lucy was still not totally confident around Dan. Dan started to dance with a very attractive colleague of Lucy's. Lucy found herself feeling jealous and insecure. Her heart started beating fast and she felt hot and breathless. Lucy's insecurity resulted in her arguing with Dan over his perceived disloyal behaviour and she went home in a taxi alone.

Let's put Lucy's experience into conceptualization format.

Situation: Lucy's boyfriend dancing with attractive colleague at company event.

Lucy's thoughts: 'He finds her attractive – more attractive than me.' 'He'd rather be with her.' 'Everybody is looking at them together.'

Lucy's feelings: Jealousy, anger.

Lucy's physical sensations: Feeling hot, increased heart rate, breathlessness.

Lucy's behaviour: Lucy accused her boyfriend of treating her badly and, after an argument, went home alone.

The personal meaning of all this to Lucy: (possibly) I'm unlovable, (or perhaps) men cannot be trusted and will always hurt you, (or maybe) my jealousy always spoils my relationships.

Making connections: joining the dots

You are now becoming familiar with the idea that CBT practice involves observing your responses to disturbing situations and then drawing your attention to the connection between cognitions, moods and behaviours. Because thoughts, feelings and actions are all connected, making changes for the better in any one area will have a positive effect on the other areas. For example, in the case study on the previous page, if Lucy notices her negative thoughts in a similar situation and then replaces them with other thoughts such as:

▶ *I have been told that I'm attractive*

or

▶ *Although Dan is talking or dancing with another woman, it doesn't necessarily follow that he finds her more attractive than me*

then she is less likely to be overwhelmed with negative feelings and take negative action. Equally, from a behavioural point of view, if Lucy had been able to take positive action, such as dancing or talking with someone else whose company she enjoyed, then she would have been likely to think about herself and the situation in a more positive light.

You will find the easiest way to develop conceptualizations of your problems is to ask yourself questions such as these:

▶ **What is the life situation that is disturbing me?**
  ▷ *Has something happened recently?*
  ▷ *Looking back over the last few years, what has distressed me most?*
  ▷ *Going back to my youth or childhood, can I identify any ongoing difficulties? For example, shyness or low self-esteem that might contribute to my present circumstances.*
▶ **How do I feel about this?**
  ▷ *Identify your emotions specifically, for example, angry, sad, anxious, depressed.*

- ▶ **What thoughts do I have about this?**
  - ▷ *About myself?*
  - ▷ *About others?*
  - ▷ *About the situation?*
  - ▷ *About the future?*
- ▶ **What do I do in regard to this situation?**
  - ▷ *Simply accept it?*
  - ▷ *Use avoidance where I can?*
  - ▷ *Act in a way that doesn't seem to make a positive difference?*
  - ▷ *Do the best I can, but it still doesn't help?*

Use your basic route map (formulation/conceptualization) to work through a variety of specific situations. You will begin to see a pattern in your responses and to identify certain beliefs (more on those later) that may contribute to the maintenance of your problems.

HOMEWORK

Your homework task for this chapter is to practise drawing a case formulation/conceptualization (or several if you have a variety of areas of your self or your life that you would like to change). Asking yourself the questions we have suggested, look for patterns in your thinking and behaviour that may explain why things are as they are and that will also help you to target areas for change.

SUMMARY

In this chapter, we have focused on helping you to understand your problems and what maintains them.

- ▶ *Formulating your problems, while normally used as a tool by psychologists, is just as effective if you work with it on your own.*
- ▶ *The formulation/conceptualization is simply a 'map' of where you are and how you got there, which will help you to identify ways out. As you notice patterns emerging – 'Ah, I notice that I always think in such-and-such a way' or 'I always do this, that and the other' – you will begin to see what it might be most helpful to work on in order to make changes.*

▶ *While you can 'tweak' any of the different areas that make up your personal map – thoughts, behaviours, feelings, circumstances – you are most likely to start with your thoughts, as these are often the most flexible part of the change process.*

In Chapter 3, we focus more specifically on your thinking and its impact on how you feel and what you do.

THINGS TO REMEMBER

▶ A formulation is a type of map to chart links between events, thoughts, emotions and behaviour. The objective is to help you understand your thought processes and their effect. It should, in essence, be telling you a story and showing you where you need to intervene to make changes.

▶ The 'negative cycle' diagram is a simple formulation you can use straight away to represent your thoughts, emotions and behaviour, and to examine what was happening in a particular situation.

▶ Formulations can take various forms and can be expanded as the therapy progresses, when deeper understandings have been reached and links made.

▶ A key point emphasized in CBT is that events themselves don't cause us problems; it is the interpretation we give to an event or situation. Two (or more) people can have the same experience, yet give different meanings to what occurred. This is what is meant by 'idiosyncratic meanings' – meanings particular to individual interpretation.

▶ The point of examining your thoughts, feelings and actions is to build self-awareness. You begin to see patterns and understand what is at the root of your problems and how the problems are being maintained.

3

Setting your goals

In this chapter you will learn:
- *how to set goals that will work*
- *about the SMART model*
- *how to evaluate the success of goals.*

Just as your car runs more smoothly and requires less energy to go faster and farther when the wheels are in perfect alignment, you perform better when your thoughts, feelings, emotions, goals and values are in balance.

Brian Tracy, US author

Insight

Stating your goals means identifying how you want things to be in your life. It engenders a sense of purpose, with the possibility of change, which encourages optimism.

Turning problems into goals

Identifying the problem is a start. Once the problem or problems are defined you are then in a position to look at what you can do to improve the situation by creating and developing your goals.

Cognitive behavioural therapy (CBT) is a structured therapy. Where you are working with a professional therapist, the early sessions will be used, in part, for working with you to define specifically and clearly:

- ▶ *what your problems are*
- ▶ *what is maintaining your problems*
- ▶ *how you would like things to be and what you will need to change to achieve this.*

This structure is an excellent one to follow, even with a DIY approach. In this chapter, the goal is to help you define your goals!

Key point: CBT is a therapy of change. Whatever you think about yourself and your life right now, however you feel and whatever you are doing, if you are not feeling good about everything then, simply, you could do better. CBT will help you achieve that.

Begin with the end in mind...

Steven R. Covey, author

As always, we emphasize that CBT is a collaborative therapy, and we have no wish to direct you to specific goals. We want to help you to work out what is important enough for you to work on yourself. However, there is one exception! We would like you to make this book one of your first goals – working through it in order to acquire the skills and techniques you will need to achieve your other goals.

SETTING GOALS ISN'T ALWAYS AS EASY AS IT APPEARS

Often, knowing what we don't want is easier than knowing what we do want. Moreover, setting goals that are too grandiose or too hard to achieve can be dispiriting rather than rewarding. So, learning the skills of successful goal-setting is extremely important, right at the start. This does not mean that your goals will be 'set in stone'. Good goals have built-in flexibility to be adjusted as you, your life and your personal desires change. What you are doing now is just a start.

When you identify areas that could be improved because they are currently causing you problems, the next step is to log them as a goal list of issues to work on.

WORKING OUT YOUR GOALS

Insight

Beware of thinking in terms of 'wishing' and 'hoping' without any defined intentions or plans. This type of thinking keeps your goals trapped as unobtainable dreams in your mind.

Exercise

Psychologists often use a skill called 'the miracle question', where you consider what it would be like to wake up tomorrow with everything as you would like it to be and ask yourself, what changes there would be in your life? This exercise will help you to work out what is wrong and what would put things right. Imagine that you live in a land where every dream comes true. Use your workbook to write down your wishes, hopes and dreams about yourself and your life.

What you have written in the exercise may give you some idea of your present stumbling blocks. For instance, you might have written very specific things, such as:

- ▶ *I wish I was in a committed relationship.*
- ▶ *I wish my finances were in better order.*
- ▶ *I wish I could get a promotion at work.*
- ▶ *I wish I got on better with my family.*

NB: If you have done this, we would now like you to change the wording slightly (this may seem 'picky', but you will come to realize how important the exact words we use in our cognitions actually are as we go along). Rewrite what you have put, taking out the word 'wish' and replacing it with 'would like'.

Why do you think that changing this one word is so important? The answer, on this occasion, is that 'wishing' is actually quite negative. Wishing and hoping get you nowhere. Stating what you would actually like is much more positive, and a better starting point for change.

It is also quite okay, and sometimes easier, to put down what you don't want, rather than what you do. So do this as well. You may find you write:

- ▶ *I don't want to keep feeling anxious.*
- ▶ *I don't want to be in the same job a year from now.*
- ▶ *I don't want to be on my own for ever.*
- ▶ *I hate feeling so low all the time.*
- ▶ *I wish I wasn't ill any more.*

These types of goals are often referred to as 'Dead Man's Goals', that is, this could be achieved by a dead man – no more anxious feelings, no more job worries, etc. You need to turn them into more positive aspirations by simply turning them around. For example, turn 'I don't want to keep feeling anxious' into 'I would like to feel more confident and worry less about things' or turn 'I wish I wasn't ill any more' to 'I would like to feel less defeated by my illness and live life to the full in spite of its limitations'.

You will now have quite a list of things that you would like to be different. These are your *goals*.

SETTING PRIORITIES

Now prioritize your goals. Revise your list so that what is more important to you is at the top of the list, and the things that are less important to you – or less urgent – are of a lower ranking. One of the mistakes people can make when trying to change things is that they become grasshoppers, hopping from one thing to another the whole time and never giving total focus to one specific thing. The result can often be no change of any consequence in any area. So focus is important.

We now want you to divide your goals into two sub-sections. Look through them all and consider the following questions:

▶ *Which of these goals can only be achieved by my doing something?*
▶ *Which of these goals might be achieved if I thought differently about them?*

To give you an example, if your partner has a bad habit that consistently irritates you, your options are either to work with him or her to eliminate the habit, or to work with yourself to not allow the habit to keep disturbing you.

Making decisions about your goals in this way will help you to decide whether you want to work cognitively or behaviourally, or both. This will then be built into your plan of action.

Insight

Realism in goal setting is very important. The idea is to get encouraging results that give you a sense of achievement and spur you on further to tackle other problematic areas of your life.

THE SMART WAY TO SET GOALS

Some of you may have used the SMART goal-setting tool before – it is extremely helpful in your quest to focus, to make things specific, so that you can be sure that a goal is exactly the goal that you want and can weigh up whether it is realistic. SMART stands for:

Specific
Measurable

Achievable
Realistic
Time frame.

SMART goals have all of these qualities:

▶ **Specific.** *This means rejecting generalizations, such as 'I would like to be happier', 'I would like to feel better about myself', and focusing on exactly what you want. For example, if someone says to you that they would like to lose weight, that doesn't really mean anything on its own. To make this goal specific, they need to tell you how much weight they want to lose, when they want to have lost it by and how they plan exactly to do so (diet, exercise, both?). Thus the specific goal could be that they would like to lose 5 kg in weight, for their sister's wedding at the end of next month, and to do so they are going to join a gym, attend three times a week, and follow a low-calorie weight-loss plan. In fact, once you really set your goals in motion, even this is not as specific as it could be (Which gym? When will they go? How will they calculate calories?), but it is still a good start.*

▶ **Measurable.** *How will you know if you have achieved your goal? What will be different? In the previous example, weekly weigh-in sessions would be a good measure, as would trying on clothes that previously didn't fit. Where your goals are more to do with adjusting aspects of yourself, that is, becoming more confident, then a measurement might be challenging yourself to do something that you would not have done previously, and to note the outcome. In the land where dreams come true, if you could wake up tomorrow and find that your dreams (now goals) had become realities, what would have changed? For example:*

  ▷ *I would feel more confident in my ability to achieve success at work.*
  ▷ *I would find it much easier to talk to people, and they would respond well.*
  ▷ *I would be facing my fears, no matter how worrying.*
These are your measurements of success.

▶ **Achievable.** *Wonderful though it might be to play in the Wembley Cup Final, perform in the leading role at La Scala, or be the president of the United States, people waste a great deal of time and energy wishing and dreaming about things that, for the huge majority of us, are just never going to happen. Don't waste your energies here. Always ask yourself, 'If all else goes as it should, is this within my grasp?' If the answer is 'Yes', you have something to work with. If the answer is 'No', then your goal is not achievable, and needs to be relegated to the rubbish bin.*

▶ **Realistic.** *If you want to lose 4 kg in a week, or you would like to go from being chronically shy to the life and soul of the party by next Saturday night, you are setting yourself unrealistic goals. This is a dangerous thing to do as it means you are 'setting yourself up to fail'. Unless you realize that your expectations are out of kilter with reality, you will condemn yourself to being a hopeless failure and a variety of other similar, worthless descriptions. Where your goals are realistic, not only do you achieve them, but you get a 'feel-good' factor from the achievement, which boosts your confidence.*

In the 1960s, when computers started to become big business, computer salespeople found that their employers set them hugely competitive targets and, as soon as they achieved them, the goalposts were moved again, so that even more was required of them. Many of these salespeople suffered from stress and burn-out. In this era, IBM sold more computers than any other company. Why? Were they better computers? Perhaps, but that was not the reason. The reason was that IBM's salespeople scored better than those in any other company. Yet these salespeople were consistently set easy targets, which they regularly reached without difficulty. What was going on? IBM had applied motivational psychology – and one of the things that motivates people is success. They encouraged their employees to be easily successful – this made them very confident and, with this confidence, they achieved even more sales.

*Do remember this story when you are setting goals for
yourself. Break down the goals into realistic steps so they
build to an achievable whole, and your confidence will soar.*

Another way in which your goals need to be realistic is that
they have to be within your control. For example, focus on
changing things about yourself, rather than other people, or
on finding a new job – which should be possible – rather than
focusing on a specific job, which might not be possible due to
circumstances outside your immediate control.

▶ **Time frame.** People are often extremely impatient about
achieving things, from getting rid of negative emotional states
to accomplishing skills and gaining the prizes of workplace
promotion or personal relationship success. This is natural.
Who wants to wait? Yet waiting may be the key to success.
Very often, when people decide that something is not working,
or that they cannot achieve it, all that has happened is that
they have not done it:
  ▷ often enough
  ▷ for long enough.
The well-known expression, 'Timing is all', is popular for a
reason. It's the truth. Always set a time frame – if you don't,
then your motivation will slip away and you won't feel the joys
of succeeding as you had planned. Procrastination will set in and
little will happen. However, don't set unrealistic time frames or,
again, you will give up. If someone asks whether you might like
to train with them for the London Marathon, and they tell you
that it is on Sunday week, you would (unless you are used to
running marathons and were free on that day) tell them that you
couldn't possibly. Yet if they tell you that it is 12 months away,
and that there will be many training opportunities in the interim,
suddenly that might sound more tempting. Timing is all. Set
good, realistic time frames for your goals.

WHAT TO TACKLE, WHEN

Now that you have a list of goals, and you have prioritized them,
we would like you to place one further set of stats in the margin on

the page. Rate the goals from 'Hardest to achieve' to 'Easiest to achieve', and those in between. The issue of which goals to tackle first will be resolved by the Easy/Hard ratings you give them. It is helpful if you initially tackle easier goals and those where change is likely to occur quite rapidly, in order to give yourself hope and confidence.

There is nothing remotely wrong in doing things the reverse way around and going in 'cold turkey' to the hardest thing on the list. If you succeed there, then everything else suddenly becomes easy. However, bear in mind what we have said in this chapter about setting yourself up for failure if you try to achieve too much too soon. Ask yourself how you would be able to handle that, compared to the more 'sure-fire' successes of getting easier goals off the list first.

> **Key point:** The extent to which, and the preciseness with which, you break down large goals into small, manageable, easily achievable components will be a key predictor of success.

HOMEWORK

Use what you have learned in this chapter to work out, in a structured and tightly focused way, what changes you would like to make in your life. Write these down clearly in your workbook.

At the moment, you don't need to worry about how you will do this – this book will teach you. However, you do need to know what you want to do, and you do need to use the SMART tool to ensure that what you want is feasible and within the realms of possibility for you.

- ▶ *Define what you would like to be different (checking against SMART that it is valid).*
- ▶ *If you have several things that you would like to change, prioritize them.*

- ▸ Use the breakdowns you have learned in this chapter to subdivide your goals.
- ▸ Be comfortable that your list reflects where you would like to be, and how you would like to be.
- ▸ Ensure that this is all clearly written down in your workbook.

You could write down your goals in the form of a chart. This will give you more clarity than a simple list. You can develop your own, but here is an example that you might consider.

Main goal	Time frame	Mini goals	Time frame
To work through this book and apply my learning to my personal situation(s)	6 months	To work on one chapter at a time and have confidence in my understanding before I move on	1 chapter per week
To identify specific positive changes I wish to make to my life	Immediately	To identify the small steps I can make towards achieving my main goal(s)	4 weeks

You will see that it is not always possible to immediately identify exactly what you need to do to bring about change. One of the tasks of this book is to teach you this. This is why goal charts need to be flexible and 'pencilled in' rather than cast in concrete – you can change them and add to them all the time as you learn more about exactly how to achieve what you want.

SUMMARY

In this chapter we have focused on defining what you may feel is not right about your life as it is, and on getting your goals into a sensible order. You will now have a clear and precise idea of what you want to work on, and what changes you want to make.

- ▶ *You may have found defining your problems very difficult. One problem people often have is not being able to define exactly why they feel as they do. This, of course, makes it equally hard to express quite what they would like. If, despite your efforts in this chapter, you still feel this way, please don't worry. CBT is very good at digging out what's really going on when you are uncertain, and we will address this as you go along.*
- ▶ *This is also where the ever-popular 'miracle question' can be helpful, and why we posed it. Again, ask yourself: if, when you wake up tomorrow, everything could be exactly as you wanted it, what would be different? How would you know that your life had changed for the better? The answer to this question can be very helpful in guiding you. Do this exercise, think about it, and then look again at the goal-setting ideas and write down one or two that relate to you. Even, 'I would like to work out what is wrong' is a goal in itself! Don't be afraid to write that down. CBT skills will help you to find the answer.*
- ▶ *Remember how important it is to be clear and specific with goal-setting.*
  - ▷ *Each goal must be something that you want very much (or you won't put the effort in).*
  - ▷ *Your goals must be SMART friendly.*
  - ▷ *Your major goal should have a reasonable chance of success – say 50:50 when you start. If you have rarely achieved a major goal before, set one that has an 80–90 per cent chance of success to start with.*
  - ▷ *Your goals must be in harmony with each other. For example, if you want to overcome social shyness, you cannot have a goal of not having to go to social occasions.*

THINGS TO REMEMBER

▶ Goals are simply a list of things that you would like to be different and are willing to work at to create change.

▶ Identifying problems is important but dwelling on them isn't helpful. What is helpful is turning problems into goals, thereby starting the solution-focused process.

▶ As part of structured therapy, during early sessions you would work with the therapist with three main objectives: firstly, to clearly define what the problems are; secondly, to identify what maintains the problems; and thirdly, what changes you would like to make.

▶ Goals aren't cast in stone. They can be adjusted as your life and personal perspectives change. At the beginning of therapy it is useful to identify short-term goals that are easy to achieve. As therapy progresses, move to medium-term goals as confidence grows, then on to long-term goals encouraged by positive changes already achieved.

▶ It is important to mentally make the move from 'wishing' your life could be different to 'wanting' things to change, and owning the latter by shifting from the 'I wish I could...' perspective to a more purposeful 'I would like...'.

▶ Goals can be broken down and made more manageable by separating the problems into two categories: problems that require you to take action, and problems that can be changed by thinking differently.

4

Catch that thought!

In this chapter you will learn:

- *to identify different types of thoughts*
- *to discover where your elusive thoughts may be, and how to catch them*
- *to rate thoughts and emotions to test their strength and severity*
- *to ensure that you can capture the correct thought – and not waste time working with the wrong one!*

You cannot control what happens to you, but you can control your attitude toward what happens to you, and in that, you will be mastering change rather than allowing it to master you.

Brian Tracy, US author

In Chapter 2, you learned how to describe what is going on in a way that helps you to see that negative thoughts, feelings and behaviour simply perpetuate a problem rather than improve or get rid of it. The good thing about a formulation is that you can go into any part of it and make changes, and the changes you make to that particular area – say your behaviour – will have a positive effect on each other area. However, it is most usual to start by looking at negative thoughts and making changes there, at least to begin with. Consequently, you now need to learn how to identify, specifically, what you are actually thinking that causes you emotional distress.

Capturing thoughts

You are by now familiar with the important role that thoughts play in how you feel and what you do. Nonetheless, many people have great problems in identifying their thinking. Some even say, 'Nothing is going through my mind' or 'I can't come up with anything'. Sometimes, it really is very difficult to access your worrying thoughts, and you may possibly feel that you simply don't know what was in your mind – or even feel certain that there wasn't anything in your mind – it was simply an emotion, sitting there on its own. Don't worry about this – with practice you will gradually learn to access difficult thoughts, and this chapter shows you how to begin the process.

Firstly, how many types of thoughts do you think you have? Many people believe we simply have negative thoughts and positive thoughts. While, when things go wrong, we find it easy to identify negative thoughts, what other types of thoughts can you identify? Write them down in your workbook. Here are some ideas:

▶ **Positive thoughts:** *'Everything is going really well.'*
▶ **Neutral thoughts:** *'I wonder what to have for lunch today?'*
▶ **Evaluative thoughts:** *'Is this the best way to do that?'*
▶ **Action-oriented thoughts:** *'I'm going to solve this problem...'*
▶ **Rational thoughts:** *'While I initially believed this to be true, I can now see that there are alternatives.'*

You are now acquainted with the idea that what we think decides how we feel. However, this is just as true in reverse – how we feel decides what we think. You may therefore find it easier to identify your mood first, and then work out what the thoughts might be that have caused it.

Insight

People often identify their feelings more readily than their thoughts as, when a situation is problematic, emotions tend to dominate over thinking. Hence the saying, 'I can't think straight', when we are emotional.

Exercise

This exercise will help you to identify your thoughts through recognizing your moods. You are to create a simple 'Thought Record' like the one on page 47. You will become familiar with Thought Records as they are a basic tool of cognitive behavioural therapy (CBT) and will help you to clarify your thinking and your feelings. For the Thought Record in this exercise, we ask you to identify your moods first, rather than your thoughts.

To help you identify your mood, look for physical sensations. Remember that your moods create physical responses, so check first with any bodily changes – are you feeling tired and lethargic (when it is likely that your mood will be low, or depressed)? Is your stomach churning and your heart racing (when it is likely that your mood will be anxious or panicky)? What is going on in your body? These questions will help you identify your mood.

NB: You will find a blank copy of the Thought Record, for you to photocopy and use, in the Appendix, page 323.

Write your identified mood in the 'Feelings' column of the Thought Record – you may wish to write down more than one. Then write down what is happening or has just happened to make you feel this way in the second column. Finally, write down what is going through your mind or was going through your mind just before this happened in the third column.

We have asked you to write down your mood before anything else as it will be the strongest part of the situation. Once you have expressed how you feel, you can then write down why – what was happening, what you thought. You can ask yourself some simple questions to assist you. For example:

▶ *'What was I afraid might be going to happen?'*
▶ *'What was happening or was in my mind just before I began feeling this way?'*
▶ *'Am I recalling any past incidences where things turned out poorly?'*

What was the trigger? The 'Situation' column in a Thought Record is very important. It enables you to begin to see patterns in 'trigger points' that more readily engender negative thoughts and emotions. You may gradually recognize that a certain situation or a certain time of day, being in the presence of a certain person or, quite often, a marked lack of activity of any sort triggers particular thoughts and moods. This is excellent information for you as it allows you to adjust the situation or even, if it is sensible and possible, eliminate it. If you cannot do either of these things, you will at least be aware ahead of time of possible mood changes and you can therefore create an action plan to help you overcome your negative thoughts and feelings.

Why not begin by focusing on the mood you may be experiencing in reading this book? How are you feeling this minute? Perhaps you feel *hopeful* (about embarking on some self-help techniques) or *overwhelmed* (by what seems like a lot to learn). If you feel differently, write down one word to describe each feeling or mood that you do have.

Now think about what kind of thoughts you are having that relate to the mood. If, for example, you are feeling hopeful you might be thinking along the lines of:

▶ *'I can learn a lot of new ways to make me feel better.'*
▶ *'I'm looking forward to trying out different techniques.'*
▶ *'The book has a section on anxiety that will help me.'*

If you feel overwhelmed, your thoughts could be something like:

▶ *'I can't do this – it's far too difficult for me.'*
▶ *'I can't learn from a book.'*
▶ *'I really haven't got the time for this.'*

Now find some more thoughts and feelings of your own. In searching for examples, look first over the very recent past – the last day or so – then the last week, and then the last several weeks or months.

Jane was a graphic designer. She loved her work but unfortunately did not get on especially well with her boss. Jane did not believe this was due to poor work on her part, but simply to a personality clash. Her boss had very narrow views on the way things should be done, and wasn't very interested in flair or originality unless it tied in with her own views.

One Friday after Jane had been at the firm a year, her boss told her to expect to be called in for an annual appraisal later in the day. Jane immediately felt her body tense and her heart rate quicken. She could feel herself becoming extremely nervous about her appraisal. Moreover, she felt irritated at the short notice her boss had given her, and her boss's expectation that it was acceptable to dump this on her without giving her much chance to prepare. Jane also felt her stomach churning, and recognized this as fear. After just a year in the firm, Jane's boss might ask her to leave, or at least give her a warning if her appraisal was really poor.

Look at the Thought Record to see how this can all be recorded so that the feelings-situation-thoughts triad comes in to play. Jane circled the strongest thought and the strongest feeling, which helped her to see that what bothered her most was a fear of losing her job.

Insight

In therapy you are likely to start working with a Thought Record in a simple three-column format, as here, covering your feelings, the situation and your thoughts. As your understanding grows, the Thought Record becomes a more searching and comprehensive vehicle of exploration.

Feelings	Situation	Thought(s)
For example, *angry, sad, despairing, anxious.*	This may be an actual event, or just an image in your mind.	What was going through your mind just before you began to feel this way?
Circle the strongest of your feelings.		If you have put down more than one thought, circle the strongest.
Nervous Irritated (Fearful)	*Awaiting annual appraisal at work from a boss I don't especially get on with.*	*I'm sure my appraisal won't be good. My boss is always a difficult person who will cut me no slack.* (*Supposing it's so bad that I am given a warning?*)

Insight

It is useful to keep your Thought Records and other worksheets in your workbook, or a separate folder. Look back on them in a few months' time and compare the old ones with the more recent to see how much you have progressed.

Identifying your strongest thoughts and feelings

In the Thought Record, you should circle the strongest emotion and thought where perhaps you have written down several. This is to ensure that:

▶ *you focus on the thoughts and feelings that bother you the most; and*
▶ *your thoughts and feelings 'match'.*

Later in the book (see Chapter 5) we ask you to rate your thoughts and feelings more exactly, on a scale of 0–100 per cent. There are many good reasons for this, for example, comparison between different thoughts and feelings or 'before and after' ratings when you have made thinking and/or behavioural changes. For the moment, simply be aware of which thought and emotion stands out more strongly than the others.

'Matching' thoughts and moods is exceedingly important. Many people waste weeks and months filling in Thought Records that are of no help to them because they do not correctly identify and work on the critical thought that is engendering the emotion. Here, we teach you how to make sure this doesn't happen to you.

> Jargon dictionary: A 'causal thought' is simply another term for the thought that causes the strongest emotion.

Insight

Scaling – using a figure between 1 and 10, or 1 and 100 per cent – is used extensively in CBT. It can be used as a measuring tool to assess the severity of a problem and its effects, and to elucidate beliefs, predictions and outcomes.

IDENTIFYING THE CAUSAL THOUGHT

An excellent way to ensure that you don't waste time on the wrong thought is to rate your thoughts and emotions, either from 1 to 10, or by using a percentage figure. For example, if your mood rating is 'Panic (90%)', a negative thought on the lines of, 'My friend has forgotten our lunch appointment' is not going to be the causal thought – that is, the thought that triggers the emotion. Ask yourself, 'Why does that matter?' and you are more likely to get to the correct causal thought, which in this case could be, 'Perhaps she has been involved in a serious accident'.

Just to give you the idea, try to identify the causal thought in the following examples. For each emotion, pick the thought that you think most closely matches the severity rating of the emotion.

Emotion:	**Depression (80%)**
Thoughts:	'I haven't done enough exam revision.'
	'Failing my exams would be a disaster.'
Emotion:	**Anxiety (75%)**
Thoughts:	'I've only got 20 minutes to finish this work before the boss wants to see it, and I'm not sure I'll manage it.'
	'If I don't finish this work by the time the boss wants it, he'll use it as an excuse to get rid of me.'
Emotion:	**Embarrassment (100%)**
Thoughts:	'I totally fluffed up my lines in the speech I just gave.'
	'I can't get over having made such a complete fool of myself.'
Emotion:	**Fear (80%)**
Thought:	'I really don't like flying.'
	'I can't stop thinking that the plane might crash.'

We suspect that, had we not added a second thought option to each emotion, you would have been happy to agree that the first thought was a good match. However, now look at all those first thoughts again. There is actually nothing in them that suggests that their owner might be severely depressed, highly anxious, totally embarrassed or full of fear. They are simply comments. Thinking that you haven't done enough exam revision will only be depressing if it bothers you – it might not. Many people don't like flying; that doesn't mean that they become filled with fear and think the plane might crash. They might just find it tedious, or not especially like being in a confined space.

In each case, it is the second thought that is the causal thought – the thought that does create high emotion – and is thus the correct thought to capture and work on.

Does this make sense? Here is another technique for reaching the causal thought, which some of you may already know.

The downward arrow technique: your first view of a useful skill
This is an excellent skill for capturing causal thoughts. Here is an example.

You are feeling stressed, anxious and your head is aching. Your thought is: 'I can't seem to get on with the work I need to do for this presentation.'

Isn't that it? Many people would stop right there: you are feeling exceedingly stressed (say 80%) and the reason is that you cannot get on with the work you need to do. That makes sense. But, from the exercise you completed above, you now know that isn't the case. Not being able to get on with your work might be bothersome, but that might irritate you only a little, and not account for such a high stress level. To work out why it is the cause of such highly rated emotion, you ask yourself a further question, as shown in Figure 4.1.

> **Insight**
> Our initial thinking may not identify the cause of our distress. A little probing with the 'downward arrow technique' can bring the true cause of concern – the underlying 'causal thought' – to the surface.

Now you have a causal thought. You have arrived at a thought that makes complete sense in the context of feeling such a high degree of emotion. This is crucial – it means you have identified exactly what you need to work on, which has little to do with the worry that you can't seem to get on with your work but everything to do with your concern that you might lose your job.

You should now understand:

▸ *how helpful it is to rate your thoughts and moods*
▸ *how the strength of a mood can be an excellent indicator of the strength of the thought you should be chasing down.*

The next question is:
'Why does that matter?'

↓

The answer may be:
'If the presentation doesn't go well, we may lose the client.'

↓

Keep going. Ask yourself a further question:
'Why does that matter?'

↓

The answer may be:
'If we lose the client our department won't meet its sales targets.'

↓

Don't stop. Ask a third question:
'Why does that matter?'

↓

The answer may be:
'I'll be held responsible and I may even lose my job.'

Figure 4.1 Downward arrow technique.

USING IMAGERY

Sometimes it is much easier to capture a thought when you imagine yourself in the situation that caused strong emotion. Particularly in situations of high anxiety, the strength of the mood can be overpowering. Picture yourself in the situation. Recreate in your mind what was going on around you and how you were feeling. Close your eyes if that helps. Relive the situation as closely as you can. Notice various aspects of where you are. If you are indoors, notice pictures on the walls, for example, or the type of furniture in the room. This will help you to recreate an accurate image of the situation you were in. As you re-experience the situation and accompanying emotions, you may find it easier to identify the thoughts that were going through your mind.

HOMEWORK

Provided you understand the rationale for chasing down your causal thoughts, your best homework task is to practise chasing these causal thoughts using a copy of the Thought Record (see Appendix, page 323) until you are completely familiar with it. If you are still a little uncertain, spend the time going over the explanations and exercises in this chapter until it becomes a little clearer.

SUMMARY

We have taken time in this chapter to familiarize you with identifying the all-important causal thought. Many people have difficulty in working on their thoughts. They waste weeks filling in Thought Records and achieving little – and the reason for this is that they are working with the *wrong thought*.

▶ *We have encouraged you to think about the various types of thoughts you may have – it isn't always negative versus positive by any means.*
▶ *The strongest thought is the thought that matches the strong emotion you are feeling. Your thoughts alone will not bother you – it is the emotions they engender that cause your disturbance.*
▶ *Where you have difficulty working out precisely what you were thinking, using imagery may be helpful.*
▶ *You can rate your thoughts and moods so that you can easily identify whether you have a good match or need to look further – perhaps use the downward arrow technique to assist you (see Figure 4.1).*

THINGS TO REMEMBER

▶ In this chapter you have been introduced to the technique of capturing your feelings and thoughts by noting these down in a Thought Record.

▶ Just as what you think decides how you feel, the reverse is also true: how you feel dictates what you think.

▶ Physical responses are linked to moods, for example, lethargy with low mood or depression, and racing heart with anxiety or panicky feelings.

▶ We established that thoughts, emotions and behaviour or actions are all interlinked and when you change in one area of your formulation (your personal 'idiosyncratic' map) it changes other areas too. Therefore, when your mood changes, you think about things differently, and vice versa.

▶ Sometimes it's hard to be clear about what you're thinking. To access thoughts, it's helpful to familiarize yourself with different types of thoughts, such as: positive, neutral, evaluative and action-orientated.

▶ Learning a skill called 'the downward arrow technique' will help you unearth the underlying thoughts and beliefs that are the true cause of associated strong emotion.

Examining and responding to negative thoughts

In this chapter you will learn:
- *to understand idiosyncratic (your own style of) thinking*
- *to understand negative automatic thoughts*
- *to use a Thought Record to evaluate your negative automatic thoughts*
- *to challenge the validity of negative automatic thoughts and to talk back to them.*

A single footstep will not make a path on the earth, so a single thought will not make a pathway in the mind. To make a deep physical path, we walk again and again. To make a deep mental path, we must think over and over the kind of thoughts we wish to dominate our lives.

Henry Thoreau, US essayist (1817–62)

Testing the validity of your thinking

In Chapter 4, you learned how to identify the types of thoughts that create strong emotions within you. Now you need to learn how to test the *validity* of these thoughts. Where these causal thoughts are so powerful that they can cause you to feel a variety of strong, often negative emotions, if they are not actually true, you are channelling a lot of energy and emotional resources in the wrong direction.

We all have a natural propensity to think in a certain way. Some find it easy to have an optimistic, positive outlook. Others are more cautious and weigh up pros and cons carefully. Yet others tend to think automatically in a more negative, pessimistic way. We are not sure why this is. It may be due to our biological or genetic inheritance, but also – most often – to our environment: our upbringing, early adulthood and specific, meaningful events. All these come together to develop our thinking style.

> **Key point: It doesn't matter how strongly you believe something – even if you believe it with your heart and soul – *it doesn't make it true.*** It is simply your particular way of viewing something, your point of view. This is actually a very positive ideology as it allows for flexibility and change when that will help you to feel better.

Once you understand that not all your thinking is helpful to you and that many of your thoughts actually hinder you, it makes sense to try to find more constructive ways of viewing yourself, others and the world around you.

Cognitive behavioural therapy (CBT) is based on the understanding that people construct their own realities and have *idiosyncratic* ways of interpreting their experiences. Different people give their own interpretation to an experience. You can see this in the way that children from the same family will recall aspects of their childhood differently – the same events took place but each interprets what happened in their own unique way. People can respond differently to the same situation, and this is usually because of their own, personal, often deeply-held beliefs about themselves, other people and the world.

Unfortunately, people don't always interpret experiences in ways that help them. Negative thinking can create problems for everyone from time to time, and CBT helps you to identify unhelpful thought patterns and beliefs, and to find alternative ways of thinking and perceiving that work for you. So how do you make a start?

Introducing negative automatic thoughts (NATs)

You now understand that the way in which you think has an important effect on the way you feel and what you are able to do. Pessimistic, negative thoughts, such as 'I can't cope' or 'I feel terrible', only make you feel more anxious and unhappy and can themselves be a major cause of anxiety or depression. Some of your thoughts may be based on reality, but some will probably be 'guesswork', and you may be jumping to conclusions that paint things blacker than they are. We call these 'negative automatic thoughts' (NATs) because they are unrealistically pessimistic and because they seem to come from nowhere and 'automatically' enter your mind.

Insight

To help you get to know your NATs, keep pen and paper with you as often as you can, to quickly jot down your involuntary thoughts as a way of discovering how much of your thinking is negative. You can later transfer these notes to your workbook.

NATs are just like a chatterbox going on in your head. You haven't invited these thoughts in, and you often wish they would leave, but instead, they stay there, talking at you like a radio you cannot switch off. One error that you can make with NATs is to try to block them out. Yet the more you wish they weren't there, the more they cling to you and dominate your thinking. Why is this?

TRY A SMALL EXPERIMENT

Sit for one minute and during that time you **must not once** think about the word 'giraffe'. Not once.

What happened? We guess that your mind was flooded with giraffes – and that the more you tried to block the thoughts, the more giraffes there were. Now. Prior to this experiment, how many times had you thought of the word 'giraffe' today? We suspect you will say (unless you have just come from the zoo or have a specialist interest in these animals), 'Not once.' Why not? Why, for one full minute, were giraffes all over the place, and yet earlier in the day they had not entered your mind at all? What is the difference here?

The answer, as we are sure you can clearly see and understand, is that once you ascribe a meaning to your thought and try to block it out, it doubles and quadruples in your mind. However, when it doesn't matter whether you have a particular thought or not, when it can come or go as it pleases, you don't notice it, and it doesn't bother you.

This is a very important lesson as CBT is not about controlling your thinking and blocking out negative thoughts. You would have very little success with this (and indeed, you may have tried it in the past and found it is hard work and rarely works for long). CBT is about taking a long, hard look at the validity of your thoughts and then re-evaluating them, offering yourself more rational, balanced alternatives that will have a better place in your mind than faulty, negative thoughts and beliefs.

BECOMING AWARE OF NEGATIVE THOUGHTS

Becoming aware of these thoughts can help you to understand why your moods are negative. This is the first step towards learning to think in a more helpful, positive way. To help you to do this, you first need to know a little more about what negative thoughts 'look like'. The following is a list of characteristics that these thoughts have in common.

- ▶ *They spring to mind without any effort from you.*
- ▶ *They are easy to believe.*
- ▶ *They are often not true.*
- ▶ *They can be difficult to stop.*
- ▶ *They are unhelpful.*
- ▶ *They keep you anxious or depressed and make it difficult to change.*

These negative thoughts may be difficult to spot to start with – you are probably not aware that you have them – and the first step is to learn to recognize them.

Thought Records and negative automatic thoughts

You can examine your NATs by using a Thought Record. You used a simple one in Chapter 4, so you are now familiar with the concept. We will develop the idea of Thought Records with you now, as they are one of the most helpful basic CBT tools for thought challenging. The more you practise filling in Thought Records, the easier it becomes to spot these NATs and to understand the effect they have on how you feel.

Don't worry if you find this difficult at first. It may be quite a new idea to try to remember what you were thinking when you were worried or feeling low, and it may take some practice before you get the hang of it. Next time you find yourself becoming tense, worried or depressed, as soon as you can, sit down and fill in your Thought Record. Describe the physical sensations you experienced and the thoughts that went through your head at the time.

On the right is an example of a good basic Thought Record that we would like you to start using.

FIVE-COLUMN THOUGHT RECORD EXAMPLE

What happened?	How you felt when this happened	What you thought	Alternative thoughts	How do you feel now?
What were you doing or thinking about?	What did you feel? How bad was it? (%)	What exactly were your thoughts? How far did you believe them? (%)	What more positive alternative thoughts can you think of? Try to find as many as you can. How far do you believe each one? (%)	How far do you now still believe your negative thoughts? (%) Do you feel any better emotionally now, i.e. less downhearted? (%)
Staying away with a friend for a few days.	Anxiety (100%) Panic (80%) Fear (100%)	I shall not be able to cope. (100%) If I feel sick, I won't know what to do. (90%) The journey there will be difficult. (60%)	This is a nice opportunity to relax. (60%) I have made perfectly adequate arrangements in case I feel unwell. (60%) It will be a treat to get away to a lovely part of the country. (70%)	The journey was fine. We all got on very well. I did not feel sick or anxious. I managed well in every way. I feel fine. (100%)

Don't worry too much if you are having trouble consigning your negative thoughts to the rubbish bin. This Thought Record is just the start of learning new ways of challenging your self-defeating thinking. Your new beliefs will strengthen in time. This is also just one of many skills you will be learning that will help you to feel much better.

Action plan: Remain more relaxed in these situations, and do not always jump to negative conclusions too quickly.

Thought Records come in a variety of shapes and sizes, and for a variety of different problems. We will refer to some of these later in the book (see Chapter 8). For the moment, the five-column version on page 59 is a good basic model to get used to using. You will find a blank copy to photocopy and use at the back of the book (see the Appendix, page 324).

> **Key point: You are not trying to eliminate your NATs.** You cannot control your thinking by blocking thoughts out (when they tend to multiply instead). What you are doing is allowing the NAT to come, and then invalidating it by finding more balanced, more believable alternatives. As the new, more positive thoughts become stronger, they will become your default thinking and your NATs will fade away of their own accord. Don't fight them; beat them with balanced, rational alternatives.

COMMONLY ASKED QUESTIONS ABOUT THOUGHT RECORDS

1 Am I going to have to write things down forever?

No. The idea of a Thought Record is that, in a way, it is 'brain gym'. It is training your mind to automatically think in a more rational, evaluative way. To start with, this is not easy. Your brain will fight you and come back with all the old negative, unhelpful thoughts that it has stored away for a long time. However, gradually, it will begin to learn the new ways of thinking that you are teaching it. Once this happens, you can throw away your Thought Records and relax in the knowledge that your brain can do this work for itself. You will need to keep working with pen and paper until your brain internalizes the processes, and you find yourself able to use the skills automatically. As you practise, keep in mind the four stages of learning:

i **Being unconsciously incompetent.** *This means that you are getting it all wrong, but are not even aware of it.*
ii **Being consciously incompetent.** *At this point, you have begun to realize that you aren't getting things right, but you don't know what changes to make.*

iii **Being consciously competent.** *This stage involves the hardest work. This is where you are learning how to get things right, but this only happens when you consciously think about these things and do them (perhaps the stage you are at now, as you read this book).*

iv **Being unconsciously competent.** *Bliss! It all just happens. No more Thought Records, no more working at things. You now have a new default where your brain automatically reacts in new, helpful ways without being prodded or coaxed to do so.*

> **Key point:** 'Brain gym' is like pumping iron but instead of getting your muscles working, you are getting your brain to practise new exercises in thinking that will build mental and emotional 'muscle' and develop its ability to think clearly and calmly in difficult situations. In the same way that your physical fitness would improve, so will your mental fitness.

2 When is the best time to fill out my Thought Record?

Many people think that as soon as something relevant has happened, they must rush to find the Thought Record and fill it in. This would be ideal, of course, but we live in the real world where you and your Thought Record may not be geographically close for vast portions of the day – or there will be a variety of other reasons why it might not be feasible to fill it in immediately, such as being busy at work, or socializing with others. Simply do it when you can. As with all other tasks, the more you do it, the quicker the changes will come. Don't let it dominate your life. A good rule of thumb would be to try and take a look at your Thought Record each evening, and recall any instances in the day that you might like to record. You will still have a good enough memory of how you felt and what was going through your mind.

3 What if nothing eventful has happened for me to write down?

Don't make the mistake of thinking that you only fill in your Thought Record after an especially momentous or traumatic event. NATs can catch us at any time. You might be sitting at

home with a cup of coffee when negative thoughts come into
your mind. Write them down. The thought itself doesn't have
to be momentous. Finding yourself feeling depressed because a
friend hasn't phoned or visited is just as valid a thought to
catch and evaluate as those thoughts that accompany redundancy
worries or a relationship break-up. The more you use your
Thought Record, the more quickly your brain will catch on to
this new way of looking at things – large or small.

Talking back to your negative thoughts

Insight

Be on the lookout for the chief characteristics of negative
thinking. NATs are: automatic, distorted, unhelpful,
involuntary, and plausible and the main point is that they
are *unrealistically pessimistic*.

You will see that the Thought Record on page 59 has more
columns than the one in Chapter 4 (page 47). Not only are you
recording your negative thoughts and feelings, but you can now
keep track of them and examine how unrealistic or unhelpful they
are and whether they are useful to you. If they are unrealistic or
unhelpful, you can challenge them with what we call a 'balanced
response'. This is a reply that you can make to these thoughts,
based on firm evidence.

QUESTIONS TO HELP YOU EVALUATE YOUR
NEGATIVE THOUGHTS

It is not always easy to evaluate your thoughts and to come up
with alternatives. Below are some questions that you can ask
yourself, which will help you to uncover at least one, if not several,
balanced responses.

▶ *'Is this really true?'*
▶ *'Is there another way of looking at this?'*

- 'Have I had experiences that suggest this thought is not true all the time?'
- 'When I'm not feeling the way I do now, do I look at similar experiences differently?'
- 'When I've had feelings like this in the past, what thoughts did I have that made me feel better?'
- 'Are there things that contradict my negative thoughts that I might be discounting?'
- 'Are there any positives or strengths in either myself or the situation that I haven't thought of or that I'm ignoring?'
- 'What have I learned from previous experiences that could help me now?'
- 'Am I jumping to any conclusions about the situation?'
- 'What is the worst thing that could happen if my fears come true?' 'Could I live through it?' 'Would it really change my life?' 'Would I still care about it in a few years' time?'
- 'Am I blaming myself over a situation that is not completely within my control?'
- 'Does ... really mean that ...?'
- 'Am I really 100 per cent certain that ..., or is this just one of many possibilities?'
- 'If a close friend or another person I care about had this thought, what would I say to them?'
- 'What would the people who care about me say about this negative thought?' 'What evidence might they point out to me to suggest the thoughts aren't 100 per cent true?'

Now write down any appropriate answers in your Thought Record. By now, you should have a better idea of how answering your negative thoughts in a more helpful, realistic way can help you to cope with your worries.

'But it really is that way'

NATs are not necessarily always invalid. Many people think that the point of CBT is to identify your negative thoughts as faulty or skewed, and then to search for more positive replacements that will, in turn, make you feel better. While this can sometimes be the case, it is not always so. CBT's role is essentially to help you to critically evaluate your NATs in the light of possible alternatives, and to come to a balanced and rational conclusion about the strength of their validity.

THE DIFFICULTY OF FINDING ALTERNATIVE THOUGHTS

Sometimes it can be very hard to find balanced alternatives to the negative thoughts you have, because you actually are in a jam or a tight spot. You did give in poor work when you got lambasted by the boss, or you did behave selfishly when you might have been kind.

An action plan to help you
You will notice at the bottom of your Thought Record that there is a small section entitled 'Action plan'. When, having looked at all the options, you are faced with accepting that your negative thoughts are very close to the mark, your solution is to develop an action plan. You need to ask yourself what you might be able to do to mitigate what has happened, and identify a variety of different options for putting things right.

Insight
Sometimes negative thoughts are an understandable reaction to a sticky position we find ourselves in. At such times, rather than trying to find alternative viewpoints, it is more productive to employ coping statements as a strategy to face up to the problem.

COPING STATEMENTS AS A POSITIVE TOOL

Occasionally, simply acknowledging the truth of the predicament you find yourself in and using coping statements rather than alternative thoughts can be the most helpful thing. Here are some examples of coping statements that, while acknowledging that your negative thinking may have some validity, nonetheless still enable you to deal with your worries in a more positive and constructive way.

- 'I'm going to face this problem situation so that I can practise coping better.'
- 'It may not work completely, but the important thing is to practise and build up my confidence.'
- 'I know that worry makes me feel worse. I know that I can manage my feelings.'
- 'I've been in this position before and have come out of it in one piece.'
- 'I know things will improve the more I get used to coping with my difficulties.'
- 'I'll feel proud of myself when I feel myself getting calmer and more confident.'
- 'It feels good learning how to control worrying feelings.'
- 'I'm deliberately going to change how I feel.'

Insight

The more you get to know about your problematic thought patterns, the less hold they are likely to have over you. Don't let the fact that it may take time and perseverance deter you.

PRACTICE MAKES PERFECT

The key to being able to think in a more balanced way is to keep practising. Every time you become aware of negative thoughts going through your mind, stop yourself and think of a more balanced, realistic response. When preparing to go into a situation that makes you anxious or worried, think about how you will answer any negative thoughts before, during and afterwards.

MY ALTERNATIVE THOUGHTS DON'T HELP ME FEEL BETTER

Writing out more balanced, optimistic alternatives to your NATs may cause you to think more broadly than you have done before – but you may also find that, on balance, you don't really believe what you are writing, and your NAT stays firmly entrenched in your mind. If you find this to be the case:

▶ *Consider whether your alternative thoughts are specific and realistic, or whether they are 'Pollyanna thinking'. For example, 'I'm sure everything will turn out wonderfully in spite of everything' or 'It won't matter how bad things get, I will handle them'. Make your alternative thoughts something you have genuine belief in. If your negative thought is, 'Nobody likes me', you are more likely to believe an alternative thought along the lines of, 'I'm sure some people like me at least some of the time' than an extreme alternative such as, 'Of course everybody likes me'. Be thoughtful when considering alternatives. Ask yourself, 'Could I have at least some faith in this idea?'*

▶ *You may need to test out your alternative thoughts in order to increase your belief in them. You can do this by thinking about the evidence you may have to support them, or by using behavioural experiments that will give you more concrete evidence about them. For example, if your negative thoughts are that no one will speak to you at a function as you consider yourself to be very boring, you might wish to consider what happened the last time you went out. Were you really on your own all night? Did no one speak to you at all? What about other occasions when you have mixed socially? What happened then? Or you could treat going to the function as an experiment. You could decide that you will try to be as warm and friendly as you can, and see what the outcome is. What did you discover? Were you totally right? Did anything occur to destabilize your, 'I'm totally boring' view?*

EARLY DIFFICULTIES ARE NATURAL

We cover both aspects of looking for evidence and behavioural testing in more depth in Chapters 8 and 9. For the moment, be assured that it is not unusual to have difficulty finding any strength of belief in your alternative thoughts while this is a new skill for you. This will change as you become more experienced and your skills become more broad-based.

HOMEWORK

We suggest that you practise filling in Thought Records as often as you can. However, don't do it 'just for the sake of it'. This is about quality, not quantity. It is better to make half a dozen entries, where you have really thought hard about identifying the correct 'strong' thought and emotion and then worked equally hard on your challenges and rebuttals, than to write up pages without anything really sinking in. Refer back to Chapter 4 as you do this work, and make sure that you become familiar with the rationale behind it all.

Look again at the 'four stages of learning' on pages 60–1. Stage iii is the one that most people get stuck on. This is the 'hard work stage' where nothing seems to happen without constant vigilance and attention to the principles of change. It is also the stage where, initially, there can seem to be lots of input and little reward. This is where many people give up. You can actually use your Thought Record to record these views; for example, 'I'm working so hard on this, but notice very little change.' Is there a more constructive way of looking at this that may keep you going? Perhaps, 'Most things require a lot of input at the start without seeing much in the way of results. Eventually that changes and things all start to come together.' You can also look for other examples of things that were hard work at the start. Why did your parents not stop you when you were trying to learn to walk, for instance? All you did was fall over and hurt yourself, time and time again. What did they know that you didn't? Recall learning to drive. For most people, doing six things at once seemed simply impossible. Do you even think about any of these actions and reactions as you drive along now? Encourage yourself with examples such as these that are personal to you, and they will keep you going.

If anything is still puzzling you, read over again what we have taught you and ensure that you understand it fully before you use up precious and valuable time on the written exercises.

SUMMARY

In this chapter you have built on your learning about eliciting your thoughts and emotions, and you have learned to begin challenging the validity of the thoughts that leave you feeling bad about things.

▶ *Thought challenging is by no means the 'be all and end all' of making constructive changes – there is much more that you can do, as you will read in further chapters – but it is a powerful start, and will help you to evaluate situations far more intelligently.*
▶ *As you become acquainted with these skills and practise them more, you will find that it becomes much easier. You will be able to put aside your paperwork and rely on your brain to work in the right way of its own accord.*

THINGS TO REMEMBER

▶ In this chapter you were encouraged to test the validity of your thinking by questioning your thinking style. For instance: Are you cautious, or overly pessimistic? Are you hounded by habitual negative thoughts?

▶ Negative automatic thoughts (NATs) are unrealistic, pessimistic thoughts that come from nowhere and permeate your brain. They tell you things like, 'I'll never come to anything' or 'No one likes me' or 'I can't cope', and can be a major cause of anxiety and depression.

▶ It's a waste of time trying to control or block out NATs as they are impossible to stop. Instead, CBT recommends examining the validity of your thoughts, then re-evaluating them and creating more balanced alternative beliefs.

▶ As a main tool of CBT, the Thought Record builds thought challenging skills. Filling in a Thought Record makes it easier to identify NATs and to understand how they affect your moods. You can use them anytime you feel troubled, tense or anxious.

▶ Coping statements are a simple way of acknowledging a difficult predicament you find yourself in and are an alternative to trying to create a more positive view of a situation. As a statement of intent, a coping statement begins a process of accepting responsibility and working on the problem.

▶ You will find alternative thoughts most helpful when they are specific rather than general 'Pollyanna thinking', such as 'I'm sure everything will turn out well in spite of everything'.

6

More on moods

In this chapter you will learn:
- *to better identify your moods*
- *easy ways to differentiate between thoughts and feelings*
- *to become more emotionally aware*
- *to use a Thought Record to ensure you are working on the right mood that is a good 'match' with your thoughts*
- *to be honest with yourself about your feelings.*

> *There can be no knowledge without emotion. We may be aware of the truth, yet until we have felt its force, it is not ours. To the cognition of the brain must be added the experience of the soul.*
>
> Arnold Bennett, novelist and playwright (1867–1931)

Insight
An awareness of the idiosyncratic meanings you attribute to your experiences, and observing the constant interplay between your thoughts, moods and behaviour are central to understanding yourself, which is the foundation for positive change.

Focusing on moods

As you have learned throughout the book there is a constant interplay between thoughts, feelings and behaviour.

Chapters 4 and 5 focused on identifying, evaluating and challenging negative thoughts. Up to now, we have made a few assumptions about moods: that you will know what they are and know how to identify them. In this chapter, we look at moods more closely, since it is our moods that drive us.

> **Key point: Always keep sight of the mood/thought/behaviour connection.** Now that you have started using a basic Thought Record, keep one beside you constantly as you work through the remainder of this book. Make photocopies of the Thought Record in the Appendix (page 324), and practise writing down thoughts, feelings and situations that reflect what we are working on with you. Even though you are looking at moods now, always ask yourself what was going through your mind to engender the mood. The more you practise this, the more it will become your default.

IDENTIFYING MOODS

Moods are not always as easy to identify as you might think. Many clients we have worked with have discovered only through using cognitive behavioural therapy (CBT) detective work that they have actually suffered from low mood or depression for years. They failed to recognize it since they were unaware of what it might be like to feel differently. Sometimes, simply feeling tired all the time can be indicative of depression; or feeling constantly tense and wound up can be caused by a generally anxious state of mind.

Before you can make changes, you need to be able to do two things:

1 *Be aware of your emotions.*
2 *Identify the appropriate emotions for the particular situation you are in.*

Your first indicator

The first thing to consider when identifying your mood is how your body feels. What is going on when your heart starts beating a little fast, or your breathing is shallow? Notice changes in your body that will give you an indication that you are beginning to feel an emotion of some sort.

Although we are focusing on the detrimental effects of negative emotions in this book, considering the physical effect of positive emotions will also be helpful. Think about a time when something good happened. Perhaps you received a letter giving good news about a job application, or an unexpected invitation to a pleasurable event. Recall how you felt on such an occasion, and the effect it might have had on your body. Think about flushed cheeks, an automatic smile, tenseness deserting you, and your heart beating faster with joy rather than dread. These are all bodily sensations connected to positive emotion – and they let you know what your feelings are quickly and easily.

Simple exercises to help you

1 *Write down three (or more) recent situations when you have received some good or bad news.*
   ▷ *Recall the thoughts that went through your mind.*
   ▷ *Recall the physical sensations you felt.*
   ▷ *Identify the mood these sensations engendered.*
2 *Become much more aware of your feelings at any given point in time. Specifically, you could spend the next week stopping for a moment three times a day and asking yourself, 'How am I feeling now?' Not 'What am I thinking?' but 'How am I feeling?' Just go straight to the emotion.*

BECOMING MORE EMOTIONALLY AWARE

Becoming more emotionally aware is a huge first step in learning to manage your emotions. It is a great skill, not simply when things are going badly and you need to work on that, but in life generally. We call this being 'emotionally intelligent'. In simple terms, this means being able to:

▶ *identify correctly what you are feeling (it is very easy to get this wrong)*
▶ *evaluate the appropriateness of the emotion to the situation*
▶ *manage how you feel so that inappropriate emotions don't 'run away' with you and inhibit rational and appropriate thoughts and responses.*

Knowing how you feel

Sometimes it is not easy to ascribe emotions to your thoughts. Emotions can be a little more comprehensive than you might imagine. For example, you could describe yourself as 'happy'. Yet under the 'feeling happy' umbrella is a variety of what you might call 'meta-emotions' – jolly, playful, jubilant, thrilled, exhilarated.

Here are some suggestions to help you identify your emotions.

Happy	Sad	Angry	Afraid
satisfied	depressed	resentful	apprehensive
pleased	melancholy	indignant	scared
cheerful	sombre	wrathful	terrified
inspired	dreary	frustrated	insecure
exhilarated	flat	seething	threatened
elated	discontented	stubborn	anxious

Hurt	Doubtful	Affectionate	Fearless
injured	distrustful	loving	confident
crushed	uncertain	tender	determined
offended	pessimistic	passionate	secure
heartbroken	hesitant	warm	brave
distressed	indecisive	caring	bold
pained	dubious	empathetic	impulsive

And there are many, many more emotions.

Insight

The words we use speak volumes about the emotion that drives them. Think, for example, how much more emotionally loaded the word 'terrified' is in comparison to 'frightened'.

Key point: 'Cognitions' are usually described by phrases or sentences. 'Moods' are usually described by one word only. For example, saying 'I feel upset by what he has done' is expressing a thought, not a mood. The mood will be one word – which in this case could be anger, disappointment, despair or hurt, for example, depending on other aspects of the situation.

BE AS HONEST AS YOU CAN

A common difficulty that everyone has is being honest with themselves. Even when you are working to uncover emotions that you know will be helpful, it can still be difficult to own up to yourself that you feel guilty, selfish, angry, ashamed or jealous. You may be tempted – even within the privacy of your own mind – to excuse how you feel by giving a different label to the moods that are driving you. If you find yourself feeling this way, you can use the thought-challenging skills that you have now learned (see Chapter 5) to work through this. For example:

My NAT: 'I don't want to admit to myself that I am jealous or selfish. It simply makes me feel bad about myself, so I would rather not go there.'

My rational responses:

▶ *'There is nothing wrong in feeling such emotions. We are all fallible human beings, and we all, from time to time, succumb to selfishness, jealousy and other emotions that we are not too proud of.'*
▶ *'Simply recognizing these emotions and admitting to them is half the battle. Many people wouldn't.'*
▶ *'Once I have properly owned these emotions I can begin to make changes. If I don't do this, they will stick around and everything will stay the same.'*

Have you got the right mood?

Don't be too hasty in mood identification. Always double-check and look for a mood underneath the one that too easily presents itself.

Case study

Paula was in the waiting area of her local hospital, waiting to see the cardiac consultant. She had been suffering from breathlessness for a while, and what she perceived to be an irregular heartbeat, and so had arranged for a variety of tests to be done. She had now been called to see a consultant, and she was very aware that this might

(Contd)

mean she was about to hear some serious news. As the appointment neared, anxiety about the outcome gnawed away at Paula. Finally, as she sat waiting to see the consultant, she could scarcely breathe with anxiety and worry.

As Paula sat waiting, a young man came and sat next to her. He started chatting inconsequentially, but Paula didn't want to talk. The young man persisted, and Paula became more and more frustrated with his incessant chatter. Finally, following a particularly inane remark, Paula exploded with anger. She shouted at the young man, telling him how annoying he was and couldn't he see that she didn't want to talk, and asking whether he was completely insensitive. Finally, before the shocked and bemused young man could respond, Paula got up and marched across to another part of the waiting area, and angrily sat down.

Once she had calmed down, Paula was horrified by her anger. Why had she been so unreasonable, so intolerant? What was going on? Did she have anger management problems that needed to be addressed? Perhaps she would need to look into that.

Reading the above case study, what would you say was Paula's driving emotion? Was it anger? Was it frustration or intolerance? Now imagine setting down Paula's mood in a Thought Record.

Situation:	**Waiting in outpatient department to see a cardiac consultant. A young man starts chatting to me.**
Thoughts:	**'I wish this young man would stop nattering on. It's driving me crazy.' (60%)**
	'I wonder how much longer I'll have to wait.' (40%)
	'I am very worried about my cardiac tests.' (100%)
Emotions:	**Anger (70%), frustration (50%), distress (80%), high anxiety (100%)**

By setting the problem out as a Thought Record, can you see what were Paula's *causal thoughts*, and the emotions engendered by those specific thoughts? In spite of the fact that Paula got very angry, and was extremely distressed at having to wait to see the consultant, the strong emotion was anxiety, related not to her thoughts about the young man, but to her thoughts about her illness. Using the 'meta' label, we can say that Paula's anger, frustration and distress were, infact, caused by the primary emotion of high anxiety.

What skill was especially helpful in working this out? You can see that by rating the strength of both Paula's thoughts and Paula's emotions, we were able to discover what was bothering her the most, as well as making the right 'match' between thoughts and feelings.

HOMEWORK

If you have a problem identifying specific emotions, practise this. Look again at the list given earlier in the chapter (page 74), use your workbook and write down as many more emotions as you can think of in, say, five minutes. Give five minutes each day for a week to add to this list. If you have few new emotions to add, don't worry. This exercise is primarily to help you get used to being aware of emotions and to spend more time thinking about them generally.

Use a Thought Record to help you identify the driving emotion. Be completely honest with yourself. Practise the skill of rating thoughts and emotions to find the strongest and best match.

SUMMARY

In this chapter we have focused on moods and identifying them more exactly than you may have previously considered.

▶ *You have discovered a variety of different ways to identify moods:*
   1 *Observing your body's physical sensations and reactions to situations you find yourself in.*

2 Becoming familiar with the wide variety of emotions that exist, and the idea of meta-emotions: those underneath the initial emotion.

3 Knowing that a mood is usually described adequately in one word. Where you need a sentence, you are describing a thought – even when you begin the sentence with, 'I felt...'

▶ You can double-check the primary mood by using a Thought Record to assess the full gamut of your thoughts and emotions, and then to match the strongest of each. This highlights the importance of rating thoughts and moods to help you both measure them and match them.

▶ Always be honest with yourself about how you feel or you will not be able to make effective changes.

THINGS TO REMEMBER

▶ *To get to know your moods and emotions you need to give them some attention. When you become more aware of your moods you can then match appropriate emotions to the particular situation.*

▶ *Your bodily response is a prime indicator to consider when identifying your mood – for example, your heart may race, indicating anxiety.*

▶ *Remember you can, at any time, use a simple but highly effective three-part exercise to help you understand your mood. Thinking of a particular situation:*
  1 *Recall what you were thinking at the time.*
  2 *Recall what physical sensations you experienced at the time.*
  3 *Identify the mood associated with the above thoughts and sensations.*

▶ *Becoming familiar with moods and being able to match an appropriate emotion with the particular situation is about developing 'emotional intelligence'.*

7

....

Recognizing distorted thinking patterns

In this chapter you will learn:
- *that negative automatic thoughts can fall into a number of basic thinking styles*
- *how thinking styles can distort reality*
- *that recognizing thinking styles is a powerful tool.*

> *You are today where your thoughts have brought you. You will be, tomorrow, where your thoughts take you.*
>
> James Allen, US author

Faulty thinking styles

Building on the work you have already done on identifying and understanding your negative thoughts, we will now introduce you to a simple way of recognizing and labelling your negative automatic thoughts (NATs) within some general groups that you will find easy to spot as you practise your awareness of them.

Many of the negative thoughts and feelings that you have about yourself are caused by what we call 'cognitive bias' – patterns of distorted thinking. Learning to recognize these patterns is a useful skill as you will then be able to recognize a great many of your individual NATs as one of these thinking styles. Then, challenging them becomes much easier.

Recognizing distorted thinking is not always easy. People assume that all their thinking is rational and correct even when it is negative. In a good frame of mind it may be (though not always). Yet when you are in a poor frame of mind, your thinking can become distorted without you realizing this is happening.

Insight

Distorted thinking is inaccurate or exaggerated where people think in terms of absolutes with no grey areas.

COMPOUNDING THINKING ERRORS

The problem is that once you start making thinking errors, you tend to 'stick with them'. They become assumptions and beliefs (more on these soon) that are retained, unless an effort is made to identify and change them.

Psychologists have identified a number of common thinking errors that most people make some of the time (and some people make all of the time). If you know what these are, and recognize them, it will make your thought-challenging rebuttals much easier to formulate. Read through the thinking errors below and place a tick against any you feel apply to you.

Generalizing the specific
You generalize the specific when you come to a general conclusion based on a single incident or piece of evidence. You use words such as 'always' and 'never', 'nobody' and 'everyone' to make an all-embracing rule out of a specific situation. If you make a

mistake, you tell yourself that you are hopeless. If you get rejected, you tell yourself that you are unlovable. For example:

▸ *You have a minor car accident and you decide you are a dangerous driver (and must never drive again).*
▸ *One failed recipe means you cannot cook and wobbly stitching means you cannot sew.*
▸ *Someone treats you unfairly and you say, 'Nobody likes me.'*

Key point: We all use distorted thinking patterns a great deal of the time. With this thought in mind, look at what you have already written in your Thought Record. Have you made any generalizations about yourself or your behaviour? If so, be sure to come up with an alternative thought that is specific.

Mind reading

This is one of the most common thinking errors people make when self-esteem is low. Without other people saying so, you 'know' what they are thinking and why they act the way they do. In particular, you are able to divine how people are feeling towards you. This is fatal to self-esteem because you believe that others agree with your negative opinions of yourself. Yet you are jumping to conclusions without any real evidence – and, for some reason, you only seem to have the gift of mind-reading *negative* views. Interestingly, you never seem to develop a talent for mind-reading positive thoughts! For example:

▸ *'I know he thinks I am boring.'*
▸ *'I can tell she doesn't like me.'*
▸ *'I'm sure they don't really want me in their group.'*

Magnification and filtering

You take the negative details from a situation and then magnify them, while at the same time filtering out all the positive aspects. You focus on the one thing that went badly in an otherwise successful presentation. You dismiss all your achievements and focus bleakly on the one thing that you are not so good at. For example, you have dressed beautifully for a formal evening and your partner pays you the well-deserved compliment of saying how nice you look. However, as you leave the room they mention that your hem is not quite straight at the back. You now feel that you no longer look lovely, and that the evening will be spoiled while you worry about this hem. The fact that you look stunning apart from this quite passes you by.

Polarized thinking

Sometimes called 'all or nothing thinking', you think of people, situations or events in extremes such as good or bad – 'I must be perfect or I am a failure', 'If I'm not beautiful, I'm ugly'. There is no middle ground. The problem is that you usually find yourself at the negative end of your polarized extremes. So if you cannot be all good, you must be all bad. For example:

- ▶ *If I am not totally successful at my job I am a complete failure at it.*
- ▶ *Unless I can get top marks in the exam, there is no point in sitting it.*
- ▶ *Unless I am liked by everyone I am an unpopular person.*

Catastrophizing

You expect disaster. You believe that things will almost certainly go wrong if they possibly can – and that if they do you will not be able to cope. Not only do you over-estimate the likelihood of calamity, you multiply it by your perceived idea of the catastrophic consequences. Whenever you notice or hear about a problem, you start on 'What if's' and then decide that if this terrible thing did happen to you, you would not be able to cope. For example:

- ▶ *'What if tragedy strikes? I will lose everything and life as I know it will be over.'*
- ▶ *'What if it happens to me? Some people might cope, but I know I would not be able to.'*
- ▶ *'I know this will turn out badly. It will be just another thing I cannot deal with.'*

Personalization

This involves thinking that everything people do or say is some kind of reaction to you. For example:

▶ *Perhaps your partner mentions that the home is looking a little untidy. You will immediately 'read' this comment as a criticism of your housekeeping skills.*

▶ *Someone mentions that the work team hasn't achieved its targets this month. You instantly decide that this comment is really directed at you personally.*

▶ *You find yourself becoming unnecessarily defensive and possibly even causing ill feeling by taking someone's passing remark as personal criticism.*

Blaming

This is the opposite of personalization. You hold other people, organizations – or even the universe – responsible for your problems. You feel unable to change your views or your circumstances, as you see yourself as a victim of other people's thoughtlessness and meanness. For example:

▶ *'She has made me feel terrible.'*

▶ *'That company ruined my life.'*

▶ *'If he hadn't done what he did, I wouldn't have reacted that way.'*

Self-blame

In this case, instead of feeling a victim, you feel responsible for the pain and happiness of everyone around you. For example:

▶ *If your daughter misses a lift taking her to a special occasion, you feel totally to blame for not having chivvied her along (even though she is 17 and has taken the whole afternoon getting ready).*

▶ *If your firm loses an important client, you will find a way to believe that something you did caused this.*

Rigid thinking

You feel resentful because you think you know what's right, but other people won't agree with you. You continually attempt to prove that your opinions and actions are correct. You expect other people to change their views and actions if you pressure or cajole them enough. You try to change people in this way when you believe your hopes for happiness depend entirely on their behaving differently. For example:

▶ 'I can't understand why people don't see things my way. There must be something wrong with me.'
▶ 'I can't understand why people don't see things my way. There must be something wrong with them.'

Insight

You might identify with some or many of the above. Don't be alarmed. Once again let us reassure you that these are common types of 'cognitive bias'. We all tend to think like this to some extent or other, especially when we are in a debilitated state of mind. But distorted thinking is destructive and requires some work to shift.

A POSITIVE WAY FORWARD

While it can be hard to discover that much of your thinking is biased by negative distortions, acknowledging this is the first step to change. The next step is to use this knowledge to help you tackle your thoughts. How? By working to familiarize yourself with these cognitive distortions. Once you understand them and can recall them easily, you can begin to spot them when they crop up. They are easier for you to identify than some of your NATs because of the patterns they follow, and you can take an, 'Oh, I recognize what I'm doing!' attitude to them and then rethink what has actually happened.

Most people, when presented with these styles of distorted thinking and asked to acknowledge any that apply to them, find themselves actually smiling as they recognize these common thinking errors. They are normal! We all do it. Now you can become more aware of them and knock them on the head quite easily.

HOMEWORK

Over the next week, use your workbook to keep a diary recording your negative thoughts. Against each thought, write down which cognitive bias applies to it. For example:

Negative thought	Cognitive bias
'I cannot cook at all. My beef Wellington was so dry.'	Generalizing the specific
'I know they all thought I was a fool at the meeting.'	Polarized thinking Mind reading
'I wouldn't have acted that way if John had been a bit nicer to me.'	Blaming

SUMMARY

We have spent time in this chapter focusing on distorted thinking styles – cognitive bias – because understanding them and being able to identify them is extremely helpful for several reasons.

▶ *A great many of your negative thoughts will fall into one of the categories referred to in this chapter. This will make it much easier to recognize where you are going wrong with your thinking, and to put it right.*

▶ *The very familiarity of these thinking errors may be quite comforting. Most people make them at some point or other, many quite often. Becoming more aware of them in day-to-day life will give you confidence that you can spot them, challenge them, and re-evaluate them without too much difficulty.*

THINGS TO REMEMBER

▶ *Recognizing your distorted ways of thinking can be hard because they may have become habitual, firm beliefs and assumptions that seem rational to you.*

▶ *Familiarizing yourself with some common thinking errors will help you in the task of challenging negative, pessimistic thoughts.*

▶ *Distorted thinking categories include:*
   1 *Mind-reading – when you are convinced that you know for sure what other people are thinking, without actually hearing them say anything that would back your assumptions.*
   2 *Polarized thinking – 'all or nothing thinking' when you think of yourself, other people or a situation as either 'all bad' or 'all good'. For example, 'I must be the best at everything or I am a failure'.*

▶ *By understanding the human tendency to think in particular negative ways, you will be able to recognize these distorted thought patterns in your own thinking and learn to challenge and re-evaluate them.*

8

Where's the evidence?

In this chapter you will learn:
- *to develop solid, evidence-based, alternative views to challenge your negative automatic thoughts*
- *to use a seven-column Thought Record to help you practise*
- *to see negative thoughts as mere 'possibilities' rather than facts*
- *to seek evidence that you may presently discount as it is outside your current awareness.*

Don't accept your dog's admiration as conclusive evidence that you are wonderful.

Anne Landers, US advice columnist (1918–2002)

Checking for evidence

What goes through you, mind when you challenge your negative automatic thoughts (NATs) and write down, in your Thought Record, more balanced, rational alternatives? Many people write diligently, but the thought in their mind is, 'I don't *really* believe any of this – what I really still believe are my negative thoughts.'

HOW CAN YOU STRENGTHEN YOUR BELIEF IN YOUR ALTERNATIVE VIEWS?

There is one extremely helpful tool – regarded by cognitive behavioural therapy (CBT) practitioners as one of the most important and valuable 'thought shifters' around. It asks a simple question: 'If this is really so, where's the evidence?'

Insight

Finding evidence (hard facts) to support your thinking will strengthen a belief.

Case study

Jenny was concerned about her job. She had heard that some redundancies were possible at her firm and she started thinking about her own performance and whether her boss might find a reason to get rid of her. The more she thought about it, the more weaknesses she came up with – being late for an important meeting last week, failing to sign up a new client company that had looked promising. Was she losing her grip?

Over lunch with her colleague Anne, Jenny voiced her concerns. Anne asked Jenny why she was coming to this negative conclusion, and Jenny cited what had happened – her 'evidence' for her pessimistic thinking. Anne expressed surprise. 'But Jenny, several people were late for that meeting due to the tube strike – it couldn't be helped. And while it was disappointing to lose the client, that may not have been your fault at all – you made an excellent presentation, and there were many possible reasons why the client may not have gone ahead. Now think of all the new business you have brought in to the firm this year, which you seem to be forgetting.' In essence, Anne was presenting Jenny with evidence to contradict Jenny's self-defeating thoughts. Yet Jenny had not thought of this herself because she was too focused on her negative views of her abilities.

This is what can happen to you when your mood is low or your thoughts are filled with anxiety. You focus on the negative and ignore the positive evidence. So we want you to introduce this element into your Thought Record.

> **Key point: Always ask yourself 'What evidence do I have?'** Having to provide this will help you move towards better-balanced thinking, and to believe it more strongly.

Exercise
To help you to practise this skill, look back to your most recent negative thought.

▶ *Ask yourself what evidence you had to support it.*
▶ *If you were a barrister in a court of law, could you provide evidence against it?*
▶ *What would you say?*

GIVING EVIDENCE IN YOUR THOUGHT RECORD

We did mention that your basic Thought Record would expand and change as you learned more CBT skills and techniques. Think of your Thought Record as a 'flexible friend' – it can be adapted to accommodate a wide variety of thought challenging and behavioural testing (see Chapter 9). What you have now (see opposite) is a full, basic, seven-column Thought Record. The two extra 'Evidence' columns were developed and incorporated into Thought Records by US clinical psychologist Christine Padesky to help her clients construct a more stable, evidence-based challenge to their negative thinking, rather than simply trying to make themselves believe something purely on the basis that it 'sounded right'.

SEVEN-COLUMN THOUGHT RECORD

Look closely at the new version of your Thought Record. The first extra column asks you to find evidence to support your NATs, and the second to support your alternative, balanced responses.

What happened?	What you thought when this happened (How strongly do you believe this? 1–10)	How you felt (How strongly did you feel this? 1–10)	Evidence to support your negative thoughts	Alternative thoughts (Generate at least two or three alternatives. Rate your belief in them 1–10)	Evidence to support your alternative thoughts	How do you feel now? (Rate any possible change now you have looked at things a little more positively. 1–10)

Why look for evidence to support negative thinking first? It might seem to make more sense to simply find evidence to support an alternative, more positive thought than to search for evidence to support your negative thinking. However, we ask you to do this first because, at this stage, you will have a strong belief that your negative thoughts are true. To start by looking for evidence that these strong thoughts are not true may be difficult and you may lack conviction. It is too far away from how you may presently see things. If you truly believe that you are a bad parent, for example, you will find it easier to search out evidence to support that view, and then to question the validity of that evidence, than to simply search for opposites. For instance, such evidence might include, 'I shout at my kids a lot', 'I don't spend enough time with them', 'Other parents seem to do more', and so on. When you start to find more optimistic alternatives, you now have something to work with. You might be able to say to yourself, 'I only shout at my kids when I'm tired, and lots of parents do that' or 'When I am not actually with them, I am working for their benefit' or 'Some parents may do more than me, but many do a lot less'. You should then be able to find evidence that will support these alternatives and make sense.

You may find it harder than you think to come up with solid reasoning. Where you consider that you have evidence to support your NATs (which you may well do) then you need to support them with:

- *data*
- *facts*
- *experiences*.

You cannot support them simply with opinions – either yours or anyone else's. Good questions to ask yourself before you commit your evidence to paper are:

- *'What would a judge think of my evidence?'*
- *'Would "Oh, I just can't help thinking that way" stand up in a court of law?'*
- *'Would the judge accept it or throw it out?'*

Finding evidence for your alternative thinking will be easier when you have worked through the other Thought Record columns. For example, imagine you have looked in the mirror just before going out and thought, 'I look dreadful.' You may have several suggestions for evidence of this:

▶ *'My hair's a mess.'*
▶ *'My clothes are all wrong.'*
▶ *'I'm overweight.'*

An alternative thought might be, 'I really don't look too bad.' But the strength of your belief in this would probably be weak. Your belief will become much stronger if you write down any evidence that might genuinely support your more balanced thought. Such evidence may be along the lines of:

▶ *'My partner always tells me I look nice when I get dressed up.'*
▶ *'My best friend has asked to borrow this dress next Saturday.'*
▶ *'I have lost 5 lb in the last two weeks.'*

As you get used to finding evidence for your thinking, it will loosen your NATs' hold on your mind through tangible, logical argument, rather than simply repeating optimistic alternatives that you don't *truly* feel hold water. This is a very powerful skill.

SEARCH HARD

Finding evidence can – and should – involve effort on your part. It is the most important tool you will have among your CBT skills for successfully challenging and replacing invalid thoughts. Don't simply give it lip service. Think of the painstaking way that detectives search for clues and evidence to help them come to the correct conclusion about a crime.

Focusing bias

When people think in a negative way about something, they tend to focus on and believe in data that supports this view. Evidence to support an alternative view can often be outside of their awareness and they need to search hard for it. It will be there, but they will have been by-passing it and discounting it. Unless you activate your memory, unless you really get it to work hard for you and encourage it to search for other experiences and explanations that may contradict your negative view, your mood will also remain negative.

Become a 'Columbo'

Some of you may recall a popular 1970s TV detective – Columbo. His trademark was weighing up evidence in a very simple way. As he would stand, scratching his chin in puzzlement, he would say, 'Hmm ... now. If that was thus, and this is so, then how can such and such be right?' Columbo usually knew exactly where he was going with his reasoning, but his goal was always to make the villain become involved in the idea that, whatever story he had made up, the evidence simply and indisputably contradicted it. Become your own Columbo.

Insight

When you weigh up evidence, you become aware of contradictions in your assumptions – thoughts you have held to be true. You look at your idiosyncratic interpretations of events, question your rationale, and learn to base your beliefs on factual evidence. Techniques you can use in your investigations include a version of the Thought Record and conducting a survey. You will find a simple way of conducting a survey in Chapter 11.

David lived in the countryside with his family. While he loved it there, as a young man he wanted to activate an independent social life and be free of asking his parents for lifts everywhere. So he was keen to learn to drive as soon as he was old enough. David's parents suggested that, if he worked to save for a second-hand car himself, they would match his savings 50/50, and as soon as he could afford a car, they would also pay for his driving lessons.

Finally, the day arrived for David's first driving lesson. Because of his lifestyle circumstances, this was hugely important to him and he set great store by it. He had 12 lessons in all, practised with his mum and dad between times, and his driving instructor was extremely complimentary about David's abilities.

On the day of his driving test, David was extremely nervous and anxious. This unfortunately prevented him from doing his best, and although he tried hard, he was devastated to be told he had failed. He simply couldn't come to terms with it. All those lessons and all that practice, and now this. In a fit of disappointment, he threw his car keys over the hedge and decided to forget the whole thing.

Let's now put David's negativity and disappointment onto a Thought Record

Seven-column Thought Record for case study: David
From the Thought Record on page 96 you can see where David could take his negativity and disappointment, using the option to find evidence to support his thoughts, rather than simply making presumptions about their validity. You can also see how David could help himself feel a lot better – and hopefully retake and pass his test next time.

What happened?	What you thought when this happened (How strongly do you believe this? 1–10)	How you felt (How strongly did you feel this? 1–10)	Evidence to support your negative thought	Alternative thoughts (Generate at least two or three alternatives. Rate your belief in them 1–10)	Evidence to support your alternative thoughts	How do you feel now? (Rate any possible change now you have looked at things a little more positively. 1–10)
Failed driving test.	Failing my test after all those lessons and practices means I'll never learn to drive. (Generalization) (8)	Hopeless (9) Depressed (8)	After ten lessons, and lots of practice, I still could not pass.	This does not mean I will never pass (6) Many people fail their test first time and I was extremely nervous. (6)	My instructor has been very complimentary. My cousin failed his test twice and then passed. My best friend passed first time but needed 15 lessons.	A little more optimistic. I've expected too much too soon and been unrealistic. I will book another test. (9)

HOMEWORK

Practise searching for evidence using your seven-column Thought Record. Follow through the example of David and then – using the copy in the Appendix (page 325) – fill in the record using NATs you have recently had yourself. Always ask, 'Where's the evidence?' As ever, the more you practise, the easier it becomes and the quicker you will begin to feel better about yourself and your own specific difficulties.

SUMMARY

In this chapter you have learned a key CBT skill: asking, 'Where's the evidence?'

▸ *You have been introduced to a seven-column Thought Record that specifically asks you to provide evidence to back up both your negative thoughts and your alternative reasoning. We have suggested that you regard both of these as 'possibilities' rather than facts, so that you can see what evidence backs up which possibility to the greater degree.*

▸ *Remember that evidence must be based on solid data and experience. It doesn't matter how much you 'feel' this way or that; unless you can verify facts, it doesn't count.*

▸ *Searching for evidence can be quite hard sometimes, as you are often seeking information that is currently outside your awareness. If you are focused in your NATs, you will be focused on the evidence that supports them. Challenge your mind to work harder and find other facts or positive events that you may have been discounting.*

THINGS TO REMEMBER

▶ *In this chapter you have learned further techniques and skills to help you shake off NATs and build new ways of thinking that validate more realistic and evidence-based beliefs. Your skills in self-awareness are growing all the time.*

▶ *Think of Thought Records as flexible, useful tools which can be adapted to accommodate a variety of thought challenging and behavioural testing.*

▶ *You can refer to the Thought Record 'in action' as an example of how the extended seven-column version (including two evidence columns) works.*

▶ *In the new version of the Thought Record, you are asked to search for evidence to support your negative thinking first, because, at this stage, you are likely to strongly believe that your negative thoughts are realistic. Once you examine the evidence (or lack of it), you will start to find more healthy, balanced alternatives that you can build on.*

▶ *If you think that you have solid evidence that supports your NATs then you need to support your views with clinical type evidence: data, facts and experience, rather than with opinions. A lack of facts or data or other evidence would confirm the non-validity of your NATs.*

9

Testing it all out: adjusting your behaviour

In this chapter you will learn:
- *to recognize self-defeating behaviour and to start to challenge it*
- *to develop behavioural experiments to test the validity of your negative thinking*
- *to use skills you have learned to help you conduct these experiments*
- *how to evaluate any positive results that come from testing things out.*

As you begin changing your thinking, start immediately to change your behaviour. Begin to act the part of the person you would like to become. Take action on your behaviour.

John Maxwell, US author and motivational speaker

The importance of behaviour in the cognitive model

You have done a great deal of work with the thoughts and emotions developed in your case conceptualization (see Chapter 2). You have learned how to track down your thoughts, how to identify those that harm you, and to notice the strong effect they have on your emotions. You have learned how to challenge your thoughts and to replace unhelpful thinking with more balanced, alternative points of view that help you to feel better within yourself. Now it is time to look at the behavioural aspect of the cognitive behavioural therapy

(CBT) model. If you look again at any conceptualizations you drew up that reflected situations and outcomes personal to you, you will notice that how you behaved had a great effect on maintaining how you felt and what you thought. We call this 'self-defeating behaviour'. For example, if someone with low self-esteem is turned down for a job they want very badly, they may say to themselves, 'I'm useless. I'll never get a good job. There will always be other candidates far better than me.' In this negative thinking state, what is this person's most likely *behavioural* response? The likelihood is that their behaviour will mirror their *thinking*.

- ▶ *They may stop applying for jobs altogether.*
- ▶ *They may set their sights lower and apply for jobs below their capabilities.*
- ▶ *They may continue to go for interviews but expect to do badly at them, which will be reflected in the impression they make or fail to make.*

This means that this person is likely to remain unemployed – confirming that their negative thoughts and beliefs were correct. This will make the person feel emotionally low, and their self-esteem will sink even lower.

Insight

Once more we draw your attention to the connection between thoughts, emotions and behaviour (or actions). This is because it is a central CBT principle to take on board. When your behaviour is self-defeating or destructive this in turn will make you feel bad about yourself and your mood will slump.

Deciding what to do

Changing your behaviour seems an obvious way forward and upwards, but how can you decide what to do, or be sure that it will give you the results you want? The answer is that you can't – for certain. However, you can develop action plans in the form of behavioural 'experiments' – trying out ideas that you think might be helpful, and checking the result against what you were hoping for. Behavioural experiments can be used for a variety of helpful purposes:

▶ *to test the validity of your thoughts*
▶ *to discover, with an open mind, what might happen if you do A instead of B*
▶ *to observe outcomes and results of behaviour changes*
▶ *to learn to manage your emotions by graded exposure to feared situations (see page 106).*

US President Benjamin Franklin once described his definition of madness as, 'Doing the same old things, in the same old ways, and expecting different results.'

YOUR OPTIONS

In its simplest form, CBT offers three possibilities when you feel disturbed by your views of life events.

1 *You can adjust your thinking about what you perceive to be happening or to have happened, moving it from a negative outlook to a more balanced, rational point of view.*
2 *You can change your behaviour – taking a different approach to a problem to see if you get a better result.*
3 *You can do nothing, and accept things as they are. Never dismiss this option entirely. Remember, your task is to test alternative thoughts and actions and, by using the process of 'guided discovery', find out what makes you feel better about yourself and your life (see overleaf). Sometimes simply coming to terms with things is a positive way forward in itself. Nonetheless, never come to this conclusion without testing alternatives first.*

Insight

Think how actors take on a role/persona and how they do this. They are likely to move differently, take on particular affectations and mannerisms, change the way they speak and display specific emotions in their faces – to do all this they

think their way into the role and behave in certain ways. The Russian founder of the Moscow Art theatre, Konstantin Stanislavsky (1863–1938), developed the method theory of acting where actors think of their own personal experiences to help them play a role; another way of putting the thought/mood/behaviour link into practical use.

Guided discovery

Guided discovery is the process by which you test your thinking and your behaviours. You literally try something out and see what happens. You then process what you have learned and, if you consider it helpful, you may wish to continue to think and act in this new way. If you discover that it was not helpful and failed to make you feel better, you discard it. Keep in mind some wise words of eminent psychologist Petrushka Clarkson (1995): 'There is no such thing as failure. There are successes – and there are learning experiences.'

What you are doing is calling upon a previously learned CBT skill – you are checking for evidence.

You are now quite experienced in the art of experimenting with different ways of thinking about your problems, challenging your negative thoughts and finding more rational alternative explanations that fit better with reality. You can start to do the same with your behaviours. Negative, self-defeating behaviours can easily be a self-fulfilling prophecy, which is why people may continue to believe in them.

Case study

Lesley is a quiet girl and considers herself to be rather boring, with very little to say when she is in social situations. Each time she receives an invitation, her first thought is to ponder whether there is any way out of it. In her mind – understandably, given her beliefs about herself – she sees social occasions as terrible ordeals, to be avoided if at all possible. The thought of spending hours in the company of others, who all seem to be chatting and laughing while Lesley fears she will find very little to say and be judged as tedious and boring, is almost unbearable. Lesley's number one technique for dealing with this is to refuse as many invitations as she possibly can. Lesley sees this as a good solution to her problem as it prevents her from putting herself 'through the mill'. However, occasionally, avoidance as a solution won't work. Family occasions, office functions, friends' birthdays – there are many things that Lesley feels she simply cannot avoid.

In these instances, Lesley's plan B is to stand quietly in a corner and hope that no one speaks to her; anyone talking to her, she feels, would provide evidence of her belief that 'Everyone will find me very boring'. Provided she can avoid as much eye contact as possible, Lesley has learned well the art of pretending to look out of the window, to study the food table, to gaze at paintings on the wall – people keep their distance, and somehow or other, Lesley gets through the evening until she feels that she can leave.

Avoidance and *escape* work very well for Lesley. Yet they maintain her problem. Lesley's actions (or inactions) simply confirm her view of herself as a boring person. Because she hides herself away at parties, of course no one speaks to her (or if they do, Lesley will tell herself that they are only feeling sorry for her). In Lesley's mind, this proves that her theory is right. Lesley never learns that people might in fact find her more interesting than she thinks, or that she might find chatting to people less of an ordeal than she imagines, or that she might even have a good time at a party. She never tests it out.

Using a behavioural experiment Thought Record

Look at the Thought Record overleaf (there is a blank copy in the Appendix, page 326, for you). You will see that it is a slightly 'new style' Thought Record specifically for recording behavioural experiments and their outcomes. In the example given, Lesley decides to try something new – to be just a little more social and to attempt to start a few conversations. It is a nerve-wracking idea for her, and she has no real idea what the result will be. In fact, her prediction of the outcome is very negative. However, she gives it a try and afterwards evaluates what actually happened against her prediction of what would happen. She discovers that things turn out a lot better than she thought, and she is able to learn from this and build on it.

THOUGHT RECORD FOR BEHAVIOURAL EXPERIMENTS

Date and situation	Prediction What do you think will happen? How much do you believe it will? (%) How anxious do you feel? (%)	Experiment What can you do to test out your prediction? (ensure you drop all safety behaviours)	Outcome What actually happened? Was the prediction correct? How anxious do you feel now? (%)	What I have learned Is there a more balanced view? How much do you believe your first prediction will happen in the future? (%) How can I build on this?
Walking into a party on my own.	I will feel very embarrassed and no one will speak to me. I'll just want to go home as soon as possible. 80%	I will get myself a drink and then look around for someone I can talk to. I will ask one or two basic questions and then focus on listening to the responses.	I did as I'd planned and, although I felt a little self-conscious, I realized that others felt the same and were very pleased to speak to me. I enjoyed the party and stayed later than I had intended.	Firstly, not to avoid difficult situations. Secondly, that, if I plan a little and stop listening to my negative chatterbox, I can cope with these situations better than I had thought, and actually have quite a nice time. 20%

Don't wait for situations to arise before you test things out – deliberately *create* them so that you get lots of practice.

Designing your own experiments

Think about your own problems – perhaps, like Lesley in the case study above, you suffer from social anxiety. Perhaps you have more generalized anxiety – you simply get nervous easily and there are many things that you fail to try because you make negative predictions as to the outcome. Thus, you never discover either that things don't turn out as badly as you thought, or that you have more resources to cope with them then you realized. The problem here is that you maintain the problem (usually a faulty belief) and that you *compound* it. As with anything, the less you do it, the less confident you become that you could possibly attempt it. Sooner or later, your nervousness about driving on motorways becomes nervousness about driving anywhere. Your worries that you'll play badly when invited to play tennis causes you to give away your rackets and never play again.

WHAT MIGHT YOU LIKE TO CHANGE?

Think about any perceived weakness you consider you have. Now think how you would like to be. Finally, think about what you could try to see if you can make a positive change.

YOUR ACTION PLAN

In Chapter 3 you learned to set goals. Behavioural experiments require you to use some of these goal-setting skills.

Plan your steps
Your experiment should push you a little way outside of your comfort zone, but not too far. Your goal is to succeed, not to set yourself up to fail. For example, if you are nervous of going in lifts

(perhaps fearing claustrophobia and panic attacks), your first experiment might be to stand in a lobby where lifts are operating. You might be willing to stand very close to the lift door, or even step inside for a moment. Record how that feels. You are putting yourself in a situation where no harm can come to you, but you may be experiencing some anxiety and you are testing the consequences. You may discover that you did not feel as bad as you thought you would. If this is the case, you may be willing to try another, slightly harder experiment next time – perhaps to go up one floor in a lift and become aware of how you feel. This is called 'graded exposure'.

> **Jargon dictionary: 'Graded exposure' means taking several small steps, rather than one big one.**

Plan ahead

Begin to become aware of all the negative predictions you make. Perhaps you don't confront your work colleague about sloppiness because you predict that they will fly off the handle and turn your argument around. In situations like this, advance planning can help you. Decide ahead of time how you might tackle the problem in the best way – and then be willing to test it out.

Visualize it

If the idea of a particular behavioural change seems especially frightening – standing up to your boss or someone who is taking advantage of you; saying 'No' for the first time when you've always said 'Yes' – then use visualization to practise in advance. Sit quietly, close your eyes, and imagine the situation and the behaviour change you would like to make. Picture yourself acting in a different way. See a very clear picture in your mind – notice the surroundings, the details, the colours. This will help to make the visualization more real and accurate. Focus on your feelings after you have visualized yourself dealing with your problem in a new way. Does this make you feel a little more confident? Practise your visualization as many times as you need to in order to feel more comfortable with testing it in reality.

Be proactive

Conducting behavioural experiments requires you to become proactive. It means actually *doing* something a little different to see if you can get a better result. You have to challenge negative assumptions and predictions, rather than presuming them to be correct (sometimes, of course, they might be; be prepared for this – but never accept them without validation). It means identifying self-defeating behaviour and seeing whether there isn't a better way – a way to make you feel better, to lift your mood, to give you more confidence.

HOMEWORK

Make testing negative predictions a regular habit. Each time you find yourself thinking, 'Oh, that won't work' or 'I'll never be able to do that' – test it out. See what happens. Even a negative result is of interest. You have learned not to approach something in that way again, and you can evaluate whether you need to accept things as they are or find another way of tackling things.

Use the behavioural experiment Thought Record in the Appendix (page 326) in order to do this. Keep an open mind. Be genuinely curious about the results. Where they are positive, determine to continue with them rather than revert to self-defeating ways.

SUMMARY

In this chapter we have looked at how negative behaviours can play a big part in maintaining negative thoughts and moods by reinforcing them.

▶ *People maintain negative behaviours by making predictions about outcomes without any solid evidence, and thus avoid testing out the validity of the prediction.*
▶ *To break the cycle of negative behaviours, construct experiments that will test the thought or assumption to check its validity and focus on what you learn from the outcome.*

► *Where trying something new might be especially daunting, break it down into small steps and try these out one at a time, moving on to the next only once you are comfortable with the last – this is 'graded exposure'.*
► *Evaluate outcomes and focus on what you might have learned from what you have done. This will help you to decide whether your previous views were at least partially invalid and if a different way of looking at things is now more substantially within your grasp.*

THINGS TO REMEMBER

▶ You have to this point done a great deal of work with thoughts and emotions and have now begun to focus on the behavioural aspect of CBT.

▶ You have learned how your behaviour mirrors your thinking, which is further evidence of the thought-emotion-behaviour link and how each impacts on the other.

▶ Behavioural experiments are a way of testing alternative thoughts and actions by various means to find out what makes you feel better about yourself and your life – in other words, what works well for you.

▶ You have seen how a Thought Record can be transformed into a highly effective tool for behavioural experimentation, as a means of discovery, to log: predictions, experiments, the outcome, and what has been learned from the experiment.

▶ Another method of checking for evidence is a process termed 'guided discovery' whereby you test your thoughts and behaviour by trying something out with interest, noting what happens and deciding whether or not it is useful to you.

10

Assumptions and beliefs: your rules for living

In this chapter you will learn:
- *about deeper layers of thinking*
- *how to identify assumptions and beliefs*
- *how to modify assumptions and beliefs or replace them with more helpful ones.*

We simply assume that the way we see things is the way they really are, or the way they should be: and our attitudes and behaviours grow out of these assumptions.

Stephen R. Covey, *Everyday Greatness*, 2006

Insight

After a number of sessions of CBT, working hard on her core beliefs, assumptions and 'rules' for living, a client said that she felt as if she was thinking like a child again. She explained that she didn't mean that her thinking was immature but rather that she was looking at her life anew, thinking in an 'anything *may* be possible' way and enjoying, once again, the challenges that life presents.

Deeper layers of thinking

You can now identify your negative thoughts and challenge their validity through a variety of cognitive behavioural therapy (CBT) skills and techniques. You have learned how to recognize self-defeating behaviours and to adjust these to get better outcomes and results. This is an essential starting point for making changes. In fact, for many, these skills are *all* that are needed to help cope with problems effectively. However, for others, this may not be enough. In this case, you need to investigate the deeper layers of thinking – your assumptions and beliefs – that give rise to your negative thoughts. The hierarchy of your belief levels is shown in Figure 10.1.

Automatic thoughts

(Your 'day–to–day' thinking, usually in response to a specific trigger)

↑

Assumptions

(Ideas that you have about yourself, others, and life in general.
You develop 'rules for living' that support and respond to
these assumptions)

↑

Core beliefs

(Basic, solid beliefs that you can sometimes misinterpret as
truths and facts)

Figure 10.1 Hierarchy of beliefs.

THE 'TOP LAYER': AUTOMATIC THOUGHTS

One of the features of negative automatic thoughts (NATs) is that they are *event-specific*. That is to say, there is usually a trigger event, which might be something negative you can clearly identify, such as losing a job or a partner, having a quarrel with a friend or having a car accident, etc. The trigger event can be as straightforward as suddenly having an image or idea when you are sitting at home alone in the evening time or doing a spot of gardening. It is the event (in whatever shape or form) that, for one reason or another, engenders negative thoughts in your mind that you then have to deal with. A further feature of NATs is that they may spring from, and therefore match with, deeper and more absolute beliefs that you hold.

THE 'MIDDLE LAYER': ASSUMPTIONS AND RULES FOR LIVING

Assumptions link your beliefs to your day-to-day thinking. In this sense, they are the 'middle layer' of your thinking. They also create your 'rules for living'. For example, if you hold a negative belief that you are a boring person, then you may make an assumption that, 'If I talk to people socially, they will find me dull and uninteresting.' Such an *assumption* may activate your *rules for living*. When you receive a party invitation, you may think, 'I won't go. No one will want to talk to me.' Or you may go, but decide, 'I'll just stand by myself in the corner and hope no one notices me. That way, I won't have to talk to people.'

Your rules for living

You may develop a rule for living not to socialize because you consider this will prevent your 'I am boring' belief being put to the test. Anne, with her 'I'm not good enough' belief (see case study above), might hold an assumption that, 'If I stay on the bottom rung of the career ladder, doing simple work I can easily handle, then hopefully, I won't lose my job.' Anne is developing a rule for living that it is better not to do anything difficult so that her (perceived) incompetence will never be discovered.

Identifying your rules

Can you identify any rules for living of your own? Look in your workbook at the list of beliefs you identified. Ask yourself how you cope with those beliefs on a day-to-day basis. For instance, if you believe you are unlovable, one of your rules for living might be to be as nice as pie to everyone at all times, no matter how they treat you, in order to mitigate this. Assumptions tend to have an, 'If ... then ...' quality about them, such as:

- ▶ *'If I don't do everything perfectly then I'm a failure.'*
- ▶ *'If I make a mistake then I will be punished.'*
- ▶ *'If I put my trust in people then I'll get hurt.'*
- ▶ *'If I show emotion then I'll be rejected.'*
- ▶ *'If I need other people's help then I'm weak.'*

Your core beliefs will drive your assumptions, which in turn create your rules for living. For example:

My belief	Assumptions	My rules for living
I'm not likeable.	If I try to get close to people they will reject me.	Keep a low profile. Be polite but never lower my guard.
I'm no good at personal relationships.	If I get too close to people I'll simply get hurt.	Turn down one-to-one invitations where possible. Sabotage opposite-sex friendships early on, before I can get hurt.
I'm fat and ugly.	If I am physically unattractive, then no one is going to like me.	Socialize as little as possible. Hide myself in huge black clothes.

You can work on both uncovering and challenging the unhelpful beliefs and assumptions that cause you to maintain self-defeating thoughts and behaviours.

Insight

Core beliefs are *activated* by difficult experiences; for instance, failing an exam may activate a hidden, underlying 'I am stupid' core belief that hasn't surfaced for years.

THE 'BOTTOM LAYER': CORE BELIEFS

Such *beliefs* are not event-specific, but are absolute and unchanging. They may have developed from your childhood and/or have been modified or cemented by adult experiences that seem to provide you with 'proof' that these beliefs are true. For example, a partner splitting up with you might serve to confirm an 'I'm unlovable' belief that developed in childhood due to over-critical parents.

The reason we have waited until now to introduce these more deeply-held beliefs is that you will often only discover what these are once you see patterns in your automatic thoughts. For example, you may discover that, when presented with tasks in life that might be challenging, you always find yourself thinking along the lines of, 'I won't be able to do that', 'I'll probably mess this up if I try it' or 'Others find all this far easier than I do'. These thought patterns are giving you information about a possible belief you may hold, which could be, 'I'm inadequate.' This type of belief forms the 'bottom layer' of your thinking. You regard such beliefs as absolute – they are not open to debate, as they are simply (in your mind) facts. You may hold negative beliefs about:

▶ *yourself ('I am worthless.')*
▶ *others ('People always let you down.')*
▶ *the world ('Crime is everywhere.')*
▶ *the future ('Nothing will ever change.')*.

Negative beliefs can be so deep that you rarely consciously notice them. You see them as absolute truths, 'just the way things are', but they are often wrong, or at least obsolete and out of date. Usually stemming from childhood, when you rarely, if ever, question what you learn, they keep you trapped in negativity. Here are some examples of negative beliefs to help you understand and identify them more clearly.

Negative beliefs you might have about yourself
▶ *I'm inadequate.*
▶ *I'm boring.*
▶ *I'm unlovable.*
▶ *I'm a failure.*
▶ *I'm a coward.*
▶ *I'm a bad person.*
▶ *I'm ugly.*
▶ *I'm unkind.*
▶ *I'm selfish.*

Negative beliefs you might have about others

▶ *Other people are cleverer than me.*
▶ *Other people take advantage when given the chance.*
▶ *No one ever gives you a chance in life.*
▶ *No one listens.*
▶ *Everyone is out for themselves.*
▶ *Nobody loves me.*

Negative beliefs you might have about the world

▶ *The world is a dangerous place.*
▶ *The world only offers opportunities for a favoured few.*
▶ *The world is full of obstacles and difficulties.*

Negative beliefs you might have about the future

▶ *The future is hopeless.*
▶ *Nothing will ever change.*
▶ *I will never feel happy again.*

Activation of beliefs causes difficulties

Your beliefs may not be especially consequential unless they
are *activated*. For example, someone with a core belief of
'I'm worthless' may be hugely affected if they are turned
down for a job. Instead of putting this down to bad luck or
heavy competition, their belief will activate assumptions and
thoughts about themselves along the lines of, 'I'm probably
unemployable', 'I'll probably never get a job', 'Nothing I do
works out', etc.

Insight

Core beliefs can also be positive and give you something
to build on. Positive core beliefs most likely come from
a positive relationship in your life, for example, your
grandmother telling you when you were a child that you had
a beautiful smile. At a later stage, you may think that you are
unattractive but this is countered by the thought, 'At least I
know I have a great smile'.

USE YOUR FORMULATION TO CHECK ON YOUR BELIEFS

In Chapter 2 you learned to use a basic formulation (or conceptualization) of your problems, making the links between your thoughts, feelings, physiology and behaviours. Developing this formulation now will help you to consider the kind of underlying mechanisms that are maintaining your problems, and the kinds of life experiences that might have led you to develop the beliefs and assumptions you have.

Use this formulation from now on to start working through your difficulties. Where you write about your early life experiences, there is no need for any great detail. We especially emphasize this if you have suffered from any kind of childhood abuse or trauma when re-focusing on this in detail can be very painful. While you may need to deal with this at some stage if it continues to affect you, this is not the purpose of the formulation. Its purpose is to help you to understand the beliefs you may have formed, and to ensure that you are making the right connections, increasing your understanding of your problems, recognizing what the activation triggers are, and what resulting thoughts and behaviours maintain your difficulties.

Let's look at a case study first, and then put it into a formulation that will help you to develop one of your own.

Case study

Anne's parents loved her very dearly, but decided that telling her that whatever she achieved she could do even better would have a positive effect. However well Anne did, instead of being praised, she was told to 'try even harder next time'. If she got 80 per cent in a test, that was a failure and she must get 90 per cent next time. If she got 90 per cent then only 100 per cent was good enough. Not surprisingly, Anne developed a negative belief about herself along the lines of 'No matter how hard I try, I'm just not good enough.'

Anne did get a good job. Nonetheless, she was never able to fulfil her potential since every time she started a piece of challenging work her 'I'm just not good enough' belief kicked in and she would think, 'I won't be able to do a good job. I'll get it wrong and everyone will see how incompetent I am. I'll let someone else take it on, and stick to simple tasks I can't mess up.'

Telling Anne to think more positively and that she will do a good job won't help her at all because it flies in the face of her basic belief that she isn't good enough.

We can formulate Anne's problems in the following way.

Anne's early life experiences Anne's parents constantly tell her that she must always try harder, no matter how well she appears to do.
Anne's beliefs 'No matter how hard I try, I'm just not good enough.'
Anne's assumptions and 'rules for living' Assumption: 'If I get things wrong, then everyone will know how hopeless I am.' Rule: 'I won't put myself in challenging situations. That way I can't get things wrong.'
Trigger events that cause Anne's assumptions and rules to be activated Being challenged or stretched in any way. Being asked to do something new.
Negative thoughts and behaviours that maintain Anne's problem Thoughts: 'I can't cope.' 'People must see I'm incompetent.' 'I'm really worried about being asked to take that on.' Behaviours: Avoidance of situations, keeping her head down at work, passing opportunities to others.

Adapted from Beck, 1995

As you read through this chapter and learn more about assumptions and beliefs, try filling in a case formulation/ conceptualization of your own – there is a blank one in the Appendix, page 327. You need to learn to identify unhelpful beliefs about yourself and your abilities, and to replace them with more realistic beliefs that will be more helpful to you.

You can transcend all negativity when you realise that the only power it has over you is your belief in it.

Eileen Caddy, author

Uncovering beliefs

Uncovering core beliefs isn't necessarily difficult. Sometimes you are only too well aware of the strong views you hold, and sometimes a core belief can simply be expressed as a NAT – you fail in some way and your first thought is, 'I'm hopeless' or 'I'm stupid'. However, to discover those beliefs that tend to lurk outside your consciousness, start by identifying patterns of thinking from your NATs (you can achieve this by looking through your Thought Records), and ask yourself: 'What beliefs do I hold that might make sense of these thought patterns?'

Once you have made a start on this list of beliefs, you can test them by looking back through childhood and early adult experiences for evidence that might make sense of how you came to think that way.

▶ *Anne, for example, was able to track her, 'I'm never good enough' belief down to her parents' attitude towards her.*
▶ *An 'I'm unlovable' belief might come from being heavily criticized in childhood, or perhaps from one or two disappointing adult relationships that were terminated by the other party.*
▶ *Beliefs about others – 'Others cannot be trusted' – might come from past experiences of being let down time and time again.*

Key point: People are less aware of their negative beliefs than of their negative thinking. This is because they convince themselves that their beliefs are 'truths'. Constantly remind yourself that negative beliefs are no more than a point of view and that they may not be true at all, no matter how strongly you believe them.

Exercises

To help you uncover your basic beliefs:

▶ *look for and identify patterns of thinking in your Thought Record*
▶ *ask yourself what belief(s) might fit with your thinking styles*
▶ *look back at past experiences from childhood onwards and see if you can find a 'fit' – either a specific or ongoing experience or a set of experiences that would make sense of you developing this belief*
▶ *use a formulation sheet to jot these down – don't try to keep all this in your head – and gradually formulate a set of negative beliefs that makes sense to you in the context of maintaining your negative thinking and behaviours. If you find it easier, draw up a chart like the one below.*

Patterns of negative thinking	Likely belief(s) that have activated these thoughts	Past experiences that might have formulated such beliefs
'Hardly anyone spoke to me at the party.'	'I'm dull and uninteresting.'	Being bullied at school.
'Work colleagues rarely consult with me.'	'I'm socially inept.'	Finding it difficult to express myself in class.
'I haven't received a social phone call in ages.'	'I'm not especially likeable.'	Parents compared me unfavourably to vivacious elder brother.
		Partner dropped me as he said we had nothing in common.

A 'discovery tool': the downward arrow technique

Remind yourself of the technique we used in Chapter 4 to help uncover specific negative thoughts. The downward arrow technique is also extremely useful at uncovering beliefs. You can use it in almost the same way as before, but the question you will be asking yourself on this occasion is, 'What does this say about me (or others, the world or the future)?' For example, see Figure 10.2.

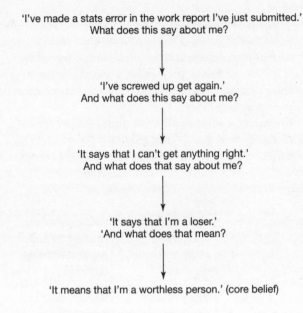

'I've made a stats error in the work report I've just submitted.'
What does this say about me?

'I've screwed up get again.'
And what does this say about me?

'It says that I can't get anything right.'
And what does that say about me?

'It says that I'm a loser.'
'And what does that mean?

'It means that I'm a worthless person.' (core belief)

Figure 10.2 The downward arrow technique for beliefs.

In your workbook, write down the beliefs you discover. They will be the beginning of your 'Blueprint for change'.

Rating the strength of your beliefs

Once you have a list of basic beliefs, a vital task is to rate the strength of your belief in them. This is critical *before* you start any work on changing them as you don't want to waste precious time and effort working on beliefs with, say, only a 20 per cent belief rating. Once you have given a subjective rating to each of your negative beliefs (just an approximate figure based on your personal views about the belief), rank them in order of strength of belief, and choose one or two with high belief ratings to work with. You only have so much time and so much energy – don't waste them on the wrong things. You may like to group your beliefs into three categories:

1 *Those needing immediate attention (just place one or two here).*
2 *Those that you might work on in the future.*
3 *Those that don't, at this moment in time, warrant great effort and attention.*

Insight

Neuroscience has proved the human ability to build new neural pathways as a method of developing a more creative and expansive view of our lives and coping with the world around us. As the physician and author Deepak Chopra puts it: 'To think is to practise brain chemistry'.

Challenging core beliefs

Don't assume that beliefs are necessarily hard to change. Sometimes the transition can be quite speedy, and may even take place as you challenge your thinking. However, some beliefs are quite rigid and deeply held, and this, in turn, can be why thought challenging is not an especially helpful exercise. No matter how many times you tell yourself that there is a different, more positive way of viewing your thoughts and feelings on a relationship break-up, if these thoughts are quite contrary to an absolute belief that you are worthless, you will not be able to make any progress. In such a case, you will need to work on the belief, rather than the thoughts.

It can also take longer to work on belief change than on thought change. Where you have deeply-held beliefs that have been around for a long time, they will fight you to stay in the frame. Be prepared to work hard if you need to. You may get a pleasant surprise and find the beliefs go quite quickly but if not, that's fine. It simply means you need to work harder for longer, not that they are immovable.

TECHNIQUES FOR CHANGING BELIEF PATTERNS

Changing belief patterns falls into two, linked, categories:

1 *Weakening and loosening old beliefs.*
2 *Strengthening new, more helpful beliefs.*

There is a variety of techniques that can help you to achieve this. Try them all – you may find that some work better for you than others.

Weighing up the pros and cons

Ask yourself what the advantages are of hanging on to your old belief. Then ask yourself what are the disadvantages of continuing to hold such beliefs.

Belief	Advantages	Disadvantages
I'm incapable.	Others help me out. I don't make myself do too much.	They may get fed up with helping. I'm gradually losing my basic life skills.
I'm exceedingly boring.	I stay home a lot – it's less effort.	I rarely go out. I have few friends. My social and conversational skills are drying up.

Working in this way can help to loosen the idea that your negative belief(s) are helpful and encourage you to look at things with a wider perspective.

> **Key point:** You are not trying to make yourself believe that something is true or not; you are considering what is the most useful belief on balance.

Using a continuum

People are often undeservedly hard on themselves with their beliefs. First, select a negative belief. For example, 'I am completely stupid'. Now look at the continuum below:

Someone who cannot read or write				Nobel prize winner
0% _____	25% _____	50% _____	75% _____	100%

Where will you place yourself on the continuum? You will probably place yourself in a far more reasonable position than at the bottom of the scale. You can expand on this by thinking of others you know – where will you place your work colleague on this list, for example? Your best friend, your uncle, the dustman? As you complete the continuum, reflect on what you find. What does this exercise tell you about the reality of your belief?

Behavioural experiments to test old belief and new belief

Chapter 9 showed you how to set up experiments to test the validity of your thoughts. You can use exactly the same skill with your beliefs.

Core belief: I cannot relate to people		
Behavioural experiment	**Prediction based on my core belief**	**What actually happened**
Find one thing to say to five different people – for example the person sitting next to me on the bus, the person behind me in the supermarket queue, the receptionist at work, the postman.	They will fail to respond, or may even ignore me.	Everyone responded pleasantly, and three actually engaged me in conversation, although the postman was in a rush.
Revised core belief based on result: I can get on with many people.		

> **Key point: Beliefs are usually no more than thinking habits.** You may have failed to re-evaluate something that might (or might not) have been true a long time ago, and have continued to believe this simply out of habit.

Rephrasing assumptions

In the same way that you found alternative, more balanced thoughts to challenge your NATs, you can do this with your assumptions. For example:

My old beliefs	More balanced alternatives
'If I make mistakes, then I'm a failure.'	'We all make mistakes sometimes; it simply means we are fallible human beings.'
'If I don't always do my best I'm worthless and lazy.'	'Doing my best can mean doing just what's appropriate to a situation, not aiming for perfection every time.'
'If this relationship breaks down, then I'll know I'm unlovable.'	'Relationships break down all the time, no matter who we are, and this often says more about the weaknesses of our partner than about us.'

Try this out. Remember, you are not trying to eradicate your present thinking patterns at this stage; you are simply trying to loosen them.

Abandoning inappropriate 'shoulds', 'musts' and 'oughts'

When we are capable of living in the moment free from the tyranny of 'shoulds', we will have peaceful hearts.

Joan Borysenko, author

A great many of people's negative, self-defeating thoughts come from using the words 'should', 'must' and 'ought'. These words imply personal failure almost every time you use them. They cause you to make demands on yourself, and suggest that you cannot meet those demands. For example:

- ▶ *'I should have good personal relationships.'*
- ▶ *'I ought to get top marks.'*
- ▶ *'I must get this right.'*

This is *not* positive thinking. You may believe it is, and that you are motivating yourself by saying these things. In fact, the exact opposite happens. You tend to add an unspoken corollary to your, 'I must …' statement so that it becomes:

- ▶ *'I must always be (polite, charming, clever, etc.) and if I am not, then I'm worthless (boring, dreary, not likeable, etc.).'*

Your 'shoulds', 'musts' and 'oughts' can extend to your beliefs about others:

- ▶ *People 'should' be nicer to me.*
- ▶ *Others 'must' consider me when making their plans.*
- ▶ *Colleagues 'ought' to take into account how busy I am before dumping extra work on my desk.*

We would like you to visualize gathering up all of these words and dropping them into the nearest rubbish bin. What can you put in their place? One option is using simple acceptance. Adopt the idea that it is acceptable to be fallible and that others also make mistakes; in other words, find a more empathetic approach. This approach – developing self-acceptance – comes initially from rational emotive behaviour therapy, although it is now being absorbed into CBT.

You can also replace 'shoulds', 'musts' and 'oughts' with softer, less absolute and critical language:

- ▶ *'It would be great if I can achieve this, but it's not the end of the world if I don't.'*
- ▶ *'It would have been better if I'd remembered to … but I am as fallible as the next person.'*

Did you find that easy or difficult? You will find that your
assumptions will soften considerably or change altogether as you
continue to practise this simple skill.

Observation: measuring yourself against others

When you set yourself standards through dysfunctional beliefs –
'I must be perfect at all times or I am a failure', 'I must always be
charming and articulate or people will dislike me', 'If I am not kind
to others at every opportunity, I am selfish and unlovable' – try
observing others around you or consider the behaviour of friends,
family and work colleagues. Ask yourself whether they also set
themselves these standards. Consider:

▶ *why they might be content with different views*
▶ *whether you personally judge them negatively for these more
  relaxed views*
▶ *whether you consider that others judge them negatively for
  these different views, these more relaxed ways of being.*

What might this suggest to you about the way you look at things?

_____

Creating more helpful beliefs

Weakening negative or inappropriate beliefs is a good start, but
you need to develop some alternative, more helpful beliefs to take
their place and then work to give these beliefs real strength.

To start this process, make a list of the negative beliefs you have
identified. Write them in a column on the left-hand side of a

worksheet page. On the right-hand side of the page, write what you believe would be a more helpful, more optimistic belief to replace the old one. Here is an example.

Old, negative belief	New, more helpful belief
I'm unlovable.	I am generally likeable, with similar strengths and weaknesses to most.
I'm worthless.	I have values and strengths, and make a contribution to society.
I'm unable to control my life.	I can take control over many aspects of my life, as I take responsibility for myself.
Nothing I do ever turns out well.	Many things I do turn out well, but I tend to focus on those that don't.
Others don't give me a chance.	I can create my own chances and invite other people to help me enhance them.
Life is too hard. Every step forward is followed by two steps back.	Life can have periods when things are difficult for everyone, but it also offers lots of positive, happy times.

RECORDING EVIDENCE TO SUPPORT A NEW BELIEF

Creating a new belief is one thing, believing in it is another. In the same way that you searched for evidence to support more balanced thinking, you can search for evidence to support core beliefs. You will do this over a longer time frame than checking the validity of NATs, so you may want to keep a record that you can keep updating to increase your confidence and strengthen your belief. You can do this using a 'Positive Data Log'.

What is a Positive Data Log?
A Positive Data Log is an excellent tool for making you question self-critical beliefs and bringing positive qualities into focus.

It is simple, but very effective. Take a negative belief that you hold and, to start with, find any evidence that might suggest your belief is *not true all the time*.

Positive Data Log

Self-critical belief: I am not likeable
How strongly I believe this: 80%

Alternative, more helpful belief: I am quite likeable
How strongly I believe this: 20%

Evidence to support your new belief and weaken your old belief:

1 I do have a few friends.
2 I have been invited to several social occasions so far this year.
3 In general, people are pleasant to me.
4 My work colleagues are friendly.
5 I get invited to workplace social functions.
6 I do my best to be kind and thoughtful.
7 My neighbour thanked me for my helpfulness.
8 I normally have a steady partner, and I have been in two long-term relationships.
9 Although I said 'no', I have had a marriage proposal.
10 I am close to my family.

Rating for how much I now believe my old belief (%):
And my new belief (%):

We do not suggest too big a swing from negative belief to positive belief to begin with. Changing beliefs can take several months, so a 'middle-of-the-road' alternative will serve you better than an unrealistic 'I am totally likeable'.

This is a useful tool, and you will find a blank Positive Data Log in the Appendix (page 328) for you to copy and fill in.

Measure the improving strength of your new beliefs

We suggest that as you work on your core beliefs you rate how
confident you are in the strength of the new belief. You will see a
space at the bottom of the Positive Data Log where you can, on
a regular (perhaps weekly) basis, give yourself a rating between 0
and 100 per cent for how strongly you now believe. Alternatively,
construct a rating scale like the one shown below.

▸ *Don't expect to see speedy gains. This may take many months.*
  Small positive shifts will have great meaning.
▸ *Don't expect to reach 100 per cent. Simply an 'on-balance'*
  view will be effective and enable you to view situations
  realistically, rather than falling back on unhelpful and
  invalid negative beliefs.

A rating scale

Desired belief: 'I am likeable most of the time'
Initial strength of that belief:
(Place an X over the percentage)
  X
0%	25%	50%	75%	100%

Desired belief: 'I am likeable most of the time'
Strength of belief after two weeks of skills practice:
       X
0%	25%	50%	75%	100%

Of course, the ratings you mark on a rating scale like this are subjective, but you will have a good 'feel' for how you are progressing. By continuing to use your Thought Record and Positive Data Log you will find that you are gathering more and more evidence to support your new beliefs. You are training your mind to re-focus on your more positive characteristics, and to re-evaluate the accuracy of your negative beliefs.

> **Key point: Be patient as you work for change.** Don't expect overnight success and then give up because of the lack of it. Rating any changes is a helpful way of seeing some improvement; even if it is only slight, it is a success.

Rate your self-critical beliefs as you see them now. You may find that you don't really want to put your X over the zero. Place it on the scale as accurately as you can. What does the fact that not all your crosses are on zero tell you about your thinking?

HOMEWORK

Identify (and, as always, write down) the negative core beliefs that you have discovered drive your NATs. You may find this quite easy or you may need to use some of the exercises in the chapter to help you. Look for the assumptions that emanate from your beliefs – and the rules for living you adhere to that maintain them. Use a formulation approach to make this easier.

Once you have done this, make a plan for how you intend to work on altering or eliminating your old beliefs. The skills we have suggested are all helpful, but some may suit you better than others. Test them out and base your plan on using those that suit you best. We would recommend, for the quickest and most solid results, that you use them all. You will find a case formulation/ conceptualization worksheet in the Appendix (page 327).

SUMMARY

In this chapter we have looked, for the first time, at the deeper levels of thinking that drive people's moods and outlook.

▶ *Beliefs develop in the main from early formative experiences, or from events that have had a great impact on you, and from which you have retained negative memories.*

▶ *Beliefs can be identified specifically by using skills such as noticing patterns in your NATs and considering what beliefs these patterns might support, and the downward arrow technique.*

▶ *There are techniques for developing new, more positive and helpful beliefs that can replace, either partially or wholly, your old negative, problem-maintaining beliefs.*

THINGS TO REMEMBER

▶ Negative assumptions feed 'rules' for living. Assumptions can usually be identified by an 'If... then...' pattern. For example, 'If I let my guard down, then others will take advantage of me'. A rule created from this outlook might be something like, 'I won't ever let others see me vulnerable'.

▶ Core beliefs are thought patterns that lie beneath your assumptions, personal rules and negative automatic thoughts (NATs) as absolute and rigid truths. They may have developed in childhood and been fortified by experiences from other times in your life which have, in your mind, confirmed them as true.

▶ Negative core beliefs relate not only to yourself but also to other people and the world at large. Examples of core beliefs include:

  ▶ 'I am unlovable' (about the self)
  ▶ 'Everyone is out for themselves' (about other people)
  ▶ 'The world is an unfriendly place' (about the world)
  ▶ 'My life is going to be a hard slog from now on' (about the future).

▶ In this chapter we have encouraged you to add to your basic formulation (or conceptualization or 'map', see Chapter 2) as a means of increasing your understanding of the underlying mechanisms that maintain your problems, and helping you to make connections between your thoughts, behaviour and activating triggers.

▶ The downward arrow technique is a questioning tool of self-discovery that reaches deeper into your thought processes to access your core beliefs.

▶ Look out for the words 'should', 'must' and 'ought' in your thinking, as these are self-imposed demands that are *very difficult to meet. They may seem useful as a motivational tool but usually they have the opposite effect, giving a sense of failure and being 'not good enough'. Instead, try adopting inner self talk that is accepting of human fallibility.*

▶ *You can use the Positive Data Log to support new, more helpful beliefs that contradict your harsh negative beliefs. (You will find a copy in the Appendix.)*

▶ *This chapter is rich in techniques to help you challenge your rigid, deeply-held views. By using skills of assessment and deduction, such as rating your conviction of the belief, rephrasing your assumptions and carrying out behaviour experiments, you are gradually developing a repertoire of skills to deal with your problems.*

Additional CBT techniques

In this chapter you will learn:
- *further basic cognitive behavioural therapy skills*
- *to review some of the skills already described and look at them in more detail.*

Practice is the best of all instructors.

Pubilius Syrus, Roman author, first century BC

More skills to help you

So far we have covered a variety of cognitive behavioural therapy (CBT) skills and techniques that are helpful in uncovering key thoughts, emotions and behaviours, and that assist you in making changes and adaptations to unhealthy beliefs.

In this chapter, we cover a few more general skills to help you pursue your own, specific life changes. We also give extra focus to skills that have already been covered but for which further 'stand-alone' commentary could provide more clarification on their best use for you.

AN EMPHASIS ON OPEN-QUESTIONING TECHNIQUES

It is interesting how often people have helpful, enquiring
conversations with others, but rarely with themselves. 'What's gone
wrong?', 'How did that happen?', 'Is it really as bad as all that?',
'Why don't you consider...?', 'Have you thought about...?' These
questions come easily when empathizing with someone else's
difficulties, yet you rarely use these same skills – for that's what
they are – on yourself.

These are the type of open questions – questions that engender a
thoughtful and considered answer – that you need to use when
trying to understand and resolve any emotional or practical
difficulties that you have yourself.

> **Jargon dictionary: In CBT terms, this type of open questioning
> (aimed at guided discovery towards solutions for problems)
> is called 'Socratic enquiry' – named after the Greek philosopher
> who lived in Athens in 400 BCE.** Socrates was famed for his
> questioning enquiry that encouraged his students to reach conclusions
> about their concerns without him directly instructing them.

We have already encouraged you to use this type of questioning
when working out your thoughts and beliefs, but it is worth
drawing your attention to it as a specific skill in order to enhance
your use of it.

Have good conversations with yourself

While it is a method of enquiry that forms the cornerstone of
professional therapy, there is no reason at all why you should not

have Socratic conversations with yourself – either in your head or, where you have time, responding in your workbook.

How does it help?

Socratic enquiry – open questioning – encourages you to consider aspects of your difficulties that you might have dismissed. It works on the principle that you have a great deal of valuable information known to you but 'outside your awareness'. That is, you are failing to take the information into account when formulating negative thoughts and beliefs. Socratic enquiry asks you to consider this in a variety of ways. It gives you the opportunity to bring into your conscious awareness all the information you have, to weigh it up and evaluate it in a way you might not have done previously – ask yourself questions that cause you to think about validity and certainty – and to draw conclusions from this, which are likely to have a depth of conviction.

Learn to have dialogues with yourself

In a sense, you need to become both Socrates and his student. Simple questions will be very helpful when you review a negatively perceived event. For example:

- ▶ *How did I feel?*
- ▶ *What went through my mind when I felt that way?*
- ▶ *What was my reaction?*
- ▶ *What was the personal meaning to me?*
- ▶ *Did any other thoughts or emotions cross my mind?*
- ▶ *What else do I know about this?*
- ▶ *Have I evidence to support my thoughts?*
- ▶ *Have I evidence that might invalidate my thoughts?*
- ▶ *How do other people deal with this situation?*
- ▶ *How would I advise someone else who had to deal with this situation?*
- ▶ *Are there any other ways of looking at this, good or bad?*
- ▶ *What conclusions might I draw from the extra information I now have?*

Essentially, you are looking for answers that will encourage you to explore the situation further and possibly revise your current conceptualization (your map) of the problem.

Socratic questioning moves you between the concrete (factual information) and the abstract (your views and interpretations) and encourages you to draw a conclusion from your assessment. You ask informational questions first, and then you make an evaluation, or look at what options there are, based on the knowledge that you have.

Insight

Cultivating a habit of questioning immediate thoughts and beliefs frees people to think outside their preconceived ideas. To return to the child analogy: children tend not to accept just one answer to their questions – they will probe deeper in layers of curiosity.

Using Socratic enquiry to challenge beliefs

Beliefs often seem like facts, with little room for manoeuvre. Making some simple enquiries of yourself will help you. For example:

- ▶ *'How helpful is it to me to hold such a belief?'*
- ▶ *'What are the disadvantages to me?'*
- ▶ *'If this belief is a truth, how do other people deal with it?'*
- ▶ *'What evidence do I have that this belief is true?'*
- ▶ *'What evidence do I have to suggest that it might not always be true?'*

This sort of enquiry will loosen your unhelpful belief and give you an opportunity to generate alternative, more helpful, possibilities. Ask yourself:

- ▶ *'Now that I have considered the bigger situation, how do I view what worried me originally?'*
- ▶ *'Do I still view my original belief as the worst thing that could happen?'*

Socratic questioning is not about 'changing minds'.
Finally, retain the idea that this type of questioning is not necessarily to get you to change your mind about something. It is to allow you to explore all the alternatives and options to thinking, feeling and acting that will encourage you to develop a view of your own, through guided discovery, that may be more hopeful and optimistic than your previous negative thoughts or beliefs.

RELIEF OF PHYSICAL SYMPTOMS

There can be times when you do not feel good at all – when your mood is low or your anxiety high – when your first desire is simply to relieve the immediate physical symptoms of your distress.

There is some argument about the usefulness of symptom relief as a CBT technique. The reason for this is that it can maintain the problem and thus become a 'safety behaviour'. For instance, if you learn how to reduce the physical sensations of a panic attack, your thinking may be, 'Great. Next time I have a panic attack, I can use my symptom relief techniques.'

Can you see anything wrong with that? Many professionals can, and their view (with which we agree, in principle) is that they don't want your confidence to be placed in a symptom relief element of subsuming your next panic attack. They – quite rightly – want you not to have any more panic attacks.

> **Jargon dictionary: A 'safety behaviour' is one that you adopt that you feel helps but that actually prevents you from facing and tackling your difficulties.** For example, someone with a fear of having a panic attack in a lift might take the stairs instead. While that works quite well for them (where the flights are not too many or too steep), it is not helping to overcome their fear of panic in any way.

In Chapter 13 we deal with physical symptoms in more detail but, for the moment, we offer an option of relieving symptoms to use while you are working on getting rid of the problem totally. Some people simply feel that they cannot face the challenges of overcoming anxiety, for example, without a little symptom relief help first. It is your choice. If you choose to try symptom relief, there are three main strategies:

1 *Deep breathing.*
2 *Relaxation techniques.*
3 *Distraction.*

Details of relaxation and breathing exercises are in Chapter 13. Here we look at distraction.

Adjusting your focus

The use of distraction is based on the view that you can only think about one thing at a time. Therefore, focusing on relaxing, pleasant thoughts may prevent your negative worries dominating. However, many people find distracting themselves from their worrying thoughts extremely difficult. Distractions that work best, therefore, are those that require absorption and mental stimulus. This may be something as stimulating as a crossword puzzle, as absorbing as a jigsaw puzzle, or – if you are trapped on a train and have nothing around you – a simple nonsense such as picking a number and counting backwards in 3s or 7s, down to zero. Chatting to someone, with the focus on listening to what they have to say, can work very well. Other forms of distraction, although perhaps less effective, can include listening to music, watching a favourite television programme, reading a book, counting the number of red cars going by or blue front doors that you notice. Develop what works best for you.

Remember that the above are temporary relief to give you some immediate respite while you tackle your problems more productively. Do not let them become safety behaviours in their own right.

FLASHCARDS

Flashcards are a simple technique to help you bring into your mind
your balanced, alternative thoughts when your negative thoughts
are crowding them out. Some people find 'thinking straight' in
moments of crisis that may be accompanied by high anxiety quite
impossible. Thoughts that come clearly and easily in the comfort
of home or in a quiet moment can desert you totally when negative
emotions overwhelm you or your mood is so low that your brain
feels like cotton wool. Flashcards can be extremely helpful here.

Simple to make

Buy a pack of small, lined index cards from a stationery shop.
Cut them in half if you wish to – some people like to put them in
their pockets and feel that they are unobtrusive. On one side of the
card write down the most common, negative thoughts and feelings
that you have in any situation that causes you distress (this could
actually be as simple as getting up in the morning). On the reverse
side write a strong, balanced rebuttal to your negative thought.
Write two or three alternatives if you can.

Keep these tiny cards with you and the next time your negative
emotions overwhelm your rational thinking, take out an
appropriate card and read the more positive, encouraging
alternative that you have written on the other side.

As with Thought Records, you won't need to do this forever but
you are training your brain to identify a balanced view more easily,

and to recall what those views might be without having to read
through them.

IMAGERY AND ROLE PLAY

Imagery as a technique in CBT is a powerful, diverse tool.
It is not within the remit of this book to describe imagery
techniques in depth because many of them need the guidance
of a qualified professional to be effective. However, we would
like to give you a summary of when these techniques might
be useful to you.

You may have a good visual memory

You may be someone who has a clearer awareness of situations
and emotions by thinking in images: you can easily access visual
recall, and this helps you to identify thoughts and emotions.
You are better at 'seeing' something than at 'thinking' about it.
If this is the case, then develop this skill as it will give you better
access to what is going on in your mind than trying to express
your thoughts without a picture in your mind.

Imagery enhances the positive and sublimates the negative

Imagery can be used both to visualize positive, successful
outcomes and to sublimate negative, distressing images from the
past. In this context, it is a valuable tool to assist those suffering
from post-traumatic stress disorder when the sufferer experiences
traumatic flashbacks that continue to haunt them. Revisiting the
trauma through the use of imagery is sensitively undertaken,
not to re-hash a nightmare, but to enable the sufferer to become
comfortable with the image and to possibly see it differently
with the benefit of extra knowledge and distance.

Visual manipulation

Visual manipulation techniques can help a person to reconstruct
a traumatic situation through, for example, imagining the image
on a television screen and learning to 'fade the image', change the
ending or 'turn the volume down'.

These are CBT skills that would be of most benefit to you by working through them with professional help (see Chapter 22).

A visual image of the future

In less traumatic situations, you may find that you can recall event details more clearly in pictures than in words. You may also prefer to use images when looking ahead and picturing how you would like things to be. This type of positive imagery can provide a more vivid, pictorial goal for some people than thoughts in the mind or words on a page.

IMAGINAL EXPOSURE: A MENTAL REHEARSAL

The use of imagery can provide an excellent mental rehearsal for a feared or anxiety-provoking experience. Fear of speaking in public or fear of flying are two areas where using what CBT would call 'imaginal exposure' can be exceedingly helpful. You create a mental image of yourself in the feared situation, handling it calmly and well. This is enormously helpful for people whose fears literally paralyse them from action – someone suffering from agoraphobia, for instance, may find even opening the front door too frightening. Using imaginal exposure, they can visualize this in their mind as many times as they like until they finally feel the anxiety decrease, at which point they may be able to manage the actuality of opening the door.

This technique, incidentally, is used a great deal in sports psychology to encourage competitors to envisage themselves winning the game and holding the trophy aloft.

> **Jargon dictionary: 'Imaginal exposure'** is the use of imagery to experience a feared or stressful situation – picturing the situation in your mind and seeing yourself dealing with it positively and well.

Role plays

Unless you are working with a therapist, you need a willing partner to assist with role plays. However, role plays can be extremely useful in working through feared or difficult situations – you and your partner can take turns in playing the different parties in the event and testing your actions and reactions in a safe place. Many people find that using this technique gives them great confidence when they face the real thing.

For example, if you have to find the courage to ask your boss for a rise, ask your partner to play the boss while you practise voicing the best way to approach the matter. You can then reverse the role play and play the boss yourself so that you can see how someone else might deal with them.

Insight

Further to what we have suggested, you can write down what you would like to say from what you have practised with your role play partner. Read it a few times as preparation – like rehearsing a script – so that words come to you more easily when you are in the anticipated feared or difficult situation.

CONDUCTING A SURVEY

This is a useful tool for loosening the validity of unhelpful negative thoughts and beliefs. Your survey can be conducted in a variety of ways to test out any number of things. In its simplest form you can survey, say, a dozen friends or work colleagues to ask their views on something that worries you. Do they think that 'only doing your absolute best at all times is acceptable', for example? Do they consider it a heinous fault to make a 'reasonable' attempt at something rather than always striving for perfection? Why do they see things this way? What is their view on such and such? What might you conclude by finding that many people don't see things as you do, or worry about things as much as you do?

Self-surveys

Another type of survey can be undertaken by you, yourself. If you worry, for instance, that your hands shake when you get nervous, and that people will notice this and judge you adversely, try it out.

Deliberately make your hands shake when you pass over change in a shop, or accept a carton of milk from the milkman. Do this a dozen times and review the outcome. Who seemed to notice? Who seemed bothered? How did that affect how they dealt with you? What do you conclude from all this?

VIDEO YOURSELF

While not always easy to set up, this is a good technique for discovering whether your views about your mannerisms and automatic behaviours are accurate. For example, many people fear blushing, twitching, showing embarrassing habits, such as inappropriate laughter, to such an extent that they avoid situations where others might view these idiosyncrasies. One of the authors has a client who suffers from Tourette's syndrome, where involuntary tics and twitches are a great problem. We agreed an experiment where he had a video camera fitted in a corner of his lounge that filmed him while he was sitting with his partner watching television. When he viewed the video, he was delighted to discover that his tics – which he had thought were so obvious that people would find him quite strange – were hardly noticeable at all.

'ASK A FRIEND'

Almost everyone has a tendency to be far harder on themselves than on others. You make allowances for the mistakes of friends and work colleagues; you understand that for others a 'bad step' doesn't make a 'bad person', yet when it comes to yourself, you show no leniency. An excellent tool for rebalancing your views of yourself or your problems is to ask yourself the following questions:

- ▶ *'If my best friend was feeling this way, rather than me, what would I say to them?'*
- ▶ *'What evidence would I point out to my best friend to help them see that their pessimistic thought or negative self-assessment was not 100 per cent true?'*

The answer you come up with will usually be quite different to your own negative thinking. People are always much wiser and more constructive at finding positive qualities in others than in themselves. Use your evidence-gathering skills to prove your point, and – almost certainly – show how little evidence there is for the self-defeating thoughts that your 'friend' has. Another good question to ask yourself is:

▶ *'Would my best friend agree with my negative views of myself? If not, what might they say about me?'*

Most importantly, then ask yourself:

▶ *'Why would my friend see me differently to the way I see myself?'*

Become your own 'best friend'. Use the questions above regularly and you will find they will really help you to see yourself and your situation in a more balanced way.

> **Exercise**
> Pick three negative aspects of yourself, or events where you feel you did not come up to scratch. Jot them down in your workbook. Now imagine that your best friend is describing these worries to you. Write down exactly what you would tell them in response. Does this give you a new perspective on your views about yourself?

DEVELOPING COPING SKILLS

Do not think we are guiding you towards the idea that all negative thoughts are incorrect. On many occasions they are 'spot on'. You are in a jam or a tight spot, things have gone terribly wrong, you have made a huge error and, while trying to see things in a positive light – 'At least nobody died' or 'Thank goodness it wasn't a total disaster' – you need to develop a sense of realism and ability to put together a 'disaster relief' action plan.

Define the worst-case scenario and how you might cope

Asking yourself, 'What is the worst outcome I could predict and, in that case, how would I feel and how would I cope?' is a superb question for developing your coping skills. It invites you to name the problem and the emotion, which you can then work on, but, more importantly, it invites you to develop a coping mechanism. You may surprise yourself by considering how rarely you do think about 'managing' when things go very wrong. People are often far too wrapped up in thoughts and emotions that lead them to think in terms of 'It would be unbearable' or 'It doesn't bear thinking about', and they don't go beyond that into the realms of what they actually would do.

Insight

Asking people to identify their 'worst-case scenario' is actually asking then to state their worst fear: what is the worst thing that could happen? How would you cope with it if it were to happen? It is a hugely beneficial aid in helping people face up to fears. Once they have stated the dreaded scenario, they can then begin working on coping mechanisms or action plans. Sometimes our worst fears sound ridiculous when we state them out loud, which in itself can be revelatory.

Develop an action plan

Don't spend too much time trying to find more positive cognitions. Become action-oriented, and ask yourself:

▶ *'What can I do – if anything – about this now?'*
▶ *'In what way can I make things better?'*
▶ *'If this cannot be undone, will openness/honesty/apology be beneficial?'*
▶ *'If the worst comes to the worst, how will I cope?'*

You will derive great confidence from this.

Think constantly in solution-focused mode, rather than trying to see things differently. Becoming active will help you to cope better emotionally with a difficult problem.

DECONSTRUCTIVE AND CONSTRUCTIVE THINKING

US psychologist Christine Padesky describes deconstructive and constructive thinking as extremely helpful to good outcomes in CBT. What are they?

Looking at the detail

Deconstructive thinking is something we talked about under another name earlier – being specific. A great deal of people's thinking, especially negative thinking, tends to be vague – 'I feel terrible', 'Nothing is working out', 'Work is stressful'. Deconstructing these thoughts into meaningful parts gives you something concrete to work with. Ask yourself 'What do I specifically mean by that?' 'What part of my work is stressful?' 'When is it stressful?' 'What causes the stressfulness?' etc. This will help you to formulate exactly what is going wrong.

Putting the detail back together with a different perspective

Constructive thinking will then help you to develop the problem in positive terms. Instead of ruminating on the awfulness of your workplace stress, construct questions that may be helpful to you: 'What can I do about this?' 'Who might help me?' 'What are the good things about my job?' Or find positive statements such as 'This won't go on forever. It is just a temporarily busy time.'

DEVELOPING VISUAL AWARENESS

When your mood is low, your focus of attention will be on your negative thinking. We call this *negative cognitive bias* (leaning towards a pessimistic point of view) – not only are you over-focused on pessimistic thoughts; you are also discounting optimistic, positive viewpoints and events.

Open your eyes

One simple tool you can use to correct this is to develop increased visual awareness of what is going on around you. For instance, you may be driving your car from A to B, and ruminating as you go over your difficulties and concerns. What are you missing?

Have you noticed how blue the sky is, the wonderful colours of the trees in autumn, the laughing children playing in the park? Probably not. You will need to practise this, so develop a behavioural experiment that might require you to focus on at least three positive things the next time you go out. What did you notice? What did you see? How did you feel after increasing your visual awareness of positive events in this way? Did your mood lift at all? Were you less focused on your worries? Did they seem less severe in relation to the small positive events you were noticing around you? What did you learn from trying this out?

We are not diminishing genuine problems and concerns that need addressing in any way, but practise balancing this with a visual awareness of the joys of life. It may give you a different perspective and raise your mood.

Don't give up
Albert Ellis (1988) is famous for saying (rightly) that one of the main reasons that people don't change – or not as much as they would like to – is that they give up on the hard work and effort required to make positive changes. For example, it is natural to hope that when you open a self-help book, glancing through it or reading it once will 'do the trick'. Yet, like everything else, it is practice that is important. You may give yourself permission to give up by saying:

▶ *'It's too hard.'*
▶ *'I don't have time.'*
▶ *'It doesn't make sense.'*
▶ *'It doesn't work.'*

Dr Robert Anthony (2004) cites research that shows it takes approximately 21 days (of daily practice) to break an old, destructive habit or form a new, positive habit. Please keep this in mind.

In order to *really* know something, it must become part of your thinking, your emotions, your actions and reactions. This is about taking responsibility for your development. When most people give up on something, citing one of the reasons given above, it is normally because they have not done it *often enough*, for *long enough*. To make changes in your life that are meaningful and positive, persevere.

HOMEWORK

Think about what you have given up and why in the last year. Write these things down and think about each one in turn for a moment. There will no doubt be good and valid reasons for some, but not for all. Have you used any of the negative excuses we have suggested above in order to give yourself permission to give up? Do you have any regrets about some of the things you gave up? How has this affected your self-esteem? What do you learn from this?

SUMMARY

CBT techniques and skills are developing all the time, and the more you read and study, the more you will come across. We have in no way covered them all here, but we have focused on those we consider to be most useful as self-help tools.

▶ *Socratic enquiry is the key to change. It means having a conversation with yourself that is as empathetic, as curious, as thoughtful and as constructive as those you might have with other people.*
▶ *Skills, such as imagery and role play, while useful, would need you to have a greater in-depth knowledge than we can provide here. Do read further (see 'Taking it further') if this area of CBT especially interests you.*
▶ *Don't give up. While not technically a CBT skill, this is vital to success. You may require encouragement to keep practising some new ideas that can seem hard, and where positive results are not immediately forthcoming.*

THINGS TO REMEMBER

▸ You will find that developing the skill of having a dialogue with yourself, asking yourself probing 'open' questions to build self-understanding and explore your problems and options from different perspectives, is an invaluable aid. Questions that could help could be: 'Is there another way I can look at this?' 'What was going through my mind?' 'What was I feeling when I behaved that way?'

▸ CBT calls this type of open questioning Socratic enquiry, after the Greek philosopher Socrates, who encouraged his students to develop their own thinking powers rather than learn parrot fashion from a teacher.

▸ Various techniques can be employed to relieve the physical symptoms that accompany the stress and anxiety associated with problem dwelling. They include breathing techniques, relaxation exercises and distraction methods.

▸ Distraction gives respite from ruminating over your problems by absorbing you in mental stimulation and focusing your attention. Tasks like crossword puzzles, sudoku or jigsaw puzzles fit the purpose well. Distraction, in a lesser way, can involve other pastimes like watching television, listening to music and reading a book. While distraction techniques are useful, they can become a way of avoiding taking problem-solving action.

▸ Another method of brain training adopts the use of flashcards. These are a convenient and simple way of reminding yourself of more helpful, alternative thoughts when you become overwhelmed with negative thoughts and moods.

▸ Imagery takes many forms in the CBT toolkit and we have introduced a few simple ideas in this chapter. You may find it easier to represent your thoughts in visual form. Visualization skills can be adapted to many situations; you can rehearse in your mind an anticipated difficult or feared situation and see things going well and coming to a satisfactory conclusion.

▶ Surveys are ways of getting to know more about your own and other people's thinking and behaviour. Use a survey to explore something that is bothering you – put together a questionnaire and ask a number of friends, family members or colleagues their thoughts on issues that concern you. You could also take video footage of yourself, viewing yourself in action, noting your behaviour and mannerisms or anything that worries you about your appearance, and how you may come over to other people.

▶ CBT is an endlessly inventive approach to therapy and simple coping mechanisms and action plans enable you to come at problems from a fresh angle. You can put yourself in an imaginary 'best friend' role, or look at the 'worst-case scenario' that your mind can conjure up and ask questions like, 'How would I cope if this happens?' 'What action could I take?'

▶ Thinking in more detail, deconstructing your negative thoughts and constructing more helpful thinking, and cultivating visual awareness by fully concentrating on your surroundings are further techniques that widen your scope in problem-solving.

12

Thinking and behavioural errors that preclude positive change

In this chapter you will learn:
- *to identify some common thinking and behavioural errors that prevent you from moving forward*
- *how to correct common thinking and behavioural errors.*

Mistakes are a part of being human. Appreciate your mistakes for what they are: precious life lessons that can only be learned the hard way – unless it's a fatal mistake, which, at least, others can learn from.

Alan Franken, US political commentator

The difficulty of spotting errors

In a self-help book you do not have the benefit of professional assistance to help you pick up various thinking and behavioural errors that are easy to make but which maintain your problems, rather than resolve them. Some of these errors are hard to spot as they appear to be solutions. In fact, on a temporary basis, for a limited time period, they may be solutions since they seem to bring you symptom relief. Eventually, however, in many instances, it is the 'solution' itself that becomes the problem.

In this chapter, therefore, we address a few further errors, of both thought and action, that are commonly made.

Errors of thought and action

> **Insight**
>
> You may be totally unaware of your thought and behaviour errors of the type we draw attention to in this chapter. These errors are common to us all at times of difficulty and they feel as if they help. However, they either create a problem in themselves or hinder our problem-solving skills.

Reducing activity

When your mood is low, you often find that making any sort of effort is, well, an effort. The answer seems obvious. Do little and wait until your low mood passes and you 'feel more like it'. Yet you are trapped in another maintaining behaviour. The less you do, the less confident you feel. If you don't go out, your social skills diminish and your friends give up on you. If you don't try, you lose the pleasurable feelings of stretching yourself and possibly succeeding. If you don't exercise, your body will close down. You then feel physically worse – which confirms your view that you are too tired (or ill) to do much. Your motivation disappears and you are in a vicious circle of maintaining your low mood. If you feel this may apply to you, read Chapter 14 for skills to break out of this cycle.

Negative focusing

HYPER-VIGILANCE

If you have a worry – perhaps about developing some sort of serious illness, for example – it might seem natural (a good idea, in fact) to keep extremely vigilant at all times, to ensure you don't miss an early indication that your fears may be about to materialize. The problem with focusing so strongly in this way is that you constantly look for evidence to support your worries.

That is, if you worry excessively about your health, a twinge in your leg (which might be simply dismissed or go unnoticed by someone else) will cause you to focus on what it might mean. Perhaps you search the internet for possible causes of leg twitches – and discover many different diagnoses, some of which are quite serious. Does this reduce your worries? On the contrary, it will increase them as you now have something new to worry about. You are constantly watchful, and your hyper-vigilance maintains your fears.

SELECTIVE FOCUS

Imagine we ask you to go out into the street and count how many red cars you see. The chances are that, after a few minutes, you would report back that there were either a lot more or a lot less than you thought.

If we then asked you, 'And how many silver cars did you see?', you would no doubt tell us that you had no idea because you were not counting silver cars, only red ones.

You may use this type of selective focusing in all sorts of ways. Imagine you have concerns about your popularity with others. You may focus on every negative nuance of people you are with – noticing if someone doesn't smile at you broadly enough or turns away a little too quickly to speak to someone else. You will quickly give a negative interpretation to this, and you are so busy doing so that you miss the friendly girl sitting next to you, or the drink offered by someone you were speaking with earlier. Your focus is selective and negatively biased – as such, it maintains your problem.

PERFECTIONISM

Where your negative beliefs in yourself are very strong, you may set yourself targets and standards that you feel you must achieve in order to regain self-validation – but which are often unreasonable. Thus, you set yourself up to fail, and the worthlessness belief is maintained, rather than reduced, for example.

Perfectionism is an extremely common problem (perhaps it is ringing a bell with you as we describe it). We have devoted Chapter 18 to it, which we hope you will find helpful in overcoming it.

PROCRASTINATION

Procrastination involves putting things off that you should be facing and dealing with. You know you have a problem and you probably also know you should be doing something about it. Instead, you give yourself reasons for not taking action, even when this would vastly improve your situation: 'I'll sort it out in a few weeks' time', 'I'll get a job soon', 'I'll wait and see what happens – maybe things will change'. The trouble is that none of these things can happen on their own. Negative thinking strategies tend to have a crippling, disempowering effect and the problem with procrastination is that it engenders a sense of helplessness. You start believing that you can't do anything – that it is beyond you – and you fail to trigger problem-solving skills that would move you forward.

DEPRESSIVE RUMINATION

Insight

Depressive rumination is a real problem for many people whose problems become very much part of how they see themselves, as a victim of others or fate. There can be a reluctance to let go of a 'hard done by' mentality and perseverance is needed to break habitual, heavily ingrained, cognitive patterns.

Rumination involves going over the same old ground again and again without adding any new or positive thinking to it. Perhaps you constantly replay past negative, upsetting or even disastrous events in your mind, turning over the idea that perhaps you could have done something differently or 'If only things hadn't worked out that way'.

This is understandable, as it is hard to put upsets and disappointments behind you. However, you then become entrenched in your problems, with the mistaken idea that going back over past events again and again is somehow helpful. In fact, it makes the problem worse as there are no positive strategies involved in this thinking, simply negative reminiscing when depression sets in. One way of breaking this depressive, maintaining cycle is to ask yourself questions such as:

▶ *'What have I learned from this experience?'*
▶ *'In what way am I now stronger, as a result of this experience?'*

While not changing reality in any way, these questions provide access to some sort of positive or learning experience to be gained from past misfortunes.

HOMEWORK

Identify any thinking or behavioural errors that you have made, as described in the chapter, either occasionally or regularly. Now think of an action plan to eliminate these errors or replace them with more helpful thoughts and actions. For example, if you realize that inactivity is a problem for you, make a weekly activity schedule to ensure that you are keeping busy and active (see Chapter 14, pages 184–6). Try this new regime for a week and then reflect and observe any changes in your thoughts and your moods as a result of it. Make similar action plans with any of the other errors described that you think might apply to you.

SUMMARY

While we have attempted to flag up thinking and behavioural errors that you might be making in each chapter of the book so far, there are a few more that you need to be aware of, and we have included them in this chapter.

▶ *Reduced activity can increase a negative mood, and depressive rumination – going over the same old thing again and again – also keeps your mood low, rather than getting active in some way to improve how you feel.*

- *You may have recognized procrastination and appreciated how you succumb to this.*
- *It is easy to focus in a narrow, negatively biased way, and there are dangers of over-focusing too.*
- *All these errors can be easily adjusted, but first you need to recognize them and identify how they negatively impact on your life.*

THINGS TO REMEMBER

▶ *Errors in your thinking and behaviour can maintain your problems rather than resolve them and it can be hard to recognize faulty strategies. Try action-related strategies.*

▶ *Avoid sabotaging yourself with unreasonable standards and targets, setting yourself up for failure and confirming your negative self-beliefs.*

▶ *When we are worried or anxious about something it is easy to focus our attention on it and relate everything back to it however this serves to maintain the problem. Try not to interpret everything you experience negatively or be too selective in your focus.*

▶ *Do not dwell on upsetting, embarrassing, disappointing or disastrous past events with regret. Instead try to gain something positive from them.*

13

Techniques for reducing negative physical symptoms

In this chapter you will learn:
- *about the physiological component of the cognitive model*
- *how working to reduce negative physiology will impact positively on your emotional health*
- *skills to reduce negative physiology.*

Inward calm cannot be maintained unless physical strength is constantly and intelligently replenished.

Siddhartha Gautama, founder of Buddhism (1st century BCE)

Is physiology part of CBT?

Yes, definitely. Physiological responsiveness is one of the four interacting systems (with thoughts, moods and behaviour) central to the cognitive behavioural therapy (CBT) model. For this reason it is important for CBT to include the development of skills that relate to improving physiological symptoms.

Think about physiological symptoms that can affect you:

- ▶ *General tiredness.*
- ▶ *Sleep difficulties.*
- ▶ *Lethargy.*

- *Exhaustion.*
- *Stomach churning.*
- *Shortness of breath.*
- *Dizziness.*
- *Sweating.*
- *Palpitations.*
- *Bodily aches and pains.*
- *General physical discomfort.*

These symptoms can all have an effect on your mood, and can also be caused by your mood. In this chapter we will encourage you to ensure that, physically, you are in good shape. This in turn will make you more resilient to dealing with negative emotions.

Sleep difficulties

One of the most common problems when your mood is low and your thoughts negative and ruminative is getting a good night's sleep. Using a CBT formulation or conceptualization (see Figure 13.1), it is easy to see how this can affect other areas of your life.

UNDERSTANDING SLEEP PATTERNS

Specific worries, general anxiety and depression can all trigger sleep problems. These difficulties can exacerbate other symptoms – being regularly exhausted makes it harder to fight negative thoughts and feelings.

What makes a good night's sleep?
In order to assess the extent of a sleep problem you need to know a little about sleep itself.

- *An average night's sleep can be anything from 3 to 11 hours. If you feel awake and well the next day, you are getting enough.*
- *It can take, on average, about 20 minutes to fall asleep.*

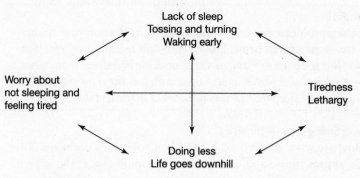

Figure 13.1 Sleep formulation.

There are four main stages in the normal sleep cycle:

▶ **Stage 1 (drowsy sleep).** *This is the transition period between being awake and falling asleep and makes up 5–10 per cent of your total night's sleep.*

▶ **Stage 2 (light sleep).** *This makes up 55–65 per cent of your night's sleep. It brings together all the important stages of sleep, including rapid eye movement (REM), known as dreaming sleep, during which information is processed, memories are fixed and the nervous system is restored.*

▶ **Stages 3 and 4 (deep sleep).** *During these stages, your brain activity and metabolic rates slow down, while growth and other tissue-building hormones are secreted. Deep sleep is the most restorative time for your body, yet it makes up only 30–35 per cent of your night's sleep.*

The first REM period comes after 90–120 minutes of sleep. It can last just 5 minutes, but as the night progresses the REM sleep periods get longer and can last up to 60 minutes. The rest of the night – up to 50 per cent – is made up of deep sleep, then further REM sleep, interspersed with short awakenings of which you are not aware.

The above describes an average, normal sleep pattern. When you have sleep problems, this pattern is thrown into disarray. Let's look at what you can do to restore your sleep pattern to a better and longer night's sleep.

Overcoming sleep difficulties

Below are some suggestions for tackling your sleep problems. They may appear simple and basic, but bear in mind that at the same time as you are following these simple rules, you will be dealing with underlying, troublesome psychological difficulties; each will reinforce and have a positive effect on the other.

▶ *Relax before going to bed. Have a warm bath, listen to music, or practise meditation or yoga.*

▶ *Write a list of things to be tackled tomorrow. This will relax your brain as it will not have to keep a mental note of what needs to be done. It's all down on paper.*

▶ *Take regular, moderate exercise such as swimming or walking – but leave a three-hour gap before going to bed.*

▶ *Cut out evening coffee. Caffeine is a stimulant that kick-starts the metabolism and keeps you awake. In the evening, drink herbal teas or warm milk instead.*

▶ *When your mood is low, or you feel anxious and worried, having an alcoholic drink may seem like a helpful antidote. However, alcohol causes sleep disturbance because your body, particularly your liver, detoxifies it. Reducing your alcohol consumption will have a positive effect on your ability to sleep.*

▶ *Don't eat heavy meals close to bedtime. The energy your body will generate to digest the meal will keep you awake.*

▶ *If you cannot avoid irregular hours, you can keep your biological clock tuned in by having four hours' sleep at the same time every day.*

▶ *Don't lie in bed worrying that you can't sleep. Get up and do something relaxing until you feel sleepy – then go back to bed.*

Reducing the physiological symptoms of worry

One of the reasons that worry and anxiety can affect you so badly is that the physical symptoms are quite extreme. Stomach churning, shortness of breath, dizziness, sweating and palpitations are all quite frightening, and can in themselves cause meta-worry (worry about the symptoms of worry). There are two well-recognized physiological techniques for calming the physical manifestations of worry – deep breathing and muscle relaxation. We describe both to you here so you can practise them. Some people prefer one skill, some prefer the other, and some like to use both. Try them and decide for yourself.

THE BENEFITS OF EFFECTIVE BREATHING

What is the purpose of breathing? On the face of it, this sounds a ridiculous question. The answer, surely and simply is, 'To stay alive.' Well, yes, of course, but why else is breathing good for you? Stop and think for a moment.

▶ *Breathing carries oxygen into your bloodstream. The bloodstream then moves around the various parts of your body providing them with the amounts of the things that they need to keep healthy.*
▶ *Breathing carries oxygen to your brain. If you want to think faster, better, at a higher level, then breathe better.*
▶ *Breathing keeps your heart rate and blood pressure down.*
▶ *If you have studied yoga, you will have heard of the 'calming breath' – the idea that breathing is good for your soul as well as your body.*

> ▶ *Did you know that oxygen also scares cancer cells? They hate oxygen!*
> ▶ *Most importantly – for the purposes of managing emotion – breathing helps you to relax.*

DEEP BREATHING

Learning to control your breathing is a big step towards controlling the physical sensations of high emotion. Becoming physically calm rests your brain, which prevents your emotional mind from dominating the proceedings. If you learn this simple skill, and practise it regularly, you will be well on the way to feeling calmer. First, start noticing how you breathe.

> ▶ *Find some space and lie on the floor on your back, with your knees slightly bent, in a relaxing position.*
> ▶ *Place your right hand on your stomach, just where your waistline is.*
> ▶ *Place your left hand in the centre of your chest.*
> ▶ *Now, without changing your natural rhythm, breathe in and out. Look out for the hand that rises highest when you breathe in – is it your right hand (on your stomach) or your left hand (on your chest)?*

This will tell you, in simple terms, whether you are a deep breather (when the hand on your stomach will lift the highest) or a shallow breather (when the hand on your chest will rise higher). Where anxiety and worry are a problem for you, you are more likely to be a naturally shallow breather.

Insight

When we are anxious, our breathing becomes fast and shallow and we expel too much carbon dioxide. This upsets the carbon dioxide–oxygen balance in our body, which can lead to physiological symptoms such as dizziness and light-headedness. These in turn exacerbate anxiety.

Horizontal or vertical? Another option, which you can decide for
yourself, is whether you sit down or lie down. You can lie down if
you prefer. However, bearing in mind that the goal is for you to be
able to use this skill 'whenever and wherever', then sitting, or even
standing, will be a better option.

1 *Place your hands on your stomach and chest, as you did
   previously. (While this is good for practising, when you wish
   to use deep breathing away from home, or in a crisis situation,
   simply imagine this part of the exercise.)*
2 *Now breathe in slowly through your nose (if you want to
   count to, say four, please do).*
3 *Ensure as you do this that the hand on your stomach rises,
   and the hand on your chest remains as still as possible.*
4 *Now exhale slowly (count again if this helps you) and, as you
   do, feel the hand on your stomach gently fall back.*

This is a simple breathing technique that you can use whenever
you like.

Key point: Learning to breathe well isn't difficult, but it is perhaps
one of the most important skills you can use to reduce high emotion.

DON'T WAIT FOR A CRISIS

One of the weaknesses of skills, such as good breathing, is that people feel they can simply use them in a crisis. However, if you wait for a crisis, you are not going to be skilled enough, or practised enough, to be able to use this tool on an almost unconscious, second-nature basis. You're going to have to run through the above steps in your mind, try to remember what to do, and in which order you do them all – you will not have the opportunity to take all this time in the crisis. Recalling the 'four stages of learning' (see Chapter 5, pages 60–1), ensure that you are 'unconsciously competent' at breathing well.

A GOOD RULE

A good rule is the 'rule of four' – devised not because of its optimum effectiveness (although it is effective), but because it is easy to remember!

▶ *Breathe in and out to a count of four.*
▶ *Do this for four minutes.*
▶ *Do it four times a day.*

To explain…

1 *Four is a 'middle-of-the-road' number for counting breaths in and out, so it is handy to use.*
2 *Practising four times a day is also obvious – the more you do it the better it is.*
3 *Practising for four minutes is not just a number picked out of thin air. It gives your lungs a chance to do the job of getting the new oxygen into the capillaries that feed your circulatory system, and to remove the carbon dioxide that has built up. This takes around four minutes.*
4 *Good breathing will relax you, ease muscular tension, and diminish other physical symptoms of anxiety.*
5 *Good breathing is not difficult to master, but it does require regular practice.*

Make sure that by the end of today you have practised these breathing skills at least twice. Then, using the 'rule of four', for the first week use your diary and write down the time at which you practised, on a daily basis. After that, use the 'rule of four' on a regular basis.

Insight

Resting, relaxing and having fun are all essential to our enjoyment of life and in fulfilling who we are. A great deal of mental, emotional and physical problems arise from living in ways not of our conscious choosing. Remember the Chinese proverb: 'Tension is who you think you should be. Relaxation is who you are.'

Muscle relaxation for calming emotion

Firstly, a surprising, quick and easy calming trick – yawning. While we tend to think that yawning indicates tiredness or boredom, on many occasions it actually helps to calm you down. It ensures more oxygen enters your lungs and moves into your bloodstream, de-tensing muscles and de-stressing your brain. If you feel a yawn coming on, and you have enough privacy, don't stifle it – use it as the ultra deep breath that it is and let it flow right through you.

The idea behind muscular relaxation is that it will eventually enable you to relax yourself quickly and at will, thus immediately helping to reduce high emotions before they become out of control.

LEARNING TO RELAX YOUR MUSCLES

Progressive muscle relaxation involves tensing and relaxing, in succession, 16 different muscle groups of the body. To begin, practise all the exercises, and you may soon find that some seem to work for you better than others. If that is the case, select those exercises only to practise, and eventually reduce these to just one or two. These are the exercises you will have 'at the ready' when your emotions appear to need some extra management help.

Make sure you are in a setting that is quiet and comfortable and take a few slow, deep breaths before you start. Then tense each muscle group hard for about 10 seconds and let go of it suddenly, enjoying the sensation of limpness. Allow the relaxation to develop for at least 15–20 seconds before going on to the next group of muscles. Notice how the muscle group feels when relaxed, in contrast to how it felt when tensed, before going on to the next group of muscles. You might also say to yourself, 'relax', as you do so. Here are the 16 exercises.

▶ *Clench your fists. Hold for 10 seconds and then release for about 15–20 seconds.*
▶ *Tighten your biceps muscles by drawing your forearms up towards your shoulders and 'making a muscle' with both arms. Hold for about 10 seconds and then relax for 15–20 seconds.*
▶ *Tighten your triceps – the muscles on the undersides of your upper arms – by extending your arms out straight and locking your elbows. Hold, then relax.*
▶ *Tighten your forehead muscles by raising your eyebrows as high as you can. Hold for about 10 seconds and then relax for 15–20 seconds.*
▶ *Tighten your jaw by opening your mouth so widely that you stretch the muscles around the hinges of your jaw. Hold, then relax. Let your lips part and let your jaw hang loose.*
▶ *Tighten up the muscles around your eyes by clenching them tightly shut. Hold for about 10 seconds and then relax for 15–20 seconds. Imagine sensations of deep relaxation spreading all around the area of your eyes.*
▶ *Tighten the muscles in the back of your neck by gently pulling your head way back, as if you were going to touch your head to your back. Focus only on tensing the muscles in your neck. Hold for about 10 seconds and then relax for 15–20 seconds. Repeat this step if your neck feels especially tight.*

- Take a few deep breaths and tune in to the weight of your head sinking into whatever surface it is resting on.
- Tighten your shoulders by raising them up as if you were going to touch your ears. Hold for about 10 seconds and then relax for 15–20 seconds.
- Tighten the muscles around your shoulder blades by pushing your shoulder blades back, as if you were going to touch them together. Hold the tension in your shoulder blades for about 10 seconds, and then relax for 15–20 seconds. Repeat this step if your upper back feels especially tight.
- Tighten the muscles of your chest by taking in a deep breath. Hold for up to 10 seconds and then release slowly. Imagine any excess tension in your chest flowing away with the exhalation.
- Tighten your stomach muscles by sucking your stomach in. Hold and then release. Imagine a wave of relaxation spreading through your abdomen.
- Tighten your lower back by arching it up. (Omit this exercise if you have lower back pain). Hold then relax.
- Tighten your buttocks by pulling them together. Hold, then relax. Imagine the muscles in your hips going loose and limp.
- Squeeze the muscles of your thighs all the way down to your knees. You will probably have to tighten your hips along with your thighs, since the thigh muscles attach at the pelvis. Hold and then relax. Feel your thigh muscles smoothing out and relaxing completely.
- Tighten your feet by curling your toes downwards. Hold, then relax.

Now imagine a wave of relaxation slowly spreading throughout your body, starting at your head and gradually penetrating every muscle group all the way down to your toes.

Practise these exercises regularly. Return to those you find especially helpful and develop your own 'mini-routine' for relaxing your body. Keep one or two exercises up your sleeve to use 'at will' in a crisis, where relaxing will help you to deal with it better.

EXERCISE

If you find yourself visiting the doctor because of low mood, the chances are they will offer you the option of anti-depressant medication. You will do far better to manufacture your own natural anti-depressant.

When you exercise – by which we mean doing something to raise your heart rate for a period of 30 minutes or so at any one time – your brain naturally manufactures more serotonin. This is the 'feel-good' chemical that helps you to maintain a good mood. This is why you will see, for instance, athletes at the end of a long race, when they should rightfully be exhausted and down on their knees, running extra laps and jumping in the air. The increase in their serotonin is so great that they are quite 'high' at this point. Don't miss this free opportunity to improve your mood.

Focus on the benefits
You will be more motivated to exercise and to appreciate its positive impact if you are specifically aware of its benefits.

Exercise:

▶ *decreases your blood pressure*
▶ *lowers your heart rate*
▶ *slows your breathing*
▶ *keeps essential muscle groups in good shape*
▶ *keeps weight down which, in turn, helps prevent diseases of obesity such as diabetes, strokes, etc.*
▶ *keeps energy levels up*
▶ *oxygenates your body, keeping your blood and circulation healthy*
▶ *reduces stress not only through all of the above but by re-channelling your energy into something constructive for your well-being.*

How do you start?
If you don't already have an exercise programme, the question becomes more, 'What could you do?' Only you can decide on

the best form of exercise for yourself (What sports do you like? Is there a gym nearby?), but we urge you to build two things into whatever you choose:

- *Timing: ideally, 30 minutes three times a week where your heart rate rises above its normal level.*
- *Consistency: don't create a programme that exhausts you, takes over your week, and that you give up after a month. Make sure that, whatever you do, it is sustainable – you need to be thinking of exercise for life. Set yourself exercise goals, and refer to Chapter 3 on goal-setting to remind yourself about setting achievable steps and the rewards of success.*

HOMEWORK

Review this chapter and consider which of the physiological exercise suggestions we have made might be of use to you. Now make an action plan for incorporating them into your life. Use behavioural experimentation to try out breathing and relaxation skills for a period of time, and notice the results. Don't have any special prior expectations – see what happens and how you feel. Begin to incorporate the more successful experiments into your daily life.

SUMMARY

We have focused on physiology in this chapter – the fourth element of the cognitive model alongside thoughts, feelings and behaviours.

- *You have learned how to tackle any sleep problems you may have.*
- *You have learned the importance of good breathing, and the exercises available for you to work on yourself to calm your anxiety.*
- *You understand something of muscle relaxation, and how it can help you.*
- *You have been reminded of the importance of taking regular exercise.*

THINGS TO REMEMBER

▶ *Physiological responsiveness is a way of describing how your body is affected by thoughts, mood and behaviour. The four elements – physiological responses (physical bodily symptoms like lethargy or palpitations), thoughts, mood and behaviour – form a four-part interacting system of CBT methodology.*

▶ *A good night's sleep is conducive to your general well-being, and there are many simple and practical steps CBT identifies that will assure restful sleep. For example, prepare for bedtime by taking a warm bath and compiling a 'to do' list of things to be addressed the following day (to put your mind to rest).*

▶ *CBT presents you with a multitude of strategies and skills for gaining control over the functioning of your body and mind. Learning breathing techniques and a key muscle relaxation exercise are quick-acting methods that can be used anywhere and in most situations.*

▶ *There are many physiological benefits from taking regular exercise, like lowering your heart rate and maintaining healthy circulation. Most importantly, when you exercise, your brain manufactures a 'feel-good' mood-enhancing natural hormone called serotonin.*

Part two

CBT in action: working with specific difficulties

In this part of the book you will have an opportunity to see cognitive behavioural therapy (CBT) in action, working with specific difficulties.

We wish to stress that, within the scope of this book, we are only able to cover these issues in the simplest terms. We encourage you to learn more, and in greater depth, either through seeking professional help (see Chapter 22) or through further reading. At the end of each chapter in this part we give specific reading suggestions, and in Taking it further at the end of the book we give general ones.

If your object in reading this part of the book is to acquire knowledge, rather than seeking help, we offer you a good basic understanding of particular CBT treatments, which may help you decide if you wish to learn more.

If you wish to work on specific issues that are troubling you, you already possess the basic skills to tackle these difficulties. Our intention in this part is to:

▶ *offer a good understanding of specific CBT treatments if you would like to learn more*
▶ *assist you to use these skills in the most beneficial way for specific problems that you may wish to work on.*

Specifically, we will explain to you:

▶ *what causes these problems*
▶ *what maintains them*
▶ *how you can overcome them.*

Through helping you to learn and understand more about these problems, we want to normalize them for you. The more you know about your difficulties, the less they will disturb you.

We also offer some further ideas and thoughts to develop your thinking about these areas of your life, and to encourage you to see these difficulties as surmountable challenges that can be overcome by anyone with effort and perseverance. The issues we cover are:

- *depression*
- *anxiety*
- *specific anxiety disorders, including generalized anxiety, panic, phobia, social anxiety, health anxiety, post-traumatic stress disorder and obsessive compulsive disorder.*

14

Understanding depression

In this chapter you will learn:
- *how to assess your mood*
- *the causes of depression and understanding it*
- *what maintains depression*
- *how to beat depression*.

> *This is my depressed stance. When you're depressed, it makes a lot of difference how you stand. The worst thing you can do is straighten up and hold your head high because then you'll start to feel better. If you're going to get any joy out of being depressed, you've got to stand like this.*
>
> Charlie Brown from *Peanuts* by Charles Schultz

Do you actually have depression?

Not everyone is aware that the way they think and act may be indicative of depression. Some people suffer for many years without having an awareness of the problem. For others, it can hit like a truck and you are in no doubt at all that things have gone horribly wrong emotionally. We therefore suggest that you look at the symptoms listed below to see whether any of these ring a bell with you.

RECOGNIZING THE SIGNS AND SYMPTOMS

The symptoms of depression can be cognitive, emotional, behavioural and physical, and may include any (or all) of the following. Place a tick against any of these symptoms that are the same as, or similar to, ones you have noticed in yourself.

▶ *Loss of interest or pleasure in things you would normally enjoy.* ☐
▶ *Feelings of guilt, worthlessness or hopelessness.* ☐
▶ *Difficulty in sleeping; waking up early.* ☐
▶ *Finding that the start of the day is the worst, and feeling somewhat better in the evening.* ☐
▶ *Extreme tiredness, with no energy.* ☐
▶ *Increased or decreased appetite.* ☐
▶ *Weight loss or weight gain.* ☐
▶ *Difficulty in concentrating, making decisions or remembering things.* ☐
▶ *Headaches, abdominal pains and palpitations.* ☐
▶ *Anxiety, panic attacks, overwhelming sadness, bouts of crying.* ☐
▶ *Inability to make decisions, feeling inadequate and unable to cope.* ☐
▶ *Feelings of isolation and insecurity.* ☐
▶ *Thinking negatively about most things.* ☐
▶ *Lack of interest in self-care/appearance.* ☐

CAN YOU DEAL WITH THIS YOURSELF?

If you have recognized four or more of the symptoms above, it is likely that you are suffering from a depressed mood. There are great variances in the level of depression you might be struggling with, ranging from mild to extremely severe. In the latter case, you would be wise to seek professional help from your doctor, who will consider both psychological help and medication to give you the best and quickest way of defeating this low mood. However, except in severe cases, you will be able to tackle depression yourself using cognitive behavioural therapy (CBT) skills and techniques.

Insight

Sometimes depression can lift after a short time with the help of the simplest of CBT techniques and skills. For example, when a person becomes aware of their negative automatic thoughts (NATs) and introduces more realistic helpful ways of looking at themselves and their lives, they can have kinder moments where they tell themselves things like, 'Well, I may not be the best at … but I am good at…'. They can then insert positive personal attributes into their thinking, which begins a process of change.

The causes of depression

If you do suffer from depression, you are not alone. In 2000 Paul Gilbert suggested that there may have been over 300 million people in the world then who suffered from it.

There is no one specific cause for depression but rather a variety of possibilities that may come together or be present individually. These causes can include genetics, biological predisposition, certain types of upbringing, and events of adult life that can be either chronic or specific and traumatic. A major culprit of modern-day life is stress, which is one of the most common influences on our state of mind. Depression can be:

▶ **event-specific.** *This type of depression can usually be tracked back to a particular trauma or negative lifestyle change, probably in the fairly recent past. An advantage of event-specific depression is that you can recall how you felt before you became depressed and this provides a goal and a focus for you to aim for and return to.*
▶ **non-specific.** *This type of depression seems to have a life of its own, and its appearance (and disappearance) bears*

little obvious relationship to your circumstances and general lifestyle at any point in time. People find this type of depression harder to comprehend because it flies in the face of what they will probably describe as 'everything being right' in their lives.

Non-specific depression can also be chronic and the sufferer may find it hard to recall a time when they did not feel this way. This can make defeating it slightly harder as the sufferer cannot imagine how it would feel not to be in depression's thrall. A depression-free life is not something they can envisage and aim to recapture.

IT'S ABOUT HOW YOU SEE IT...

Event-specific depression is most likely to be caused by negative thinking bias or dormant negative beliefs activated by traumatic and/or upsetting events. Non-specific depression is more likely to be maintained by faulty core beliefs that have been around for a long time and drive the sufferer's assumptions, rules, thoughts and behaviours to the extent that their thinking styles, which would to most people seem pessimistic and faulty, seem to them quite rational and realistic.

Insight

The well-known psychotherapist and writer Dorothy Rowe likened depression to a self-made prison, pointing out that for most people choice is involved. You can either stay in the depressed state or make a concerted effort to get out of the depression by getting the appropriate professional help and discovering methods of self-help.

UNDERSTANDING DEPRESSION

Depression is, in simple terms, a mood disorder. This is to say that it is caused not by events (although they may trigger activation of the negative cycle that brings depression on) but by your thoughts and perceptions about specific events, about yourself, about life in general, and about the future.

Depression is occasionally described as the 'common cold' of psychological disorders, and doctors say that approximately one in three of their patients have some sort of depressive symptoms.

YOU CAN RECOVER

Depression is curable, and even in those who seek no treatment and make no attempt to try to get better in any way, it usually goes away of its own accord. However, it is a very distressing illness, and the feelings of bleakness and hopelessness it engenders need not be supported – there is a better way to live.

Negative automatic thoughts again

One of the hallmarks of depression is an extreme negative thinking bias (as always, focusing on worst-case scenarios). Where your mood is low, your thoughts will also be extremely negative and you will find it hard to motivate yourself. This will lead to a cycle of inactivity which, in turn, will increase your depression. The cycle will look something like Figure 14.1.

Low mood leads to:
a more negative view of yourself and/or others;
loss of pleasure or any sense of achievement;
fatigue, poor concentration;
increased sense of hopelessness;
reduced capacity to problem-solve;
reduced activity

↓

which leads to:
lower mood

↓

which leads to:
depression.

Figure 14.1 Cycle of inactivity.

As you study the cycle, think about how it might apply to you and to how you deal with your own problems. Does it seem familiar in any way?

BREAK THE OLD HABIT BY REPLACING IT WITH A NEW ONE

Breaking the cycle will break the hold of the depression. As you will notice, there is a cognitive element, a behavioural element and a physiological element to the cycle, and you will be able to use your CBT tools to make changes to any and all of these areas to lift your mood.

Insight

Cognitive therapy was originally developed by Beck in his work with depressed patients. He noticed that when people were depressed they had negative thoughts about themselves, others and the world. He wrote: 'The depressed person thinks in idiosyncratic and negative ways about himself, his environment, and his future'.

The cognitive component: getting your rational mind back on track

In order to break this spiral of negativity, you need your rational mind to work a little harder. This means starting to challenge the negative outlook that has crept in as a default. Your best way to achieve this is by using a Thought Record. Since you are familiar with the process (see Chapters 5 and 8), you can move immediately to a full seven-column Thought Record. Use this regularly to both dispute your negative thoughts and to discover patterns in your thinking that may flag up negative beliefs that are operating. Because negative thoughts are particularly severe in depression, you will need to use 'Where's the evidence?' strongly, starting out with the evidence you have to support your negative thinking before moving on to evidence that might support an alternative way of looking at things.

- Can you find any evidence of distorted thinking styles? (Refer back to Chapter 7 to remind yourself of these.) This is a good skill as you will often gain comfort and confidence from identifying your thinking with one of the negative styles listed. It will help you to realize the distorted thinking bias you are using, without having to search too hard on your own.

- Can you find any patterns of thinking that might help you identify negative beliefs that are operating? For example, if you find yourself having thoughts with a pattern such as, 'Everything I touch goes wrong', 'Nothing I do works out for me', 'I always mess things up', what type of belief might this throw up? Perhaps, 'I'm useless' (belief about yourself) or 'Life sucks' (belief about the world).

- What will help you to assess your beliefs? This is your formulation (or conceptualization). On a piece of paper, jot down past experiences that might have formed these. For example, over-critical parents would suggest an 'I'm useless' belief, while a few incidents in the past that failed to work out might leave you with the view that life rarely gives you a break.

Once you identify any negative beliefs, you will need to work to modify them (re-read Chapter 10). Working only with negative automatic thoughts (NATs) will not be especially helpful to you if your balanced alternative thoughts (BATs) fly in the face of the negative beliefs that you hold. For example:

Belief: 'I am weak and useless.'
NAT: 'I haven't got the guts to tackle the difficulties in my life.'
BAT: 'If I give things a try, I may find that I do better than I think.'

SHIFTING BELIEFS BEFORE CHANGING THOUGHTS

Although this alternative thought makes good sense as a rational response where the belief is 'I am weak and useless', believing such a positive option is going to be almost impossible. However, if the belief can, at first, be shifted from 'I'm weak and useless' to 'I can occasionally stand my ground', then the balanced thought becomes a believable possibility.

The physiological component: get active

Insight

It is when we are feeling our worst, when we feel anxious and depressed, that we don't do what can give us a psychological and physiological lift, like taking a brisk walk, meeting up with friends, treating ourselves to a beautiful bunch of flowers – the list is endless. Cultivate a habit of self-care.

Depression saps your energy. It can leave you feeling tired and exhausted, even at the start of the day, leading to inactivity. This in turn keeps your mood low. Where you have problems with sleep, read the section on sleep difficulties in Chapter 13. If your sleep problems are severe and ongoing, you may consider discussing medication options with your doctor. Bear in mind that such medication should only be used on an occasional basis in severe conditions. Your mind and body need to learn to restructure natural sleep patterns for longer-term good health. Medication may be used simply to give you an occasional 'break' when tiredness is defeating you.

Depression can sap your motivation and desire to do anything. Because it leaves you feeling flat and uninterested in normal activities, the tendency is not to do them. Staying home feels so much easier and safer. However, as you will appreciate, 'The less we do, the less we want to do' state of mind operates with a vengeance with depression.

ACTIVITY SCHEDULING

A basic CBT tool in dealing with inactivity in depression, and its negative repercussions, is an 'Activity Schedule'. Activity Schedules serve two clear purposes:

1 *They encourage you to structure your day and build a little more activity into it.*

2 *They identify patterns for your moods. You can record when your mood is at its lowest, and you will be able to see – over a period of, say, a week – what levels and types of activity or inactivity exacerbate your low mood, and when you feel somewhat better. This gives you valuable information on how to enhance your mood, and how to avoid letting it get too low.*

The downside of Activity Schedules is that they can seem a bothersome bore, especially when even the most interesting activities fail to rouse your interest. You can set this out in a Thought Record to help you.

Event: **Filling in an Activity Schedule.**
NAT: **This is extremely boring and dull. I just can't be bothered.**
BAT: **The reason everything seems boring just now is due to my depression. There is a point to activity scheduling. I can give this a chance for just a few days and see if it is helpful in fighting my low mood.**

Setting up an activity schedule
You can use your workbook to write up an Activity Schedule. Draw nine vertical lines down the page. The first column needs to contain the time of day, marked off in hourly divisions – 9 a.m., 10 a.m., etc. The other seven columns are the days of the week. Write into your schedule any activities that you already have scheduled immediately. If your activity schedule looks rather blank, ask yourself what else you might do to fill it up. Make a real effort here. It should look something like this:

Time	MON	TUES	WED	THURS	FRI	SAT	SUN
7 a.m.	Get up, shower, etc.	Get up, shower, etc.	Get up, shower, etc.	Get up, shower, etc.	Get up, shower, etc.	Sleep	Sleep
8 a.m.	Breakfast	Go to gym	Breakfast	Go to dentist	Walk dog	Sleep	Sleep

And so on, through the day. Place an asterisk (ideally, in bright red) against the times and situations when you feel at your lowest. Place a (bright green) asterisk against the times you feel at your best. Do you begin to see patterns in when you feel good and when you feel low? What do you make of this? What information do these patterns give you?

Don't let the fact that you have no motivation or enthusiasm for your activities be the driver. You will need to start off without enthusiasm. Be patient. Eventually it will come, but you must become active physically, no matter how lacking in motivation you are.

USING EXERCISE TO IMPROVE YOUR MOOD

In terms of activity scheduling, physical activity can mean anything from going shopping, visiting a friend or driving your car. However, you will also need to put your trainers on. Regular exercise provides your brain with a natural boost of serotonin – the brain chemical that provides the 'feel-good' factor that we have in abundance when our mood is optimistic and positive (see Chapter 13). Please take this seriously – physical exercise is one of the best mood lifters around, and one of the least used by those suffering from depression.

The behavioural component: testing things out and doing more

As you work on your Thought Records and on shifting negative thoughts and beliefs, you will eventually be able to build new behaviours into your efforts. Some of these behavioural changes will be obvious – getting out more, socializing, working, gardening – whatever increases your activity and energy levels; others will be more experimental and will help you to test out negative thoughts and beliefs to check their validity. For example, to test a belief that you are dull and uninteresting you may need to try starting conversations with people to see if you are right. These behavioural experiments can be quite difficult to begin with as they require courage from you to test a hypothesis that you won't believe in. You will initially expect a negative result, not a positive one. For this reason, return to the chapters on goal-setting and behavioural experiments (Chapters 3 and 9). Take very small steps to start with and don't set yourself up to fail. For instance, with the belief mentioned above – that you are dull and uninteresting – start by talking to people. Begin by making a one-sentence comment to people – 'I like your scarf', 'How hot it is', 'What a long queue!' – where it is relatively unimportant how they respond to you. If a dental receptionist you see just once a year fails to connect with you in spite of your efforts, you will not find that as disappointing as someone whose opinion of you is of great value. Use the SMART model to set your goals – you will gain confidence and your mood will lift (see Chapter 3).

HOMEWORK

If you feel that depression or low mood may be a problem for you, you now have the skills to start a programme of recovery. One of the keys to success is to plan well. Start with the cognitive component skills and only move to behavioural testing once you feel a little more comfortable and confident. Expect to work for several weeks to see an improvement, and don't be discouraged if it isn't immediate. Small, consistent steps forward will be more beneficial than occasional larger ones punctured by periods of withdrawal and inactivity.

SUMMARY

In this chapter you have learned more about depression, what causes it, what maintains it, and how to tackle it.

▶ *You can check whether you have depression and also the level of it.*
▶ *We have explained the origins of depression, and the fact that there is no one single universal cause for it. Depression is often brought on by an accumulation of negative components that finally trigger your low mood.*

- *There is a negative cycle that maintains depression and inactivity, and negative thoughts and beliefs can drive your mood down even further.*
- *You can link the CBT skills you have learned in previous chapters to a variety of ways of eliminating depression and lifting your mood.*

FURTHER READING

Beck, A., *Cognitive Therapy of Depression* (New York: The Guildford Press, 1979).

Blackburn, I. M. and Davidson, K., *Cognitive Therapy for Depression and Anxiety* (Oxford: Blackwell, 1995).

Gilbert, P., *Overcoming Depression* (London: Robinson, 2000).

THINGS TO REMEMBER

▸ *Checking the symptoms of depression listed at the beginning of this chapter can help you assess whether or not you are suffering from depression. If you assess that you have mild depression, then you will be able to tackle it with the CBT methods in this book; however, if you think your depression is more severe, it is advisable to seek your GP's help.*

▸ *If you feel depressed, remember you are not alone by any means. Recent studies show that many millions of people across the world suffer depression. Depression is curable and often goes away of its own accord.*

▸ *CBT understands depression as a mood disorder caused by your negative thoughts and perceptions about yourself, your experiences, life as a whole, and fear of the future.*

▸ *People become depressed for many reasons, including: biological predisposition, difficult early life experiences or events in later life, and the stress of modern life. Depression can be event-specific – meaning it can be traced back to a particular traumatic event or time, or non-specific – with no obvious source.*

▸ *Attention to your NATs is crucial in tackling the negative thinking bias that supports depression.*

▸ *When your mood is depressed, your thoughts will be pessimistic and motivation becomes difficult, resulting in inactivity which, in turn, makes the negativity and lethargy worse. Cognitive, behavioural and physiological factors interact in a perpetual self-defeating cycle.*

▸ *The seven-column Thought Record is highly effective in challenging the negative outlook that depression sustains.*

▶ *You have been introduced to another key tool in treating depression, namely, the Activity Schedule, an eight-column chart that helps you plan your days and make observations regarding, for example, your lowest times in the day, what you find difficult and what you manage well and enjoy.*

▶ *Once there is a positive shift in your thinking, you can make changes in your behaviour by embracing new challenges and carrying out some simple behaviour experiments to test your hypotheses, trying things out and noting the results.*

15

Understanding anxiety

In this chapter you will learn:
- *what anxiety is*
- *how it can affect us*
- *the difference between healthy and unhealthy anxiety*
- *how to use your cognitive behavioural therapy skills to defeat unhealthy anxiety.*

> *One ought never to turn one's back on a threatened danger and try to run away from it. If you do that, you will double the danger. But if you meet it promptly and without flinching, you will reduce the danger by half. Never run away from anything. Never!*
>
> Sir Winston Churchill, British Prime Minister (1940–5, 1951–5)

What causes anxiety?

Anxiety is one of the most distressing emotions you can feel, in part because the physiology is so severe – heart-pounding, stomach churning, shaking, dizziness and a variety of other symptoms give you further cause to worry. Anxiety is caused by the belief that situations are more frightening than they really are. The physical symptoms of anxiety play a great part in this over-estimation of the perceived threat, as they are seen themselves as significant indicators that something is seriously wrong.

WHAT DOES ANXIETY MEAN TO YOU?

▶ *Does it mean heightened concern about a positive outcome to a specific situation?*
▶ *Does it mean that you find most situations new to you stressful?*
▶ *Do you suffer from a specific type of anxiety? For example, social anxiety, health anxiety, panic, phobias or obsessional worries or agoraphobia.*

Insight

Fear is at the root of all types of anxiety: for example, fear of being shamed in public, fear resulting from trauma, fear that your health is failing or fear that something dreadful looms in the future. Facing the fear and 'talking it down' in your thought processes is key to working on anxiety.

ANXIETY AS A GOOD THING

Anxiety isn't always a bad thing. Aaron Beck (1976) refers to 'nature favouring anxious genes'. Anxiety prevents you from walking in front of buses or falling over cliffs. It keeps you safe. Albert Ellis (1979) refers to the concept of 'healthy and unhealthy anxiety'. In essence, anxiety is only a problem to you if it is inappropriate to the circumstances you find yourself in. In this chapter, we look at inappropriate anxiety.

Key point: When you start to feel anxious, ask yourself if it is appropriate to the situation and at the right level for the situation. If you are trapped in a lift, being somewhat unnerved would be entirely appropriate. Having a serious panic attack would not be, and would need remedying.

Whereas in depression your focus is usually on past and present events that disturb you, anxiety causes you to worry about events that have not – and may not – happen. Sir Winston Churchill told a story of visiting a man on his deathbed who told him, 'I have had a great many worries and troubles in my life, most of which have never happened.'

When you are in an anxious frame of mind, you not only anticipate a 'worst-case scenario', but you may also conclude that it would be quite unbearable if this scenario were to happen, and that you would be unable to cope with the consequences. You fail to appreciate that you could perhaps deal with the problem, or that someone else might be able to help you. A way of expressing this is:

$$\text{Anxiety} = \frac{\text{Over-estimation of disaster} \times \text{Over-estimation of the perceived 'awfulness' if disaster were to happen}}{\text{Under-estimation of coping skills} + \text{Under-estimation of safety factors}}$$

Normalizing the physiology

Feelings that you describe as 'anxiety' or 'tension' are simply the result of a normal bodily reaction to danger or threat in the world about you. This bodily reaction, called 'automatic arousal', helped prepare the cave people to muster the physiological resources to either fight or run away when faced with danger along the lines of sabre-toothed tigers and such like. Be assured that when you have these feelings, your body is simply trying to *help* you – not to cause you any distress.

BODILY RESPONSE TO A RED ALERT MESSAGE

When you face danger, messages pass from your brain to different
parts of the body, telling it to speed up and be prepared for
extra activity. You may experience similar sensations when
you take vigorous exercise, and many of the physical reactions
in anxiety are like those after, say, running around the block –
heart beating fast, face flushing and legs feeling like jelly.

How do you feel when you become anxious? What bodily or
physical changes do you notice? Below is a list of ways in which
anxiety can affect you, particularly if it has been going on for a
while. If you have felt any of these, place a tick beside them and
add any others that you think are important.

Common effects of anxiety or worry
- *I get irritable or touchy.* ☐
- *My eating pattern is affected.* ☐
- *My sleep is disturbed.* ☐
- *I can't concentrate.* ☐
- *I can't seem to get on with my family/partner as well as
  I used to.* ☐
- *My social life is affected and I don't want to see
  my friends as much.* ☐
- *I stay in much more than I used to do.* ☐
- *I have difficulty keeping up with important things
  in my life.* ☐
- *I lose interest in life and feel depressed – nothing seems
  to interest me any more.* ☐

Can you think of any others? The statements you have ticked show
you the most important ways in which your anxiety and worry
affect you.

Other symptoms associated with anxiety

▶ **Poor concentration and memory.** *When you are under stress, thoughts may become fuzzy and hard to organize. You can become easily distracted or unable to take in or remember information as effectively as normal.*

▶ **Sleep disturbance.** *Worry can make it particularly difficult to 'switch off' and sleep is often affected. This has a build-up effect that gets worse over an extended period of time.*

▶ **Short temper, irritability.** *If you are experiencing excessive worry and tiredness, you may find you become more easily frustrated and have little energy for problems outside your most immediate concerns. This can make you feel snappy and short-tempered.*

▶ **Tiredness and lethargy.** *Worry and tension use up a lot of energy so that it feels difficult to make the effort to cope.*

▶ **Depression.** *The feeling that worries are taking over your life or disrupting normal activities can understandably lead to feelings of depression and despair. This often makes it difficult to believe that change is possible or that life can be better. Your motivation goes and you no longer feel like doing the things you once enjoyed.*

Key point: While these may seem to be worrying symptoms, they are simply alerting you to the fact that your thinking has become conditioned to looking at things in an anxious way. They are not harmful in themselves, nor are they indications of any serious physical or emotional problems.

How anxiety develops: the anxiety spiral

Physical sensations that occur when you are confronted with an anxiety-provoking situation can often aggravate it. These symptoms may be anticipatory or they may be evoked by the memory of a past experience when you became anxious. Feeling that something is physically wrong can increase the tension and exacerbate the symptoms. The result can be seen in an 'anxiety spiral', or a vicious cycle of anxiety, as shown in Figure 15.1. Panic can ensue, as can the desire to run away or avoid the situation.

'Here I am in a situation where I usually get upset.'

↓

Physical symptoms manifest

↓

'I can't cope when i'm anxious.'

↓

Physical symptoms increase

↓

'I knew it; I'm becoming really anxious now.'

↓

Symptoms of anxiety intensify

↓

'Maybe I'm going to faint!'

↓

'I feel sick and dizzy.'

↓

Panic, run, escape

↓

Eventual subsidence of physical and emotional feelings

Figure 15.1 The anxiety spiral.

Think about a recent situation you have found stressful and whether your reaction was similar to that in the anxiety spiral.

> ## Insight
>
> You may have found your own ways to stay on top of your anxiety that seem harmless or sensible to you – and these can be idiosyncratic and highly inventive – but they may perpetuate a vicious cycle of anxiety by maintaining the problem and stopping you from tackling it.

FACTORS THAT MAINTAIN ANXIETY

Safety behaviours

Safety behaviours, as the name implies, are tactics you embrace in order – you believe – to keep you safe from threat or harm. For example, someone who fears having a panic attack in the supermarket simply never shops in one. Someone who fears being found dull and uninteresting never accepts social invitations. If you think you might fail at something, then don't even try it. These seem like obvious, natural solutions to your fears and worries – and, what is more, they seem to work. However, on the down side, they cause your worries to stay with you as you never give yourself the opportunity to discover that the perceived threat was either invalid or manageable.

You may have heard of the story of the man riding on a bus with a banana in his ear. When the passenger sitting next to him asked him about this, the man explained that it was to keep the elephants away. The other passenger was flabbergasted. 'But there aren't any elephants within miles of here,' he responded, bemused. 'I know,' said the first man. 'The banana works really well, doesn't it?' This man's safety behaviour appeared to work for him, although it may eventually have given him bad earache! Although this story is amusing, it is a real example of the type of reassurances people develop and maintain to protect themselves from unlikely catastrophes.

Avoidance

Avoidance is the most common safety behaviour of all, and one that many people use occasionally. As we have described above, simply failing to place yourself in situations of perceived threat appears to keep you safe. Yet its downfall is that it fails to allow you to discover that the threat was either non-existent or manageable, and thus avoidance becomes a *problem-maintaining* behaviour.

You may say, 'Oh, but I don't avoid things. I face up to them.' For instance, although you suffer from chronic shyness and feel like an 'outsider' in a group, you still go to the pub or attend parties and group gatherings. However, you may be discounting that you use safety behaviours once there. Perhaps you sit quietly, talk very little, fail to act in an animated way or engage others in conversation. Perhaps you leave such events early. Avoidance can be more subtle than you realize, so look closely at this. Are you really facing your fears fully or only partially?

Escape

Escape is a first cousin of avoidance. It means that you tolerate situations until you feel either physical and/or emotional sensations that worry you – then you make a quick getaway.

Escape is often planned in advance – emergency forward planning. You sit next to the emergency exit at the school play, or only accept an aisle seat in the cinema. You put yourself in a position to abscond quickly if you feel that you need to. A consequence of this is that you not only fail to discover whether the threat is real or if you might cope with it if it is – you give the perceived threat more credence than it deserves, which again maintains its hold over you.

Consider this: imagine that you have placed yourself in a position so that you can easily escape from a perceived threat. Say you are sitting near a theatre exit in case you feel a panic attack coming on. Now, imagine that this panicky feeling does start. You dive for the door, and as soon as you get to the other side of it, your panicky feelings diminish. Thank goodness! But why? Why have they reduced or disappeared? Is it the air? Is it different on one side of the door to the other? Is it hotter inside, cooler outside? Is it standing rather than sitting? Is it somehow safer outside than in? Think what it could be.

The answer is that on one side of the door you are tense, and on the other side you are relaxed. It is nothing more than that. By constantly using an 'escape hatch' you are never giving yourself the opportunity to discover that you could gradually relax if you stayed on the other side of the door (and you wouldn't miss the second half of the play!).

Over-focusing

This can involve the anxious person in either:

▶ *focusing on the anxiety-provoking thought or situation – for example, someone with health anxiety consistently checking out the meaning of every minor ache or pain; or*
▶ *focusing away from the anxiety-provoking situation – for example, an accident victim with post-trauma anxiety deliberately avoiding going anywhere near the scene of the accident.*

In instances such as these, because the anxious thoughts are not faced, it becomes impossible for them to be challenged.

The faulty logic of emotional reasoning

Emotional reasoning will follow the lines of 'If I feel it then it must be so'. For instance, someone who is highly anxious about a speech they must make, and fears that they will shake and stutter as they speak, will believe that they are actually doing this, even though these symptoms are invisible to anyone else. Someone who perceives a situation as dangerous, and feels the physical and emotional symptoms of anxiety, will presume that their anxious feelings are proof that they are in a dangerous situation, irrespective of the reality.

Overcoming anxiety

Cognitive behavioural therapy (CBT) offers a collection of cognitive, behavioural and physiological strategies for treating anxiety, all of which have been covered in earlier chapters of this book.

COGNITIVE STRATEGIES

The key error that anxious people make is that they focus on ways to *reduce their anxious feelings* by using safety behaviours. Instead, they need to focus on *reducing the strength of the erroneous belief* that drives the anxiety. As the belief strength diminishes, so will the anxiety, of its own accord and permanently.

Key point: When challenging your most anxious and worrying thoughts, you are specifically looking for an alternative, less threatening explanation for your worries. You can achieve this cognitively or by testing out your fears with behavioural experimentation.

Challenging your anxious thoughts
A Thought Record is a key aid in assisting you to re-evaluate the severity and/or likelihood of the threat causing your anxiety. Use this a little differently than with depression, as with anxiety you are making predictions about the likelihood of future events, rather than trying to evaluate the past or present. You therefore evaluate the accuracy of your predictions by assessing outcomes.

- ▶ *What did I think would happen?*
- ▶ *What actually happened?*
- ▶ *What can I learn from that?*

Theory A versus Theory B
This is an excellent technique, used especially with cases of irrational worry such as those seen in obsessive compulsive disorder (OCD), developed by Salkovskis and Kirk (1997). This theory invites the anxious person to consider two alternative propositions. The first (Theory A) is that his or her fears are correct and that the problem is therefore one of catastrophe. For example, 'If I travel in a lift, I will have a panic attack that will cause me heart failure.' The second (Theory B) is that the problem is possibly not one of catastrophe, but one of worry about catastrophe. For example,

'I worry that I might panic, and that this might cause me to be ill.'
You can then test these alternative theories using various CBT
skills – looking for evidence, testing beliefs, weighing up the pros
and cons of likelihood, and so on.

Theory A possibility	Theory B possibility
'If I travel by train I will have a panic attack and die.'	'If I travel by train I am worried that I will have a panic attack and die.'
Evidence for this view: 'I have felt as though something terrible could happen when I have travelled by train in the past.'	**Evidence for this view:** 'My thoughts do make me extremely anxious, but nothing physically bad has ever happened, nor have I heard of this happening to anyone else.'
What I need to do if this is true: Never again travel by train to ensure my safety. Warn others of the possible consequences of travelling by train.	**What I need to do if this is true:** Take steps to learn to reduce my anxiety and face my fears. I need to travel in trains more often until I am comfortable.

Imaginal exposure

Imaginal exposure is used in the treatment of certain anxiety
disorders where the fear of testing out the negative predictions
is too great. Instead, you start by simply imagining yourself, for
example, as an agoraphobic, opening the front door and going
outside. Or, with a phobic fear of spiders, you can imagine
yourself being near to one or even touching one. Begin with small
challenges and work towards the more difficult. As always, don't
set yourself up to fail. Imagine easy things to start with, and
don't move on until you can hold the image for some time and
feel quite comfortable with it. Equally, if the image is stressful,
metaphorically step backwards, and find something less anxiety-
provoking to start with.

BEHAVIOURAL STRATEGIES

Devising experiments to test out the validity of catastrophic predictions – in principle, learning to 'face your fears' – is invaluable for tackling avoidance head on. Develop an action plan for graded exposure (see Chapter 9, page 106), where going 'cold turkey' would be too traumatic. However, a note of caution: don't let graded exposure be too gentle or cautious or you will gain little sense of achievement and perhaps feel that your efforts are not working.

PHYSIOLOGICAL STRATEGIES

Learning to reduce the physical sensations of anxiety through relaxation and deep breathing is extremely useful when the consequences of high anxiety severely impair performance or the ability to face a feared situation. You have learned about these techniques in Chapter 13.

Insight

CBT acknowledges that because deep relaxation is an anxiety-inhibiting response we are unable to experience deep relaxation and fear concurrently.

HOMEWORK

If you have read this chapter to gain more knowledge of anxiety and its treatment, then we suggest you read more on the subject – perhaps using our 'Further reading' suggestions below.

If you suffer from anxiety yourself, work through the exercises described above, using the skills you have learned in previous chapters. Identify your own personal anxiety triggers and devise ways to deal with these using thought challenging, evidence finding, and behavioural experimentation. You will be pleasantly surprised by the positive results you achieve if you persevere.

SUMMARY

In this chapter we have looked at the causes of anxiety and what maintains it.

▶ *The very things that many people regard as anxiety reducers – avoidance and escape – in fact maintain and exacerbate the anxious situations.*

▶ *The key to overcoming anxiety is not to focus on reducing the sensations, but on loosening the strength of erroneous belief that is causing them.*

▶ *You can overcome anxiety using thought challenging and searching for evidence to support both your anxious views and more balanced alternative explanations.*

▶ *You can devise behavioural experiments to test out your negative predictions. In the case of anxiety, this usually means 'standing your ground' in graded steps so that you have the opportunity to see that your fears are probably exaggerated and possibly groundless.*

FURTHER READING

Beck, A., *Cognitive Therapy and the Emotional Disorders* (Michigan: International Universities Press, 1976).

Kennerley, H., *Overcoming Anxiety: A Self-help Practical Manual Using CBT Techniques* (London: Robinson, 2006).

Salkovskis, P. and Kirk, J., 'Obsessive Compulsive Disorder' in Clark, D. and Fairburn, C. (eds.), *The Science and Practice of Cognitive Behavioural Therapy* (Oxford: Oxford University Press, 1997).

Wells, A., *Cognitive Therapy of Anxiety Disorders: A Practice Manual* (Chichester: Wiley, 2000).

THINGS TO REMEMBER

▶ Anxiety manifests in different forms – post-traumatic stress disorder (PTSD), health anxiety, obsessive compulsive disorder (OCD), phobias and panic all come under the blanket term 'anxiety disorder'. GAD stands for 'generalized anxiety disorder': when a person perpetually worries and frets and their worrying moves from one area to the next, without any one particular focus.

▶ People become alarmed by the physical symptoms of anxiety as they can be extreme, such as a racing heart, palpitations, shaking, dizziness and pains in the chest. It is important to appreciate that these symptoms cannot harm you and will go away on their own.

▶ A certain amount of anxiety is built into your genes, to protect you from danger and from taking unwarranted risks, but when levels of anxiety are disproportionate to the actual threat it becomes unhealthy.

▶ Your anxiety will disappear as you challenge the validity of the anxiety-provoking belief using both cognitive and behavioural challenges rathar than simply attempting to reduce or eliminate anxious sensations.

▶ Anxiety is evident in bodily or physical changes, such as irritability, disturbed sleep, lack of concentration, exhaustion and lethargy.

▶ Psychologists call a quick bodily reaction to perceived dangerous situations 'automatic arousal'.

▶ When anxiety starts to take hold, physical symptoms can build quickly, backed up by your anxious thoughts. This creates an interacting 'anxiety spiral', taking your anxiety to crescendo levels.

▶ Look out for your 'safety behaviours' and avoidance tactics like 'escape' plans. They may make you feel safer in the short term, but this is illusionary. They will hinder your progress rather than help you conquer your anxiety.

▶ Thought Records are a central tool in addressing anxiety: they are used in a 'prediction' context to articulate your anxious thoughts and what you think is going to happen in perceived difficult situations. You can then evaluate the accuracy of your predictions by looking at what actually happened.

▶ There are many CBT techniques and skills that can help you put your anxiety into perspective and prepare you for facing up to feared situations. Examples include the 'Theory A versus Theory B technique', 'imaginal exposure' and behavioural and physiological strategies.

16

CBT for specific anxiety disorders

In this chapter you will learn:
- **to identify different types of anxiety**
- **to understand anxiety disorder causes and what maintains them**
- **about CBT treatments for overcoming anxiety disorders.**

> *Alright. Let's not panic. I can make the money by selling one of my livers. I can get by with one.*
>
> Dan Castellaneta, US actor and writer

> *Blessed is the person who is too busy to worry in the daytime and too sleepy to worry at night.*
>
> Author unknown

Anxiety disorders

In this chapter, we look at specific problems – common to many – that come under the general heading of anxiety disorders, although they have their own specific features and treatments. They will be known to you as 'panic', 'phobia' and 'health anxiety', 'social anxiety', 'post-traumatic stress disorder' and 'obsessive compulsive spectrum disorders'. A further common type of anxiety covered here – which you may be personally familiar with, or certainly know of someone who is – belongs to those who seem to worry all the time about anything and everything. This type of worry is called 'generalized anxiety disorder' (GAD).

In this chapter, we do not constantly point out to you when to use a Thought Record or another technique you have already worked on. We assume that you can apply these skills now, and here we add to this basic knowledge with more specific key facts and treatment possibilities.

Insight

Anxiety is a common response when we are overwrought, stressed and worried – it warns us something is wrong. Usually we take anxious feelings in our stride and they subside when the pressures lift. However, this isn't always the case – anxiety and its effects can persist and have a profound and debilitating impact on our lives.

WHAT IS MEANT BY 'ANXIETY DISORDERS'?

In a therapeutic sense, the term 'anxiety disorders' covers a number of psychological problems including GAD (characterized by excessive worrying and anxiousness about anything and everything), phobias (specific fears such as fear of flying, fear of heights, spiders, snakes, etc.), panic (when a person experiences intense anxious feelings and may think they are going to die or lose their mind), health anxiety, social anxiety, agoraphobia, post-traumatic stress disorder and obsessive compulsive spectrum disorders.

BASIC GUIDANCE

It is not within the remit of this book to offer in-depth cognitive behavioural therapy (CBT) help for these conditions. Our aims are to, firstly, inform you of the existence of such conditions and tell you something about them, secondly, to look at what maintains them, and, thirdly, to summarize the skills and techniques that can be used to overcome the problems. At the end of this chapter there are reading suggestions for each of the specific disorders mentioned. You can also read Chapter 22 on seeking professional help if you consider that this might be beneficial.

> **Key point: While CBT offers basic skills to address anxiety disorders, the specific treatment protocols for each disorder are, in essence, quite different.** It is for this reason that we ask you to learn more about these disorders where they are a problem for you, either through reading or through professional therapy. Do not rely on general anxiety treatment alone.

Insight

The cognitions of GAD sufferers are deeply entrenched in worrying, almost as a way of life. If this is true of you, challenge the 'buts' and 'cannots' that your conditioned mind throws at you in objection to learning new skills and techniques, in order to defeat your anxiety.

Generalized anxiety disorder

To begin with, we look at GAD. This is the most common type of day-to-day anxiety that frustrates and upsets people. However once you understand the reasons it is maintained, it is usually not too hard to break free from.

'Generalized anxiety disorder' (GAD) is a term used to describe symptoms of intense anxiety (worrying, tension, impairment) without the anxiety being focused on a specific area (for instance, on health, social situations or phobias). As with all anxiety disorders, GAD is characterized by excessive worry and anxiety that persists over a reasonably long period of time. This chronic anxiety state is difficult to control, causes distress and limits a person's activities.

GAD sufferers usually find that as one worry resolves itself, another comes along and takes its place. In other words, it is not the events that are the problem, but the sufferer's consistent perception of events as threats and problems.

EXAMPLE

Peter was 42 and felt that he should be very happy with his life. He had a lovely wife, two delightful children, a good job and a nice home. Yet Peter spent his life worrying – suppose he lost his job and couldn't pay the bills? Suppose his wife became tired of his worrying and decided to leave him? Suppose the children fell in with a bad group of friends and failed at school or got into drugs? Life seemed like one long battle to Peter and he could not remember a time when worry had not dominated it.

Peter is a good example of someone who suffers from GAD. GAD sufferers tend to hold similar views about worry, such as:

- *beliefs that worry leads to positive consequences – it is motivating*
- *beliefs that worry can prevent negative outcomes – worrying prepares you for the worst*
- *beliefs that worry has negative effects, for example, 'I will be unable to perform well', or, on the contrary, beliefs that worry is generally helpful – 'The more I worry, the more likely it will be that a solution will present itself'.*

The vicious cycle of worry is caused when relentless worry undermines the ability to problem-solve so that a person loses confidence in their problem-solving abilities, which in turn supports further worry.

OVERCOMING GENERALIZED ANXIETY DISORDER

The best way to defeat generalized worry involves breaking this cycle by understanding it and then eliminating it by addressing the underlying fears. This can be achieved by the following.

- **Identifying and challenging unhelpful thoughts** *based on the worry beliefs cited above.*
- **Learning to live with uncertainty.** *This is a more helpful way forward than trying to estimate the likelihood of feared events actually happening. Begin to challenge the thoughts that*

relate to such an intolerance of uncertainty. Ask yourself questions such as: 'How would it be possible to be completely certain of events?' Consider the many events in your life that are uncertain – the possibility of a car crash when driving from A to B, for example – which don't disturb you, and question why that is. Learn to accept the idea of possibility (it might happen), against that of probability (it is unlikely to).

▶ **Overcoming avoidance** and learning to face the fear that the worry represents. In other words, moving from, 'What if...?' to 'If it happens, I'll deal with it.'

▶ **Learn to use strategies such as distraction** when worries flood in, or time-limit the worry period.

Phobias

A phobia is a form of anxiety that has a specific focus. For example, a fear of spiders, or of being in open spaces or of heights.

Common phobias
Acrophobia: fear of heights.

Agoraphobia: fear of open spaces, crowded places or being out of a safe environment.

Arachnophobia: fear of spiders.

Claustrophobia: fear of confined or small spaces.

Emetophobia: fear of vomiting.

Haemophobia: fear of blood.

Noctiphobia: fear of the dark and night.

Using behavioural techniques to overcome phobias
The usual treatment for a phobia is graded exposure and desensitization to the fear. As we have described in Chapter 15, where the phobic fear is strong you can start with imaginal

exposure to the feared situation. Once you are comfortable with this, move on to the next stage.

Here's an example for you. Imagine that you have a snake phobia.

▶ **Step 1.** *Look at photographs of snakes for as long as you can. Let the initial anxiety wash over you, and hang on. You will find that your anxiety will subside gradually.*
▶ **Step 2.** *Now touch the snakes in the photographs. Use the same technique of continuing to touch the snake photo until your anxiety subsides.*
▶ **Step 3.** *Get hold of a toy rubber snake from somewhere (your nearest toy shop or a toy chest would be good places to look). Play with it, drape it around your neck, take it to bed with you.*
▶ **Step 4.** *What next? (This is a flexible model that you will build yourself, so we are not being prescriptive.) Find a snake programme on television that you could watch.*
▶ **Step 5.** *At this point, you might be ready to start imagining touching a snake, or having one draped around you. If that is too difficult, even just as imagery, drop it for the moment and come back to it.*
▶ **Step 6.** *This could logically be visiting the reptile house at the zoo, starting off behind the glass.*
▶ **Step 7.** *Eventually, you might ask to be able to touch a snake at the zoo (although you may be the only adult among a group of children).*

You can see that the task of graded exposure can be adjusted and modified to suit you. Become comfortable with one step before you move on to another. Incidentally, there is no rule that says that simply plunging your hand into a basketful of snakes isn't just as effective – research shows that it is. However, this is not the easiest effort to make and most people prefer the staggered approach.

Insight

Graded exposure and desensitization to the fear are the usual treatment for phobias. These are methods of facing the fear by acclimatizing you, in gradual manageable stages, to the feared object or situation.

Panic

Panic is extreme anxiety where the physical symptoms become so marked and frightening that the person misinterprets these sensations and believes some harm is going to come to them, or that they are going to lose control completely.

> **Jargon dictionary: A 'panic attack' is a sudden increase in anxiety.** 'Panic disorder' describes the presence of repeated panic attacks over a period of time.

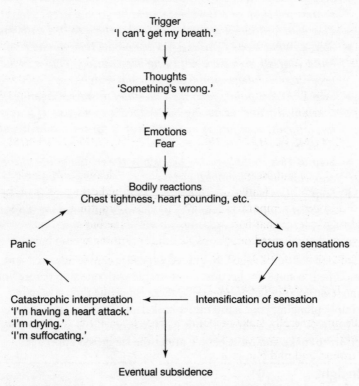

Figure 16.1 The panic model.

Panic can start from a small, indiscriminate trigger – perhaps a missed heartbeat or a momentary breathing difficulty. The anxiety is initially created by a misinterpretation of what that small trigger means. For example, look at the panic model in Figure 16.1.

MISINTERPRETING THE SYMPTOMS

The individual's misinterpretation of the meaning of the symptoms leads to the anxiety increasing, until the physical symptoms are so bad that the person 'cannot stand it' and escapes from the situation.

RETAINED MEMORY OF THE FEAR CAN ACT AS A TRIGGER

A common source of panic is claustrophobia – very often in lifts, perhaps in trains or other confined spaces. However, once someone has had a panic attack, the retained memory of how unpleasant it was can trigger a further attack, simply, for example, by being in the same place that the first attack happened or by seeing or hearing something that recreates the negative memory.

DEALING WITH PANIC IN A WAY THAT MAINTAINS THE PROBLEM

Avoidance and escape are the usual ways of dealing with panic. Once out of the feared situation, the individual calms down. While this causes a temporary reduction in panic symptoms, the person does not learn that had they not fled the scene but stood their ground and waited out the panic attack, nothing would have happened and the attack would simply have died away.

THE COMMON PREDICTIONS

People generally make one of two predictions about the outcome of their panic attack, neither of which they are prepared to wait around and find out about.

1 *The physical feelings they have will get so bad that they will be seriously ill and perhaps die.*
2 *They will 'lose control' and behave in a way that will be extremely embarrassing and simply not bearable.*

In reality, neither of these things is going to happen to any great extent. The physiology does no physical harm at all, and no one ever becomes maniacal. What actually happens is that the panic dies away of *its own accord*.

OVERCOMING PANIC

Overcoming panic involves challenging the negative predictions and looking at less threatening alternative explanations for the marked physical sensations. For example, this would mean recognizing that the sensations are due to anxiety, which is not harmful, rather than to impending heart failure, which is.

You can face up to the feelings panic engenders using behavioural experiments. Make your prediction about what you think will happen and then test it out to see if it does. As with phobias, graded exposure usually works the best (see Chapter 9). If, for example, a person thinks they will have a panic attack if they go into a supermarket, then:

▸ *step 1 could be to stand outside the door of the supermarket for as long and as often as it takes for the anxiety to die away*
▸ *step 2 could be to go inside the supermarket, but just briefly and not far in. They would need to do this regularly until they become comfortable with it*
▸ *step 3 might be picking up a shopping basket.*

You will understand the process by now. You keep facing the fear, but in graded steps, becoming comfortable with each one before moving on. Letting a full panic attack come on, and refusing to use escape but waiting to see what happens is totally effective, but not a popular first choice for breaking panic's hold.

Insight

Feelings of panic escalate as thoughts become more extreme, adding to the fear. Therefore, controlling negative fearful thoughts by replacing them with more balanced self-supporting thoughts and using breathing and relaxation techniques can be helpful.

Health anxiety

In the case of health anxiety, you make the assumption that, because you have pain or another physical symptom then you must have a serious health complaint. Even when health is checked, tests are carried out by doctors and specialists, and the individual has been assured that nothing is medically wrong with them, they are still not reassured and a preoccupation with health problems persists. This preoccupation may cause significant distress and difficulties in relationships and other areas of the worrier's life. Medical checks that show no evidence of ill health are disbelieved and the person remains convinced that something has been missed. Health anxiety is maintained through:

▶ *avoidance (failure to learn that the problem is not physical)*
▶ *reassurance seeking (repeated medical tests)*
▶ *scanning for symptoms (constantly checking both the person's body and external confirmatory sources such as the internet).*

Insight

It is the irrational interpretation you give to bodily symptoms or the focusing on possible future threats to your health that maintain health anxiety.

OVER-FOCUSING ON THE WORRY

Often a person who has anxiety concerning their health will believe that their complaints have been diagnosed incorrectly and this can add to the anxiety. They may insist on repeated medical tests and constantly consult their doctors, or they may avoid having tests for fear 'of hearing the worst'. They usually need to talk about their health over and over again with other people. The constant focus on the physical symptoms can cause a cycle of anxiety as the anxiety maintains the bodily tensions (physiological signs) that result in further symptoms, anxiety and stress.

Such people tend to trawl the internet and/or medical books looking for symptoms that match theirs. Instead of reducing their fears, this tends to increase them because the more they read, the more they come across other symptoms to worry about. Or they notice that their original, perceived symptoms have other possible meanings and interpretations that could suggest different and even worse prognoses. Following from this, the person spends enormous amounts of time ruminating over what they have discovered, trying to interpret and re-interpret what it could mean.

OVERCOMING HEALTH ANXIETY

Challenging the content of the prediction
As with other types of anxiety, it is the interpretation of the worrying thoughts that needs to be identified. Some people may hold the following belief:

▶ *'If I stay vigilant for the signs and symptoms of illness, I will be okay.'*

Others may think:

▶ *'Just thinking about my illness will bring it on.'*

TESTING UNHELPFUL BELIEFS
You can test your fears and beliefs by various methods. One is to investigate the evidence and ask yourself, 'What evidence is there that I have a serious health problem or disease?'

Evidence for:

▶ *'I have pain in my body on a regular basis.'*
▶ *'I have other symptoms – I have no energy. I feel lethargic and tired.'*
▶ *'I read about someone who had symptoms similar to mine and they died of (for example) cancer.'*

Evidence against:

- ▶ *'I have been to my doctor and had various tests and they assured me there are no medical reasons to suggest I have a serious medical complaint.'*
- ▶ *'I have been to a specialist who carried out tests and they didn't find anything significantly physically wrong with me either.'*
- ▶ *'When people are around I sometimes forget my symptoms – they seem to go away.'*
- ▶ *'I know that aches and pains can be a common result of bodily tension and when I practise relaxation techniques it seems to help.'*
- ▶ *'Although I worry a lot about my health, I still seem to be in good shape.'*

CONDUCTING A SURVEY

Ask a number of people, perhaps colleagues, friends and family members, whether they have similar pains or sensations in their bodies at times and what kind of thoughts they have if they do. What do you think might be the outcome?

- ▶ *You may find that they have similar thoughts to you but that they then dismiss them and stop worrying.*
- ▶ *You may find that when they do have symptoms they consult a doctor and accept the doctor's explanation or diagnosis of the complaint.*
- ▶ *The findings of your survey may reassure you that your worries are normal or you may discover that you worry more about your health than other people – which suggests that you might be worrying unnecessarily.*

REDUCING SAFETY BEHAVIOURS

This includes eliminating the practice of reassurance seeking from medical tests, consulting friends and family, medical books and the internet.

Ellie was a 32-year-old single mother who worried constantly. If she had a bad headache she thought she had a brain tumour. If she had aches in her arms she interpreted them as an impending heart attack. She had palpitations and dizziness when she was in anxiety-provoking situations, which strengthened her belief that she had heart weaknesses.

Ellie had seen a doctor who referred her to specialists and she was found to be in overall good health. However, she couldn't agree with their diagnosis and was convinced that they were missing things. She repeatedly asked for more tests.

Three years previously, Ellie had a spate of bereavements: a close friend, an aunt and her mother had died in a little over a year. The loss of her mother in particular was very hard as she had been a great source of support to Ellie, helping her with the children, housework and finances. All this came to an end with her mother's death as Ellie's father had health problems and was unable to be supportive.

Ellie was well aware of the stress she was under as the mother of two young children. She lay in bed at night with thoughts running through her mind such as, 'How will I manage?' and 'How will my children manage if something happens to me?'

Ellie's health anxiety was improved by:

- *making notes of her thoughts and moods and writing them up in a Thought Record*
- *checking out the evidence for and against her having a serious illness (doctors/specialist diagnosis, results of her tests and predictions)*
- *planning daily activity sheets (including pleasure, mastering and achievement activities which demonstrated to Ellie both that she was capable of managing her affairs on a daily basis and that she was able to enjoy many aspects of her life)*

- *testing her predictions (for example, about how she could manage on her own when she might feel physically bad)*
- *imagining herself well, happy and coping*
- *taking practical steps by arranging childcare to improve her support network, and making provision for her children in case she became ill.*

Once Ellie appreciated that her fears about her health were unfounded and that, even if there was a problem, she would cope, her fears faded and her life returned to normal.

Social anxiety

THE DISCOMFORT OF MIXING SOCIALLY

'Social anxiety' is a term used to describe feeling extreme anxiety and discomfort in social situations. There is a fear of being judged harshly by other people, behaving in an inappropriate or embarrassing way, or being humiliatingly publicly exposed. The person may not actually do anything that is embarrassing but they feel that they have done so or fear that if they do expose themselves to the scrutiny of others, humiliation and disaster will follow. Research shows that social anxiety affects both men and women equally. It often begins in adolescence and in its early stages it will show as extreme shyness.

Social anxiety may cause an individual to avoid social interaction as much as possible, especially social gatherings where they will be exposed to a large number of people. When social events can't be avoided, the person might attend functions but feel a high level of distress before and during the event. It is a typical feature of social anxiety that over time the person will increasingly focus attention on themselves and their social failings, making negative self-evaluations and catastrophic interpretations of either imagined or actual events and comparing themselves unfavourably to others.

POTENTIAL PROBLEMS OF SOCIAL ANXIETY

People who are affected by social anxiety tend to:

▶ *worry overly and relentlessly about what other people think about them and assume that any thoughts will be critical or negative*
▶ *worry about their performance in social settings and make negative assessments regarding this*
▶ *have persistent negative thoughts about the physical signs of anxiety such as sweating, palpitations and blushing.*

For someone with social anxiety, their negative beliefs about themselves, such as, 'I'm dull/boring/no one ever likes me', can turn into self-fulfilling prophecies, leading to:

▶ *Isolation and loneliness, meaning fewer opportunities to develop intimate relationships with others.*
▶ *This lack of opportunity to socialise, in turn, will prevent the person developing – or even maintaining – their social skills.*
▶ *Thus, they are more likely to avoid social situations, exacerbating the problem and further lowering their poor self-esteem.*
▶ *In time, this can lead to depression, as the sufferer becomes ever more isolated and believes more firmly that there is something wrong with them.*

OVERCOMING SOCIAL ANXIETY

What happens
One of the problems for someone suffering from social anxiety is that, when in company, their focus is totally on themselves and their negative thoughts. Wonderings such as, 'How do I look?', 'What is this person thinking about me?', 'What will I say next?', 'How will I handle a gap in the conversation?' flood the mind of the sufferer, and actually prevent them from focusing on anything else. This can mean that the person *does* come across as not clearly present and interested/interesting. They will seem preoccupied

and may not properly contribute to the conversation. Part of the person's mind is listening; while another part is feeding themselves negative self-talk.

The solution
The way out of this is to literally 'turn off the radio' of self-talk. Become an active listener. If you focus totally on what someone else is saying you will forget your own concerns. Ensure you concentrate to the extent that, if there is a lull in the conversation, you can simply pick a word from the last sentence spoken, and say, 'Tell me more', 'Tell me more about Istanbul, I've never been there', 'Surfing, I have never tried that. Tell me more about what it involves', and so on.

Becoming a good listener is an excellent skill for anyone suffering from social anxiety, as it takes away the focus from negative self-thoughts and puts it on really hearing what the other person is saying.

Insight
Self-consciousness typifies social anxiety, where you concentrate on yourself and worry about how others view you. A helpful method to assist you in overcoming social anxiety is to focus outwardly on other people and your surroundings.

Other strategies, skills and techniques
▶ *Deal with anticipatory anxiety – examining predictions, anticipating problems – and work out how these can be minimized.*
▶ *Carry out experiments to help focus your attention.*
▶ *Conduct a post-mortem of the situation – 'What did I learn from it?', 'How did I do?', 'What could I do in a similar situation that could help me in the future?'*
▶ *Construct a balanced appraisal of the situation and consider the thoughts and assumptions it shows up. Consider their validity. Look for evidence for an alternative thought. Consider how else you might look at the situation.*
▶ *Observe other people, noting how they behave and what they say. Develop ways into conversations that you feel at ease using.*

- *Practise introductions. 'Hello, I'm Angela – It's good to meet you', for example, will help to relax you. Also practise ways of ending a conversation. This might be something like 'It's been nice talking to you; I think I'll get myself something to eat/to drink.'*
- *Practise managing situations in your mind by using imaginal exposure (see page 201).*
- *Slow your breathing and relax your body.*

Post-traumatic stress disorder

Post-traumatic stress is an anxiety-related condition caused by an adverse reaction to a traumatic or extremely stressful event. Many different kinds of events can lead to post-traumatic stress disorder (PTSD), including being a victim of crime or abuse (physical or sexual) or being involved in a serious accident. People who work in high-risk safety professions, such as soldiers or fire officers, may experience PTSD as they are more likely to witness traumatic events or to experience personal danger or injury. Others who are susceptible to developing PTSD may include:

- *those who have had a shocking event in their lives such as the sudden, violent or suicidal death of a loved one*
- *someone who has either witnessed or inadvertently been involved in an accident. For example, a driver, passenger or witness in a car crash, a train driver where someone has thrown themselves into the path of the train*
- *people who have either been directly involved or been innocent victims of war.*

Symptoms of PTSD include:

- *insomnia*
- *flashbacks and nightmares*
- *general anger and irritability*
- *vivid memories arising as if the danger was in the present time*

▶ *memories recalled by visual images as well as sounds, physical sensations or smells.*

Insight

A feature of PTSD is immobilizing anxiety following shock or trauma. It used to be called 'shell shock', which described the traumatized condition of soldiers suffering from the after-effects of warfare. Common symptoms are flashbacks, hyper-arousal and being overly alert.

OVERCOMING POST-TRAUMATIC STRESS DISORDER

Because of the nature of the treatment of PTSD, professional help would normally be the best way forward for overcoming this anxiety problem. We can nonetheless give you brief details of the treatment so that you have some understanding of what would be involved.

Normalizing the experience

It is firstly important for sufferers to understand that they are not 'mad' for feeling this way, and that their response to trauma is quite rational and makes sense in view of the distress they have experienced.

Restructuring the experience

This can take the form of both imaginal and *in vivo* (actual) exposure. The goal is to reduce the amount of stress caused by the trauma by allowing the sufferer to become gradually more comfortable with what happened, and to be able to better deal with the emotional aspects of it – perhaps guilt at personal responsibility or anger at how the trauma was caused.

Using imaginal exposure, the sufferer is encouraged to relive the experience in as much detail as possible, relaying the content of memories, starting with those that cause least distress and moving on to the more distressing ones as they become easier to deal with. It is possible to audio-tape these accounts, although this needs to be treated sensitively. Where the content is too distressing, the sufferer will be advised not to listen to the tapes on their own.

The idea is to enable the sufferer to become *habituated* to the details of the trauma.

> **Jargon dictionary: 'Habituation' means getting used to something until it becomes less fearful.**

Where specific memories of the trauma concern the site of a disaster, or certain places have become associated with the trauma through conditioning, then encouraging the sufferer to become less fearful and avoidant by *in vivo* exposure is helpful. A hierarchy of difficult situations is created so that the sufferer can deal with the easiest ones first and move on to those that are more difficult as the fear subsides.

Eye movement desensitization and reprocessing
Eye movement desensitization and reprocessing (EMDR) is a desensitization process that elicits rapid lateral eye movements in the sufferer to alleviate trauma. It is not yet quite certain how EMDR exerts its effects, and it does require specialist professional training to carry out the treatment. It is presently not widely available. However, it is highly regarded as a helpful process for PTSD because it means the sufferer can avoid re-experiencing the trauma through relating it on a one-to-one basis to a professional.

Thought challenging and discouraging safety behaviours
Key unhelpful beliefs and assumptions about the event can be addressed and challenged using a Thought Record, and avoidance and escape behaviours can be discouraged.

Encouraging anxiety management techniques
Using deep breathing and relaxation techniques can be helpful to encourage the sufferer to face up to exposure tasks.

Obsessive compulsive disorder

Obsessive compulsive disorder (OCD) is the most commonly known of the OCD spectrum disorders, which include body dysmorphic disorder (feelings of revulsion about physical appearance), obsessive behaviours such as trichotillomania (where the sufferer constantly pulls their hair out) and Tourette's syndrome (where the sufferer has involuntary tics and twitches and occasionally shouts out nonsense).

It is only in recent years that the extent of the prevalence of OCD has been understood. It has been called 'the hidden epidemic', and in the UK alone there are over 2 million known sufferers.

Sufferers always, quite naturally, want to understand why they have this particular disorder. The present answer is that no one knows. Research undertaken in 2007 shows that there may be a genetic link to OCD. The work is in its early stages at present, but it may in the future lead to a wider range of options for overcoming the illness. What we do know is that OCD is triggered or worsened by trauma. Most sufferers can track back the origins of their problem to some kind of traumatic event after which the obsessions and compulsion either started up or became more noticeable.

CHARACTERISTICS OF OBSESSIVE COMPULSIVE DISORDER

OCD is characterized by persistent, repetitive and disturbing thoughts, ideas or impulses. For some individuals the response to these thoughts is to assign a fearful meaning to them, indicating that if they do not pay attention to them or act on them in some way, something bad will happen and they will be responsible for this. The anxiety caused by these worrying thoughts becomes so intense that, in order to manage it, the sufferer will engage in a variety of safety behaviours such as avoidance, reassurance seeking and/or performing rituals, which may be either mental (for example, repeated counting) or physical (for example, checking).

An essential difference between OCD and other anxiety disorders lies in the irrational content of the negative predictions made. The individual also usually appreciates this – 'I know it's all nonsense', 'I know this couldn't possibly really happen' – but nonetheless, once the anxious thoughts take hold, the desire to reduce the anxiety by any means becomes paramount and overtakes rationality.

OCD sufferers often wonder if they are 'going mad' or think, 'There must be something very wrong with me to even have thoughts like this.' On the contrary, most people with OCD are caring, intelligent people – and therein lies the problem.

A feature of OCD is an over-developed sense of responsibility, so that a conscientious concern for the well-being of others takes on problematic proportions. Many sufferers are also hugely ashamed of the content of their thoughts, which can include those of a sexual, blasphemous or harming nature. There is no need to be. These thoughts are far more common to most people than is often realized.

COMMON NEGATIVE PREDICTIONS

Negative predictions made by those with OCD can be very specific. For example, 'Unless I ensure that every spoon in my kitchen is laid face downwards then my mother will die.' Or they can be quite vague: 'I simply know that something bad will happen.' There can also be a supernatural element to the prediction: 'The devil will cause something dreadful to happen.'

The most common obsessional worries that people have concern:

- *contamination that can only be avoided by excessive cleanliness*
- *a desire for everything to be 'just so', which can only be achieved by repeating actions again and again until things feel 'right'*
- *potential danger, which can only be avoided by constant vigilance and checking, for example, locks and electrical sockets, etc.*
- *a fear of discarding something important – leading to excessive hoarding and an inability to part with anything*
- *a fear of harming someone (often a child), which can only be prevented by avoiding being near, say, children or by hiding possible aids to harm such as kitchen knives, etc.*

THE PROBLEM OF SAFETY BEHAVIOURS

As with other anxiety disorders, the safety behaviours people adopt maintain the problem and strengthen its hold. These include the following.

- **Rituals** *that can be physical, such as checking, washing, repeating certain actions over and over, or mental, such as repeating mantras or prayers or counting in specific sequences.*
- **Reassurance seeking** – *constantly asking others to validate or disconfirm their OCD thoughts.*
- **Avoidance** *of situations that might trigger obsessional worries. This might include not doing something that the individual thinks may lead to a bad thing happening, for example, not wearing a particular dress as this might lead to a specific catastrophe.*

Insight

Intrusive thoughts in themselves are not unusual – most of us have them from time to time. It is the meaning that OCD gives to these thoughts – e.g. "If I have had this thought, it must be important. Therefore I must act on it, or I will be responsible for any untoward outcome if I don't" – that is a problem for sufferers.

OVERCOMING OBSESSIVE COMPULSIVE DISORDER

Exposure and response prevention

There is a variety of techniques for getting over OCD, but still the most widely regarded is the behavioural technique of exposure and response prevention. This requires the sufferer to expose themselves to the irrational fear (in a structured and graded way) and to resist engaging in the usual ritualistic safety behaviour. This can be achieved by gradually increasing the time delay before ritualizing until the level of anxiety reduces and the ritual becomes unnecessary, or by reducing the length of time that the ritual takes on a consistent basis, until a feeling of 'normality' is reached. Professional guidance may be needed to overcome OCD.

Elimination of reassurance

This may involve family members and friends who may tend to unwittingly collude with the sufferer by offering the reassurance requested. They will need to be instructed to discontinue this and to encourage the sufferer to challenge their negative beliefs more strongly themselves.

Reducing the significance of the thoughts

We cannot emphasize strongly enough that OCD thoughts are just meaningless nonsense, and it is important for the sufferer to reinforce this to themselves.

Let the thoughts come. They are not harmful. Trying to fight them or banish them will only cause them to multiply. Your goal is to reduce the *significance* of the thoughts. Techniques to achieve this include the following.

▶ *Thinking of nothing but the obsessive thoughts for defined time periods – say one hour. If your thoughts wander, bring them back to the obsessive thoughts. Eventually, you will become quite bored with them and see that there are better things to do with your day.*
▶ *Make a loop tape of the worrying thought(s). Pop in your earphones and listen to the feared thought again and again as you carry on with your day.*
▶ *Label the thoughts. Tell yourself 'These are just my OCD thoughts', 'They don't matter', 'They don't deserve a moment of my attention'.*

Insight

Remember, a thought is just a thought (however dangerous a thought may seem) and you don't have to act on it.

Re-evaluating obsessive compulsive disorder as a problem of danger

Challenge the idea that OCD can actually cause any harm and replace this with the idea that it is simply a problem of *worry* that harm can be caused. The 'Theory A, Theory B' model described in Chapter 15 is ideal for this.

Reappraisal of unhelpful beliefs

Use the thought-challenging skills described in early chapters to reappraise such beliefs as, 'Thinking something can make it happen', 'I must take full responsibility for the safety of others', or 'Simply thinking of it is as bad as doing it'.

Do the opposite

Simplistic though this may sound, this is an excellent and well-grounded technique for defeating OCD. On the principle that OCD is a liar and never tells the truth, if you always do and think the opposite of what your OCD is telling you, you will beat it. Try it. With practice it will work very well.

THE PROBLEM OF DOUBT

OCD is very good at bringing doubt into things. It will suggest, 'Are you really sure that this is an OCD thought?', 'Are you really certain that you can risk that?' and so on. Use the principles above for recognizing these doubtful thoughts as OCD and treat them in the same way as all other OCD thoughts.

OCD can seem an especially worrying problem because of the irrational nature of the thoughts and rituals. However, it is simply a problem of anxiety, not danger, and can be defeated by using standard CBT techniques.

HOMEWORK

Your homework depends on whether you have difficulties you would like to work on, or whether you are purely interested in understanding more about these common problems. If it is the former, then, with the specific knowledge you now have about these problems, your skills can assist you in defeating them. Use your goal-setting skills to make an action plan and your CBT techniques to carry it out. If it is the latter, a more appropriate homework task is to read one of the many good books on CBT for anxiety disorders so that you can learn about them in more depth. We give you one or two suggestions in this chapter's 'Further reading' section.

SUMMARY

You now have an understanding of some of the specific worries that many people are familiar with, and battle with on a day-to-day basis. We have given brief outlines both of the disorders and their treatments, and would urge you, if you have reason to be specially interested in any specific disorder, to do further research and reading to increase your knowledge of the full range of treatments available.

▶ *People may maintain these problems rather than overcome them. Their natural 'leaning' is towards a solution that actually becomes a problem in itself.*
▶ *It is difficult to move away from safety behaviours unless you possess good alternative skills and techniques that you can be confident will work for you.*
▶ *Always look first for a less threatening explanation for the worry and fear, and then test that new, more helpful explanation with CBT skills and techniques.*
▶ *All anxiety disorders are quite common problems, and all are treatable.*
▶ *CBT offers specific treatment protocols for each anxiety disorder, rather than a general 'one-size-fits-all' model. You therefore need to learn and understand the different skills required, depending on the disorder identified.*

FURTHER READING

Butler, G., *Overcoming Social Anxiety: A Self-help Guide Using CBT* (London: Robinson, 1999).

Fennell, M., *Overcoming Low Self-Esteem* (London: Constable and Robinson, 1999).

Ingham, C., *Panic Attacks: What They Are, Why They Happen and What You Can Do About Them* (London: Thorsons, 2000).

Kinchin, D., *Post Traumatic Stress Disorder: A Practical Guide to Recovery* (London: Thorsons, 1994).

Lampe, L., *Take Control of Your Worry: Managing Generalised Anxiety Disorder* (Australia: Simon & Schuster, 2005).

Mansell, W., *Coping with Fears and Phobias* (Oxford: Oneworld, 2007).

Purdon, C. and Clark, C., *Overcoming Obsessive Thoughts: How to Gain Control of Your OCD* (Oakland: New Harbinger, 2005).

Taylor, S. and Asmundson, G., *Treating Health Anxiety: A Cognitive Behavioural Approach* (New York: Guildford Press, 2004).

THINGS TO REMEMBER

▶ *The term anxiety disorder is a generic term which covers an array of anxiety complaints, some of which you may have already been familiar with. These include: phobia, panic, health anxiety, social anxiety, post-traumatic stress disorder (PTSD), obsessive compulsive disorder (OCD), and generalized anxiety disorder (GAD).*

▶ *Relentless worrying serves no useful purpose. Rather than being motivating or preparing you for a 'worst-case scenario', constant worrying undermines your problem-solving abilities.*

▶ *Continuous worrying sabotages your ability to problem-solve, causing your confidence in dealing with problems to diminish. This, in turn, creates further worry in a self-perpetuating vicious cycle.*

▶ *It is not the anxious or irrational thoughts themselves that disturb us, but the* meaning *that we give them. For example, 'If I think this will happen, it will', or 'I must act to prevent this happening' and so on.*

▶ *In this chapter we have added more specific details about what techniques and interventions are used to address particular anxiety problems, building on your knowledge of CBT and its wide-ranging applications.*

Part three

CBT for developing strengths

In Part two, we looked at ways in which cognitive behavioural therapy (CBT) skills can help you to overcome adversity and provide solutions to emotional problems. However, CBT is also an excellent model for developing strengths. In other words, rather than taking you from minus nine to zero, where zero is feeling okay, it can take you from plus three to plus ten (or higher, if you wish). In Part three, therefore, we look at some of the strengths that you can develop with CBT.

▶ **Increasing self-esteem.** *Most people feel that their self-esteem could do with a boost from time to time. You may be someone for whom good self-esteem seems a distant or impossible goal. These skills will change this for you.*

▶ **Developing a more relaxed outlook.** *Getting rid of a drive for perfectionism in everything will increase your sense of self-confidence and well-being, and encourage you to develop a better balance in life.*

▶ **Building resilience** *or mental strength can make an enormous difference to your ability to deal with difficulties and setbacks in life.*

▶ **Overcoming anger.** *You can learn how to prevent this extremely strong emotion getting the better of you and causing damage to both yourself and your relationships with others.*

▶ **Developing assertiveness.** *Every time you say the wrong thing, respond aggressively or fail to secure the outcome you want, you recognize that you have not acted in the calm, assertive manner you would have liked. Learning to develop assertiveness will help you to achieve outcomes and results that are positive rather than negative or disappointing.*

In this section our intention is to integrate CBT skills into your everyday thinking, reflecting, questioning and acting so that they become helpful to you without you constantly thinking, 'Ah, that's CBT.' We encourage thought development and challenging, constructive questioning, reflecting, reviewing constructive and destructive behaviours, and action planning to become your 'way of being'.

17

Improving your self-esteem

In this chapter you will learn:
- *what creates low self-esteem*
- *what maintains low self-esteem*
- *the problems low self-esteem presents for you*
- *how to overcome low self-esteem using cognitive behavioural therapy skills.*

> *Never think that you're not good enough yourself. A man should never think that. People will take you very much at your own reckoning.*
>
> Anthony Trollope, English novelist (1815–82)

Low self-esteem

Do you feel that you suffer from low self-esteem? Do you run yourself down, lack belief in your abilities to achieve much, consider yourself not very likeable, and feel that others take no account of you?

WHERE MIGHT THIS COME FROM?

Low self-esteem can be traced back to a variety of factors, most probably your upbringing, when you may have been heavily criticized and given little confidence in yourself. Perhaps you were bullied at school or found it hard to fit in. It may also have been caused by events in adulthood that have made you revise your view of yourself, for example, being fired from your job or a relationship break-up.

How you perceive what goes on around you and how you interpret your abilities to deal with things has a great impact on self-esteem.

Insight

Abuse is another possible root cause of low self-esteem. The four main commonly cited categories of abuse are: neglect, physical injury, sexual abuse and emotional abuse. Experiences of abuse, either in childhood or adulthood, can lead to feelings of low self-worth.

Skills to improve your self-esteem

To start with, formulate your problem. Using one of your basic formulation or conceptualization plans, find a recent incident when your self-esteem felt very low. Write into the plan what you were thinking, how you were feeling, and what happened. Next, begin to look for patterns. Is this how things always go? For example, perhaps you wrote something like:

Event:	Office party
My thoughts:	I will be sure to say and do the wrong thing
Feelings:	Nervousness, anxiety, fear
Physiology:	Felt a little sick physically
Behaviour:	Spoke to very few people and left early
Outcome/Meaning to me:	Very few people showed an interest in me

It just proves that I am regarded as a nonentity at work

Now translate these negative thoughts and feelings to a Thought Record. Begin to challenge your thoughts and feelings about your low self-esteem. Start to ask yourself some thoughtful and enquiring questions – look back to the section on Socratic enquiry (Chapter 11) if you cannot think of many – and use the skills you have learned, especially examining the evidence, to test the validity of these negative thoughts.

What can maintain low self-esteem and how to raise it

Case study

Jenny was in a troubled relationship, and her partner, James, had recently moved out of their shared home. Although James had treated Jenny quite cruelly at times – having several affairs and behaving in a moody and erratic way – her self-esteem was so low that she interpreted this as simply a response to her own hopelessness and unlovability.

Jenny spent a great deal of time telephoning and emailing James, begging him to come home. She felt that, without him, she was totally unlovable, and that she needed him desperately to restore her confidence. In the end, James reluctantly agreed to Jenny's pleading, and returned home. However, the relationship continued to deteriorate as James did not really want to be there, and he continued to see other women.

DON'T DEPEND ON OTHERS MAKING CHANGES

Jenny's despair came from feeling absolutely stuck. She felt she had tried as hard as she could in the relationship, and that it was James' cruel treatment that made her feel so poorly about herself. If only James would change, she would feel okay about herself again. Without his input, Jenny felt unable to deal with her life.

It was Jenny's low self-esteem that defeated her. Her thoughts, for example, 'I feel so badly due to someone else's behaviour, and need that person to change in order to feel better', precluded her from taking any action herself that might have improved things – certainly, in as far as she perceived herself.

> **Key point: If you feel that the only way forward is for someone else to change, you may have a long wait.** Only by making changes yourself can you take charge of your life and take responsibility for good outcomes.

DON'T LOOK TO OTHERS TO PROVIDE YOUR 'FEEL-GOOD' FACTOR

One of the key features of low self-esteem is that you crave approval from others. But you cannot rely on this. The moment you say, 'If he had not done that, I would not have felt this way', 'I only acted that way because of the way she behaved', 'If she would only treat me with more respect, I'd feel so much better', you remain trapped in your view that others are responsible for how you feel and what you do.

You risk suffering from low self-esteem forever when you blame others for making you feel the way that you do. You may be right – so-and-so may be rude, may have run you down terribly, may have landed you in it, made you look a fool – but it is not about what other people do, it is about how you respond to what they do that decides how you feel about yourself.

TAKE RESPONSIBILITY FOR YOUR FEELINGS

Case study

Paula was walking down the corridor at work when a colleague coming the other way jostled her, resulting in hot coffee being spilled over Paula's new suit. Instead of apologizing, the colleague made a weak joke about it and rushed on, calling back to her that he was late for a meeting but that Paula should send him the bill for the dry cleaning. Paula was really upset. She was left to clean up the mess, dry herself off, and had to walk into a meeting looking a wreck rather than her usually smart self. In response to a jokey comment made by someone in the meeting concerning Paula's appearance, she started to cry and was asked by the chairperson to leave the room and calm down. Paula's negative emotions had taken over. She blamed her colleagues for both her wretched day and the distress it had produced that seemed to alienate her from several of them.

Was she right?
As we are sure you realize, the only person responsible for Paula's distress was Paula herself.

> **Key point: No one else can make you feel a particular emotion.** You choose to feel that way – and you have an opportunity to take responsibility for your emotions and decide not to.

Once you realize that no one else has control over how you feel and that you have excellent control over how you feel, you can put the lid on negative emotions. You don't have to. If you wish to be angry or upset, you can be. Yet acknowledge that you are choosing to feel that way and make this choice through evaluative thinking, not using 'I couldn't help it' as an excuse.

With the exception of reflex actions, such as a knee jerk or blushing, you are able to learn to control your responses. It is hard, but it can be done.

Exercise
Do you always take responsibility for your emotions? Look back over the last two weeks (longer, if you need). Was there a time when you felt extremely emotional about something? If so, can you recall what thoughts were in your mind? Did they perhaps include the idea that someone or something had made you feel that way? How could you look at that now, taking responsibility for it yourself? You will feel better if you take responsibility.

OVER-PERSONALIZATION

Somebody makes a comment about liking long hair, and you immediately think they are criticizing your new short cut. Your boss tells you that the department is lagging behind on completing an important project on time and you assume he is commenting on your own poor performance. You suggest to your friend or partner that you get takeaway pizzas tonight, and they pull a face and say, 'No, I really don't fancy pizza.' What you hear is, 'What a rotten choice – can't you think up anything better than that?'

Insight

If you have low self-esteem, you may have little confidence in your views and opinions; yet you find yourself sticking doggedly to them when they are opposed to those of others.

When you over-personalize, you erroneously feel that you are to blame for the perceived negative reactions of others. 'If someone disagrees with me, then I must be wrong, and that makes me stupid.' These types of thoughts will maintain your low self-esteem.

You need to identify these thoughts and counteract them. Here are some suggestions for broadening your thinking skills to prevent over-personalization:

▶ *Have respect for the opinions of others in the same way that you hope they will respect yours. Tell yourself that you are not stupid if you disagree with them as they are not if they disagree with you.*
▶ *Distinguish between opinion and fact. However strongly either you, or the person talking to you, believe something, that doesn't make it true. There are many different opinions on almost every subject. Opinions are exactly that – simply points of view.*
▶ *Have confidence in your own views. Tell yourself that you don't need to be right all the time – simply having a view shows thoughtful intelligence on your part, and you may have valid reasons/past experiences that mean you are more likely to have formed your opinions in a certain way.*

▶ *Others have their own problems. Your boss may have been under a lot of pressure from his superior to get this work out, and the friend who didn't want pizza may have been preoccupied with a relationship difficulty.*

▶ *Other people don't always react in the best possible way. This has nothing to do with you.*

> **Exercise**
>
> Think back over the last week. Can you identify an occasion when you might have erroneously taken something too personally? What went through your mind?
>
> In your workbook, jot down some alternative ways of thinking about this using some of the skills we have mentioned above. How do you feel now?

GETTING RID OF SELF-PITY

Every time you run yourself down by letting negative thoughts about yourself dominate your mind, you are indulging in self-pity. Self-pity is similar to being locked into victim mode, except that on this occasion you are not blaming others as much as you are blaming yourself.

Self-pity thinking
▶ *Why do bad things always happen to me?*
▶ *Why am I such an idiot?*
▶ *I'll never be any good.*
▶ *I always draw the short straw.*
▶ *I can't get anything right.*
▶ *I got a bad deal on good looks.*

Use your cognitive behavioural therapy (CBT) skills to strongly challenge these thoughts. Check back to Chapter 7 on distorted thinking styles and ask yourself which of these self-pity thoughts fit with those descriptions. Apart from thought challenging, use the 'pros and cons' skill to review the disadvantages of running yourself down all the time. Some of these include the following.

▶ **Low self-esteem is destructive** *because it robs you of an opportunity to make changes. It can also lead to depression. What could be more likely to take you into dark despair than the idea that everything is against you and that there is nothing you can do about it?*

▶ **Low self-esteem is unattractive.** *Others may feel sorry for you, but they may also think you are self-absorbed and poor company. They may consider you to be a negative pessimist, someone to avoid.*

▶ **Low self-esteem wastes energy.** *The energy that you waste feeling sorry for yourself could be much better used in problem-solving. Self-defeating worry is physically tiring, without serving any useful purpose.*

▶ **Low self-esteem prevents you from moving on.** *Self-pity gives you an excuse to indulge your 'stuckness'. You lose yourself in self-oriented thoughts instead of action-oriented thoughts and nothing positive happens. You stay where you are.*

Exercise
When did you last feel sorry for yourself? Why? Do you still feel that way? If not, why not? What did you do to stop your self-pitying thoughts? How did you feel once they had disappeared?

BRINGING POSITIVE QUALITIES INTO FOCUS

If your self-esteem has been low for some time, you will probably have difficulty in identifying your strong points and qualities. This does not mean that you do not have any – it means that you are out of the habit of noticing and giving weight to them.

When you have self-critical thoughts, instead of simply accepting them, challenge them, look for alternatives and create a more balanced view of yourself. You will almost certainly find that you are discounting a lot of positive points about yourself and acknowledging them will help to raise your self-esteem.

Self-critical thoughts	Alternative thoughts
I shouldn't be taking the evening off. I haven't done enough.	Doing things I enjoy helps me feel better about myself and then I relax and think more positively.

'I cannot find anything positive about myself'

When your self-esteem is low, you are excellent at focusing on all your negative traits, and find it hard to see your good points. Here is an exercise to help you redress the balance. Write the answers in your workbook as they will be valuable for you to keep and refer to again in the future.

Exercise

Questions to help you identify your good points:

▶ *What do you like about yourself, however small and fleeting?*
▶ *What positive qualities do you possess?*
▶ *What have you achieved in your life, however small?*
▶ *What challenges have you faced?*
▶ *What gifts or talents do you have, however modest?*
▶ *What skills have you acquired?*
▶ *What do other people like or value in you?*
▶ *What qualities and actions that you value in others do you share?*
▶ *What aspects of yourself would you appreciate if they were aspects of another person?*
▶ *What small positives are you discounting?*
▶ *What are the bad things you are not?*
▶ *How might another person who cared about you describe you?*

Did you find this hard? If you did, and have not written very much, simply add to it as you work on your self-esteem. Eventually you will find it easier to identify your good qualities. Keep this exercise in your workbook and look at it from time to time to remind you to take a more balanced view of yourself.

POSITIVE EVENT LOG

Another 'self-esteem lifter' can be to keep a daily 'Positive Event
Log' (see below). Each evening, take a moment to write down
three positive things that happened during the day. These can be
big ('I got a promotion at work') or small ('The milkman said
hello'). They all have equal value. Next, write down why you think
these positive things happened. For example, 'I got a promotion
at work because my employer considers me to be good at my job'
or 'The milkman smiled at me because he sees me as a friendly
person'. Don't worry that your answers are sometimes subjective
viewpoints – simply write down what you think. If you think there
is more than one possible explanation, write them all. You will find
a blank 'Positive Event Log' to use in the Appendix (page 329).

Positive Event Log

Date	Positive event	Why this happened
3 Jan	1 Promotion at work 2 Friend invited me for lunch 3 Letter from my niece	1 Good at my job 2 She likes me! 3 She has remembered her aunt
4 Jan	1 Noticed the sunshine 2 Postman smiled 3 My mother rang	1 My mood is better 2 He must think I am okay 3 She's no longer cross with me

Improving your self-esteem is essential to developing other life
skills. Once you feel at ease with yourself, you will have the

confidence to tackle more and you will not be too disturbed by risk of failure.

HOMEWORK

Review the CBT skills that can help you to overcome low self-esteem. Write your own list of the skills that will help you to feel better about yourself. We have covered them all in this book and discussed some of them in this chapter. To start you off:

- ▶ *formulate the problem*
- ▶ *challenge your thinking with a Thought Record*
- ▶ *look for evidence both for and against your views*
- ▶ *develop some behavioural experiments to test your views out*
- ▶ *work on behavioural changes that you might make as a result*
- ▶ *work on assumptions and core beliefs to make a gradual shift*
- ▶ *don't expect overnight success but be thrilled with small gains.*

What can you add to this list? Now set yourself some goals and develop your plan to achieve them.

SUMMARY

In this chapter we have looked at many different ways that you can increase your self-esteem.

- ▶ *Many things maintain low self-esteem, including hoping that others will make you feel good about yourself and failing to take more responsibility for your own behaviour and reactions.*
- ▶ *You can improve your self-esteem immeasurably by challenging your negative assumptions and thoughts and by focusing on the positive aspects of your self and your life.*
- ▶ *You can overcome low self-esteem by using a variety of CBT skills such as a Positive Event Log and exercises to bring your positive qualities into focus.*

THINGS TO REMEMBER

▶ *Low self-esteem can originate from many sources: for instance, having overly critical parents or authority figures as you grew up, adverse experiences in the educational system or workplace, relationship break-ups, poverty or any type of abuse. These are the kind of experiences that may have considerably affected your confidence.*

▶ *Your perceptions of what goes on around you (with other people and events) and your sense of your abilities to cope with what happens impact on your level of self-esteem.*

▶ *You can begin to explore your thoughts, feelings, behaviour and physiology by using the basic formulation format and the Thought Record to uncover any long-held negative beliefs you have about yourself that you can then work on challenging and disputing.*

▶ *No one else can make you feel or behave in a particular way. Ultimately, it is your choice whether or not you retaliate negatively in response to other people's actions or words.*

▶ *Beware of the nullifying impact of over-personalization and self-pity, when you think you are to blame for the perceived negative responses of others and the source of all ills.*

18

Defeating perfectionism

In this chapter you will learn:

- *to understand more about perfectionism and its origins*
- *to identify the source of your own perfectionist tendencies and the self-defeating beliefs they engender and maintain*
- *skills for challenging these beliefs and re-evaluating their usefulness to you*
- *how to develop healthier values.*

Striving for excellence motivates you: striving for perfection is demoralising.

Dr Harriet Braiker, US psychologist (1949–2004)

What is perfectionism?

Many people's negative views of themselves are driven by unhelpful thinking about the standards they should be able to reach in order to feel good about themselves. These are often bright and intelligent people, doing well in their lives, but they are not reaching the 'perfect way of being' that they believe they should attain.

Perfectionism has become the bane of modern life. In our competitive, ultra-fast lifestyles, we find ourselves feeling dissatisfied and upset when we fail to achieve the ultimate in 'just so-ness'. You drive yourself to be the perfect home-maker, cook, parent or property magnate – and feel a failure if you aren't. It is much healthier (but, it seems, increasingly harder) to accept your imperfections, cut yourself some slack, and simply relax.

Insight

In connection with genius, the Irish novelist James Joyce (1882–1941) denied anything was an out and out mistake. Instead he purported "errors are volitional and are the portals of discovery".

PERFECTIONISM CAN MEAN SETTING YOURSELF UP FOR FAILURE

This is because it is almost impossible to achieve a perfect score. In many cases, it is impossible to know what that score would be. For example:

▶ *Is there a cast-iron, concrete definition for perfect beauty?*
▶ *Is there a cast-iron, concrete definition for being a perfect pianist?*
▶ *Is there a cast-iron, concrete definition for being a mathematician?*
▶ *Is there a cast-iron, concrete definition for being a perfect parent?*
▶ *How would you even know if you had reached perfection?*
▶ *Even being the best in the world at something doesn't mean that you are perfect at it.*

In aiming for perfection, you will almost certainly fail every time.

Key point: Perfection is impossible to quantify, and therefore very much in your mind. Don't see yourself as a failure; see yourself as someone who is very able but setting the bar too high.

Why perfectionism is a common problem

Perfectionism as a psychological problem has increased in proportion to the increased activity in people's lives generally. Many people work hard to achieve a great deal in a limited time, and this puts pressure on them to achieve more with less. Working life especially can be very competitive, and the desire to succeed, to be measured positively, to be liked and respected has moved, within the minds of many, from a preference to a highly pursued desire – something to be achieved at any cost.

A female sufferer describes it in this way: 'I always have an image in my head of exactly how I want everything to be, and drive myself to attain that. This can be anything from the colour scheme in my lounge to my Christmas decorations. I exhaust myself trying to attain this perfection, which makes me tense at home and leads to rows with my family. I recently had a terrible argument with my husband because he was cutting the carrots for a supper party into circles, when the recipe said, "Cut carrots into matchsticks". This was when I realized that my perfectionism was ruining my life.'

Insight

Rather than comparing your own personal qualities, looks, competencies or achievements with those of other people, try instead to appreciate your own unique attributes, do things that give you satisfaction as well as you can, and be proud of your achievements, however small.

WHERE DOES PERFECTIONISM COME FROM?

Before you begin the task of shedding unhelpful perfectionist tendencies, it may be useful for you to understand how you got them in the first place. Experience shows that the trait usually develops in childhood, often from parents, teachers or contemporaries who drive a child to constantly do better – 80 per cent should be 90 per cent; 90 per cent should be 100 per cent. Being in the football team wasn't good enough unless you were captain. Playing an instrument required you to practise relentlessly, and then some more. The legacy for many young people is they feel that, no matter what they do, it is never good enough. You may carry this 'Nothing I do is ever good enough' belief with you into adulthood as a self-defeating belief, and – even though you are probably very successful in most areas of your life – you may constantly criticize yourself and feel worthless because you aren't doing things perfectly.

While one explanation for perfectionist tendencies is that your parents were always stretching you to achieve more, there are of course many others:

▶ *Desperately needing to please a parent. This might be out of fear or even love where, for example, financial sacrifices were made to ensure you received a good education.*
▶ *Sibling rivalry.*
▶ *Scholastic rivalry – perhaps being in competition with one or two other pupils to 'always be the best'.*
▶ *Feelings of inferiority, either at home or in adult personal relationships that taught you conditional love ('Unless I am perfect, my family/partner will not care for me').*
▶ *Being heavily criticized. Either, 'I'll show them!' or throwing yourself into work or academia with a determination to be the best.*
▶ *The pressures of living a fast-paced life where everyone else does seem to manage ten things at once and still finds time to make their own hand-embroidered cushion covers. This fosters the view that you must be able to achieve at the same level to have any sort of self-worth.*

If you wish, use a formulation/conceptualization worksheet to write down:

▶ *where you feel your own perfectionist tendencies have come from*

- *what your beliefs are about yourself, others and perfectionism*
- *why you feel that you need to keep this perfectionism going – your assumptions and rules. For example:*
  - ▷ *'I must be perfect at what I do in order to like myself.'*
  - ▷ *'I must be perfect at what I do in order for others to like me.'*

Now consider whether these reasons are still valid or if you are carrying past beliefs along with you that could be more helpfully replaced.

Making changes

To help you identify and adjust perfectionist views, write down in your workbook any beliefs you have uncovered about striving for perfection. For example:

- *'I must always try to be perfect.'*
- *'Anything less than complete success is failure.'*
- *'Others will think less of me if I make mistakes.'*
- *'I cannot live with myself if I let my standards slip.'*

USING THE 'PROS AND CONS' TECHNIQUE

Now, as shown in the chart on the next page, take each belief in turn and write down the advantages to you of having this view. On the other side of the chart, write down any disadvantages to you of holding this view. For any views where the disadvantages outweigh the advantages, can you come up with an alternative view that might be more helpful? If you can, write it down. There is a template of this chart, which you can photocopy and fill in, in the Appendix.

Perfectionist view you hold (1)	
Advantages of holding this view	Disadvantages of holding this view
Could you find a more helpful view now?	
Perfectionist view you hold (2)	
Advantages of holding this view	Disadvantages of holding this view
Could you find a more helpful view now?	
Perfectionist view you hold (3)	
Advantages of holding this view	Disadvantages of holding this view
Could you find a more helpful view now?	

CHECKING THE PERFECTIONIST PERSPECTIVE OF OTHERS

Using your workbook, if perfection equals 100 per cent, rate how close you are to that for each area you have listed. Now think of two friends or work colleagues and rate what you consider their abilities to be in these areas. If their ratings are lower than yours, or the same, are they as anxious about it as you are? Do they mind as much? If not, why not?

For each answer you have given, answer another question: Why does this matter? For example, if you have put, 'My colleagues are contented with a lower standard of work', ask yourself why that matters. You can use the downward arrow technique to help you with this (see Chapter 4).

Now, this time for your colleagues' achievements, ask yourself the advantages and disadvantages *to them* of their approach. Then, for each person, make a subjective assessment of their self-esteem (1 = low, 10 = high).

View of friend/colleague (1)	
Advantages of holding this view	Disadvantages of holding this view
Subjective self-esteem rating for friend/colleague (1–10)	
View of friend/colleague (2)	
Advantages of holding this view	Disadvantages of holding this view
Subjective self-esteem rating for friend/colleague (1–10)	
View of friend/colleague (3)	
Advantages of holding this view	Disadvantages of holding this view
Subjective self-esteem rating for friend/colleague (1–10)	

What does this tell you? Write down what you have discovered and what it might mean to you.

CHALLENGING BELIEFS THAT PERFECTIONISM ENGENDERS

Look again at the perfectionist beliefs you listed above (see page 251). Now return to Chapter 7 where we looked at distorted thinking styles. Can you match your views with any of these styles? Remember that these are thinking errors. What thinking errors are you making? We suspect that 'all or nothing thinking' might be one of them. Become aware of any others.

> **Key point: Ideas about being perfect come from past experiences which, if you stop and think, are often no longer valid.** Therefore, you don't need to keep following these old rules.

DEVELOPING HEALTHIER VALUES

In the same way that you weighed up the pros and cons of your perfectionist tendencies, we would like you to do something similar with what you have now discovered about the origins of your perfectionism. Write down what you have discovered and do a cost-benefit analysis:

▶ *What are the advantages of continuing to be driven by this?*
▶ *What are the disadvantages of continuing to be driven by this?*
▶ *Is it realistic to continue to think this way?*
▶ *What is the purpose of continuing to prove something, either to yourself or to others?*

> **Key point: When answering the above questions, bear in mind that we are not asking you to list the advantages to you of being perfect.** We are asking you to consider the advantages of basing your view of yourself on your perfectionism. In other words – don't robotically continue to think, 'I must do things perfectly'. Begin to critically examine what useful purpose this serves.

Testing things out

Perfectionist thinking dictates that satisfaction from doing something is based on how effectively you performed. You can test out whether this is actually true by focusing on some of the tasks you have to do and treating them like behavioural experiments. Look for evidence of satisfaction, and rate it. Construct a chart like the one here to subjectively measure this. Use it regularly, and be aware of what you learn from it.

What you have to do	Rate the satisfaction you hope to get from your performance (%)	How much satisfaction did you actually get? (%) Comment on your rating	Now rate how effectively you consider you performed the task (%) Comment on your rating	How do you feel now?
Mend garden fence	20%	90% (can't believe I actually did it!)	30% (DIY is not my thing, so it's not the best job in the world)	Pretty chuffed!
Give monthly presentation at work	90%	40% (I do this every month, so of course I do it well. I expect it)	90% (I obviously turn in the best performance I can and am good at my work)	Pleased it went well, but nothing more
Game of tennis	60%	90% (got in a couple of good backhands, and had lots of fun)	40% (I played poorly, even for my mediocre standard)	Relaxed and happy. It's only a game. I've had great exercise and a drink with my friends afterwards

This exercise will help you to loosen the belief you may have that the only way to feel good is to do things perfectly.

HOMEWORK

A variety of thinking and evaluation tasks have been suggested in this chapter as possibly helpful in subduing or eliminating your perfectionist tendencies. Undertake them all but, using your goal-setting skills, develop a realistic time frame to give yourself the best chance of success while reminding yourself that it doesn't all need to be perfect.

SUMMARY

In this chapter we have looked at a very common problem – the desire to achieve perfection either in specific areas or in general, and the self-defeating, negative beliefs that accompany a failure to do so.

- ▶ *You can identify the origins of your perfectionist tendencies and the beliefs that perfectionism can engender, which will usually centre on a need for others to like and respect you, or a desire not to see yourself as a failure.*
- ▶ *There are a variety of skills for challenging your perfectionist beliefs, including assessing why others do not share these beliefs with you.*
- ▶ *You can develop healthier values, which will contribute far more to your psychological well-being than continuing to hold on to beliefs that encourage you to be consistently self-critical, no matter how hard you try. In other words, you can learn not to harbour beliefs that will almost always set you up to fail.*

FURTHER READING

Abrahamson, E. and Freedman, D., *The Perfect Mess: The Hidden Benefits of Disorder* (London: Weidenfeld & Nicolson, 2007).

THINGS TO REMEMBER

▶ *You are likely to fail if you aim for perfection, as there is no such thing as 'perfect' other than the meaning you attribute to it in your own thinking.*

▶ *You are likely to have adopted perfectionist ideas from significant others in your childhood, perhaps parents and teachers, who may have demanded high standards of themselves and enveloped you in their ambitions. The legacy is that no matter how hard you try, it never feels good enough.*

▶ *Other possible reasons for self-defeating, perfectionist tendencies include: sibling rivalry, feelings of inferiority, being heavily criticized, and the stress and pressure of being in a highly competitive environment.*

▶ *When you find yourself driven by standards that you find impossible to meet, ask yourself helpful questions like: 'Whose standards am I trying to meet?', 'How would I know I had reached perfection?', 'Is what I judge to be perfect the same as another person's view?'*

▶ *Once again you can use the versatile formulation 'map' to examine the origins of your perfectionism, look at your beliefs, explore your rules and assumptions, and look for alternative views.*

▶ *Here you have been introduced to the 'Advantages and Disadvantages' chart (a highly useful CBT technique) to weigh up the pros and cons of your thinking, to consider alternative views, and examine your discoveries.*

▶ *Your perfectionist ideas are likely to be backed up by distorted thinking errors like 'all or nothing thinking'.*

▶ *You can draw out a chart to test, record and rate your levels of satisfaction to prove the point to yourself that you don't need to reach standards of perfection to gain considerable satisfaction from doing tasks.*

19

Developing emotional strength

In this chapter you will learn:

- **how to overcome emotional weakness that keeps you trapped in negativity by developing resilience**
- **resilience's call on your emotions**
- **resilience's characteristics**
- **how you develop resilience.**

> *Our greatest glory is not in never falling, but in rising every time we fall.*
>
> Confucius, Chinese philosopher (551–479 BCE)

The importance of resilience

Resilience can provide protection against emotional disorders, such as depression and anxiety, and can help people to deal constructively with the after-effects of trauma. Learning how to become resilient – having the ability to stand firm in the face of adversity and to respond strongly to emotions that might be upsetting or difficult to deal with – has in recent years been signposted as an important developmental characteristic. American psychologist, Christine Padesky, has developed a cognitive behavioural therapy (CBT) skills model that enhances resilience and we look at her ideas here.

> **Key point: It is possible that by developing resilience you will be better able to resolve problems and manage your responses to adverse situations.** We introduce it as a further problem-solving skill you can develop alongside the others you are working on.

HOW RESILIENT ARE YOU NOW?

When something goes wrong, do you face it squarely or fall apart? People with resilience harness inner strengths and tend to recover more quickly from a setback or challenge – whether this is a job loss, an illness or the death of a loved one. In contrast, people who are less resilient may dwell on problems, feel victimized, become overwhelmed and turn to unhealthy coping mechanisms such as drink or drugs. They may be more likely to develop mental health problems. While resilience won't necessarily make your problems go away, it will give you the ability to see past them, find some enjoyment in life and handle things better.

If you aren't as resilient as you'd like, you can use the skills you have learned to teach yourself to become more so.

Resilience means being able to adapt to stress and adversity
Resilience is the ability to adapt well to stress, adversity, trauma or tragedy. It means that, overall, you remain stable and maintain healthy levels of psychological and physical functioning in the face of things going seriously wrong.

Resilience helps you to cope with temporary disruptions in your life
You may have a period of worry over your job security, for example. Resilience ensures that you are able to continue with daily tasks and remain generally optimistic about life.

Being resilient doesn't just mean trying to weather a storm
It doesn't mean you ignore feelings of sadness over a loss – it actually means becoming more aware of them and then dealing with them. Nor does it mean that you always have to be strong and that you can't ask others for support – in fact, reaching out to others is a key component of nurturing resilience in yourself.

- *Resilience doesn't mean that you're unable to express your emotions or don't feel them. It can provide protection against emotional disorders and help people to deal constructively with the after-effects of trauma.*
- *Resilience may even help strengthen us against physical illnesses such as heart disease and diabetes.*
- *People who are resilient have the ability to say to themselves, 'This bad thing has happened, but I have a choice. I can either dwell on it or I can do something about it.'*

RESILIENCE PROVIDES SKILLS TO GET THROUGH HARD TIMES

Resilience can help you to endure loss, stress, traumas and other challenges. It will enable you to develop many internal resources that you can draw on, to help you survive challenges and even thrive in the midst of chaos and hardship. Resilient individuals are able to cultivate a sense of acceptance (which is not the same thing as defeatism) and, regardless of the setback, they are able to let go of it and move on.

The characteristics of resilience

American psychologist and researcher Nancy Davis (1999) has identified six areas of competence that she defines as characteristics of resilience. As you read through these characteristics, think hard about those that may already apply to you, or if they don't yet, where you could absorb them and develop them yourself.

PHYSICAL

- *Good health.*
- *Easy temperament.*

SPIRITUAL

▶ *Having faith that your own life matters.*
▶ *Seeing meaning in your life even in pain and suffering.*
▶ *Sense of connection with humanity.*

MORAL

▶ *Ability and opportunity to contribute to others.*
▶ *Willingness to engage in socially and/or economically useful tasks.*

EMOTIONAL

▶ *Ability to identify and control emotions.*
▶ *Ability to delay gratification (patience).*
▶ *Realistically high self-esteem.*
▶ *Creativity.*
▶ *Sense of humour.*

SOCIAL/RELATIONAL

▶ *Ability to form secure attachments.*
▶ *Basic trust.*
▶ *Ability and opportunity to actively seek help from others.*
▶ *Ability to make and keep good friends.*
▶ *Ability to empathize.*
▶ *Good other-awareness.*

COGNITIVE (THINKING SKILLS)

▶ *High emotional intelligence.*
▶ *Good communication skills.*
▶ *Openness to a variety of ideas and points of view.*
▶ *Capacity to plan.*
▶ *Ability to exercise foresight.*
▶ *Good problem-solving abilities.*
▶ *Ability to take and use initiative.*

▶ *Good self-awareness.*
▶ *Ability to appreciate and assess the consequences of actions taken.*

Insight

Certain personal qualities and attitudes will predispose you to resilience, such as an easy-going nature, self-belief, seeing meaning in life, love of others, a sense of humour, a trust in life, a strong social network, good problem-solving skills and emotional intelligence.

Exercise

To help you measure your resilience, here is a test of your ability to bounce back from stressful situations. It is based on discovering the level of characteristics you possess, such as flexibility, self-confidence, creativity, and the ability to learn from experience, that make you more resilient.

Look at each statement below, and write beside it the number that most closely describes how much you agree with it.

1 = strongly disagree; 5 = strongly agree

1 *I don't allow difficulties to keep me down for long.* ☐
2 *I am able to be open about my feelings; I don't harbour grievances and I don't get easily discouraged.* ☐
3 *I am normally confident and possess good self-esteem.* ☐
4 *If things go wrong, I am able to stay calm and constructively work out the best course of action.* ☐
5 *I'm optimistic that any difficulties presented are temporary and I expect to overcome them.* ☐
6 *I adapt to changes in circumstances quickly and without fuss.* ☐
7 *My emotions help me to move on from losses and upsets.* ☐
8 *I can be quite creative in thinking up solutions to problems.* ☐
9 *I normally trust my intuition.* ☐

(Contd)

10 *I have a curious mind, and always ask questions and want to know how things work.* ☐

11 *I am at ease with myself.* ☐

12 *I'm a good problem-solver.* ☐

13 *I can usually find something amusing, even in the direst situations.* ☐

14 *I can laugh at myself.* ☐

15 *I try always to find something to learn from my experiences.* ☐

16 *I'm good at understanding other people's feelings.* ☐

17 *I will adapt to situations as they change.* ☐

18 *I try to look ahead and anticipate and, if possible, deflect problems before they happen.* ☐

19 *I am strong and independent, and don't tend to give in when things are difficult.* ☐

20 *I'm open-minded about other people's views and lifestyles.* ☐

21 *I am not fazed by uncertainty.* ☐

22 *I don't usually fail at tasks I am presented with.* ☐

23 *I am regarded as a good leader.* ☐

24 *I believe that the experience of difficult situations can make me stronger.* ☐

25 *I believe that something good comes out of every bad thing.* ☐

YOUR SCORE

100–120: You are extremely resilient.

75–99: You normally bounce back quite well.

50–75: You may 'wobble' occasionally.

Under 50: You find recovery from difficulties quite hard and need to develop your personal strength to deal with what life throws at you.

Don't worry if your resilience ratings weren't as high as you'd hoped or expected. It is not hard to develop the qualities that will improve your resilience in all areas of your life.

Which CBT skills will help you?

Having checked your score to the above exercise on the rating scale, what do you think you need to do to improve your resilience? Think back over the CBT skills you have learned so far, and consider which you might use here. Below are some skills that you may find useful.

▶ *Look back at other times in your life when you have had to cope with difficulties – perhaps something that you felt you would not be able to overcome. What actually happened? What helped you to resolve the situation? Was there anything that didn't help? If so, ensure that you don't repeat that mistake. Building on the way you coped well with previous difficult situations will increase your resilience when you are faced with a new problem. How might you have changed as a result of dealing with the difficulty? Are you perhaps stronger than you thought? If you really don't think so – if you feel worse as a result of your experiences – consider what changes you might make to improve things next time.*

▶ *Use your thought-challenging skills. Even when things seem quite dire, consistently ask yourself whether there is a more positive way in which you can look at things. If you can somehow encourage yourself to remain hopeful and optimistic when you're in the middle of a crisis, it will be much easier to get through.*

▶ *Resilience is not always about putting things right, but about taking an optimistic view even when you cannot change events.*

▶ *Don't discourage yourself by focusing on tasks that seem unachievable. Instead, ask yourself, 'What's one thing I know I can accomplish today that helps me move in the direction I want to go?'*

▶ *With chronic problems, take some action to put them right. Take decisive action. Once you address your problems with an action plan, you are on the way to overcoming them.*

▶ *Positive self-talk is often brushed aside as meaning little – in fact it is a powerful tool. The more you tell yourself that you are capable and strong, that you can withstand difficulties and criticism, the more control you will have over events and situations in your life and confidence in your ability to manage them well.*

▶ *Everything is relative. Sometimes people see their problems in isolation rather than against the bigger picture of the world around them. This can negatively discourage you as you may see your difficulties as acute and overwhelming. Look around you and evaluate your problems against those of the wider world and perhaps even against those you have weathered before. Once you gain a better perspective, your problem will become easier to resolve.*

▶ *Certain adverse circumstances are impossible to correct, and you cannot change the fact that they have happened and affected your life. In such circumstances, resilience offers you the chance to respond in the most positive way you can. This may simply be acceptance, forgiveness, or it may be an ability to learn and adapt in the best way you can. Sometimes, accepting circumstances that cannot be changed can help you focus on other things that you can alter.*

▶ *Always focus on solutions, rather than problems. This will give you an active focus, rather than a passive one. Always think in solution-focused mode and be determined not to dwell on the negative side of the situation.*

The most important thing is to identify ways that are likely to work well for you as part of your own personal strategy for fostering resilience.

Insight

You may be more resilient than you give yourself credit for. A key method of identifying your resilience is to think of a time of significant difficulty in your past that you managed to come through. Ask yourself questions like: 'What did I do that helped me get through it?' and apply similar coping strategies in the present.

Understanding resilience as a developing process

Resilience is not a personal attribute as this would imply a fixed and unchanging strength that some people have and some do not. It is a more complex process involving both internal cognitive and personality factors and external protective factors. Resilience is also a normal, understandable process. It arises from normal, human qualities such as the ability to rationally solve problems, the capacity to regulate emotion and the ability to form close, supportive ties with others. It is only when these systems are damaged or overwhelmed that natural resilience fails. In other words, it goes hand in hand with being emotionally intelligent. By developing one, you develop the other.

Thinking your way to being more resilient

Exercise

To help you develop personal resilience in specific areas, you will need to practise. Firstly, do the following:

▶ *Write down four aspects of your life in which you consider yourself to be resilient in general, or have specifically shown resilience recently.*

Now do the same for areas of your life in which you consider you would like to develop your resilience.

When you look at the parts of your life where you have shown resilience, what specific attributes have you demonstrated, for example, tenacity, emotional control, ability to see the problem and the solution? Use examples from what you have read so far to give yourself some ideas.

Look at the areas of your life where you would like to develop your resilience. Would any of the attributes you have identified
(Contd)

already help you? If not, what further attributes would you need to develop (again, look for examples in what you have read so far). And how will you do this?

Most importantly, developing resilience means stepping outside of your comfort zone. It means being willing to try a little harder, carry on when you might previously have given up, and feel emotions such as anxiety and fear and yet not back down.

It also means practice. The only reason most people do not master new skills as well as they would like is that they simply have not done them often enough for long enough. Keep practising, and the difficult becomes possible, and the possible becomes easy.

HOW RESILIENCE HELPS YOUR CONFIDENCE

Several additional factors are associated with resilience, including:

▶ *the capacity to make realistic plans and take steps to carry them out*
▶ *a positive view of yourself and confidence in your strengths and abilities*
▶ *skills in communication and problem-solving*
▶ *the capacity to manage strong feelings and impulses.*

All of these are factors that you can develop within yourself. Now think about your personal strategies for building resilience to manage your emotions. Think about what being resilient means to you, and identify the areas of your life where a more resilient outlook might be helpful to you.

Insight

CBT skills to help you improve your resilience include: thought-challenging skills to help you put an optimistic slant on things; taking action step by step; the use of encouraging, positive 'self-talk'; placing things into a larger perspective; and focusing on solutions as opposed to ruminating over problems.

HOMEWORK

Consider how resilient you think you are already, and – using what you have learned in this chapter – construct an action plan that will help you to develop this attribute further. This will involve making short-, medium- and long-term goals. Revisit Chapter 3 on goal-setting if you need to.

SUMMARY

In this chapter you have learned about the importance of resilience as a skill to prevent low mood, stress and anxiety.

▶ *By using a variety of CBT skills – such as thought challenging, Socratic enquiry, behavioural experimentation and developing positive strategies – you can develop your mental strength in the face of adversity.*
▶ *You can recognize a variety of characteristics present in a resilient personality, some of which you may have already, and others which you may have identified and feel that you can now develop.*
▶ *Work with those areas that apply to you. You will notice the role that self-confidence plays and you may decide that you need to work on this as well.*

FURTHER READING

Davies, N. J., *Resilience: Status of the Research and Research-based Programmes* (US Department of Health, Centre for Mental Health Resources, 1999).

Newman, A., *What Works in Building Resilience* (Ilford: Barnardo's, 2004).

THINGS TO REMEMBER

▶ Resilience is an important personal quality, sometimes described as 'inner strength', and an essential problem-solving skill that helps you cope with stress, adversity, loss or trauma. It keeps you mentally and emotionally strong, and able to respond creatively and flexibly, maintaining stability when things go radically wrong.

▶ Resilient individuals cultivate acceptance of situations such as a setback or life challenge and look for ways to cope or resolve the problem, rather that let themselves be overwhelmed and feel powerless in the face of adversity.

▶ Building resilience skills doesn't mean suppressing your emotions; in fact, being resilient involves becoming more self-aware and dealing with your strong feelings. Nor does being resilient mean you have to bear your burdens alone; reaching out to others for help, when you most need it, is crucial to nurturing resilient self-care qualities in yourself.

▶ Having the resource of resilience to draw on at trying times of loss or when dealing with the after-effects of trauma can protect you against emotional disorders and physical illness, such as heart disease, high blood pressure and diabetes.

▶ Check your own characteristics of resilience with those identified by American psychologist Nancy Davis to decide which apply to you and which you may need to develop. Similarly, the personal resilience exercise tests your ability to bounce back from problematic events and learn from experience, and gives you insight into areas to improve.

20

Increasing your assertiveness skills

In this chapter you will learn:
- *the behaviour styles you adopt that can help or harm you*
- *how to develop improved interpersonal skills*
- *to achieve desired outcomes in a positive way*
- *to feel less stressed about confrontation.*

The basic difference between being assertive and being aggressive is how our words and behaviour affect the rights and well-being of others.

Sharon Anthony Bower, US author

Are you assertive?

Many people find their perceived inability to behave assertively blocks them from being able to develop self-confidence. Where your fear of confrontation is so high that you avoid it constantly, you are maintaining the problem with such negative views as, 'I cannot cope with difficult circumstances', 'No one ever listens to me', 'People never do as I ask', 'I'm always frightened that I will get angry and so I would rather not raise an issue'.

In terms of your self-development, you need to develop assertive skills. Assertiveness is simply remaining calm but firm under pressure.

Do you currently:

▶ *find yourself getting upset very quickly when others question your opinions and views?*
▶ *avoid discussions that might become confrontational, even though it may mean you don't achieve something you need or want?*
▶ *say something you then immediately wish you had not said?*
▶ *agree with the wishes of others – when really you don't agree at all?*
▶ *feel your self-esteem constantly dented by your inability to stand up to other people's arguments?*

If you said 'Yes' to any of the above, then your assertiveness skills are not what they could be and you should consider developing them further.

Insight

Lack of assertiveness often goes hand in hand with low self-esteem and feelings of inadequacy. When you have a negative opinion of yourself you will lack confidence and be easily intimidated or offended by the sarcasm or ridicule of others. You are likely to avoid confrontation at all costs and blame others for your predicaments. If you recognize these tendencies in yourself, CBT skills can help.

WHAT TYPE OF PERSON ARE YOU?

Exercise
Take the test below to identify your own interpersonal skills style.

Give yourself a score for each statement.
1 = never or not like me; 2 = sometimes like me; 3 = always or very like me

SECTION A
1 *When I have to confront someone about a problem I feel very nervous.* ☐
2 *I am easily upset or intimidated by ridicule or sarcasm.* ☐

3 *Being liked by people is very important to me no matter what the cost.* □

4 *I really don't like conflict and will avoid it in any way I can.* □

5 *I find it hard to be direct with people if I think they will not like what I have to say.* □

Total score for section A □

SECTION B

6 *I lose my temper easily.* □

7 *I don't care if people like me as long as I get what I want.* □

8 *I'll use the tone of my voice or sarcasm to get what I want from other people.* □

9 *Patience with people is not one of my strong points.* □

10 *I often wag my finger at other people to make my point.* □

Total score for section B □

SECTION C

11 *I remain calm when faced with sarcasm, ridicule or criticism.* □

12 *I am not frightened of addressing problems directly without casting blame.* □

13 *I am confident about asking for what I want, or explaining how I feel.* □

14 *I am able to look other people in the eye when dealing with difficult issues.* □

15 *I feel confident in my ability to handle confrontational work situations.* □

Total score for section C □

SECTION D

16 *I often make my point by using sarcasm.* □

17 *Rather than speaking out directly to make my feelings known, I'll use impatient or cutting remarks.* □

18 *I show my impatience by my body language.* □

(Contd)

Case study

Marian is 42 years old, married with two teenage children, and works part-time in a local office. Her self-esteem is low, and she feels she is not a good wife, mother or work colleague. At work, she feels over-loaded and unable to keep up with the volume of work. Because she has little confidence in her work skills, she says nothing, fearful that her inadequacies will be exposed if she says she cannot manage. The problem is that her colleagues have no idea that she is struggling – they keep passing more work her way because she never says 'No'. As a result, Marian doesn't enjoy her job at all and is constantly fearful that she may lose it.

At home, her teenagers are fairly noisy and self-centred, usually untidy, empty the fridge as soon as Marian fills it, and spend more time with their friends than on their school work. Again, Marian fears her inadequacies as a mother are to blame for this behaviour. In this instance, however, she tries to remedy the situation by shouting at the children, finding fault with their lazy, noisy ways and punishing them with 'No TV' and curfews when they refuse to toe the line. As a result, her relationship with her children is poor. This convinces Marian even more that she is a bad parent.

When Marian's husband returns from work, Marian feels annoyed that he cannot see how stressed she is and does not appreciate the difficulties she has with the children. Instead of saying anything, Marian remains quiet and a little sulky – 'John should be able to tell how I'm feeling' is her view. Unfortunately, John isn't aware of this and finds Marian's lack of communication rather hostile. They spend the evening sitting in different rooms, with no warmth or affection between them at all.

The four behaviour types

The test you took above was based on identifying which of four different behaviour types you adhered most closely to. The types are:

A *Passive*
B *Aggressive*
C *Assertive*
D *Passive aggressive*.

You need to identify your present behaviour type before you can adjust to a more assertive style.

Using your scores from the above assertiveness test, identify which of the behaviour styles most apply to you – if you scored high in section A of the test, you are passive; if you scored high in section B, you are aggressive, and so on. You might find that you are a combination of two or three types, rather than always acting in the same way. Now look at Marian's story and identify the behaviour styles she was using in the various areas of her life – none of which did anything for her happiness.

A – PASSIVE BEHAVIOUR

When you behave passively, you tend to 'let things go'. You may totally disagree with what is going on, but you don't say anything because you make a negative prediction that things will go against you if you do. If you do speak, you are usually disproportionately deferential, full of premature apology, and back down too easily.

Key point: Being passive is not being easy-going; it is being a doormat.

B – AGGRESSIVE BEHAVIOUR

Bully-boy tactics, rudeness, raised voice, shouting, threats – these are all geared to ensure that the aggressor gets their way on a 'no matter what' basis. You may have behaved this way yourself on occasion, even if you usually exhibit passivity. For the passive person, never saying what they mean or asking for what they need can eventually lead to emotional overload. Something 'snaps' and suddenly Sally Shy hits the roof and becomes Betty Bully.

C – ASSERTIVE BEHAVIOUR

When you behave assertively, you do two things:

1 *You remain (relatively) calm.*
2 *You stand your ground.*

You are also happy to hear the points of view of others as you don't feel threatened or intimidated by them. Valid counter-arguments might make you change your point of view but if not, you clearly stay with what you believe in. You treat others with respect (even if they don't treat you that way). You may be willing to compromise, you speak clearly, and you are willing to persist with the discussion until a satisfactory outcome is reached.

D – PASSIVE-AGGRESSIVE BEHAVIOUR

One of the most common examples of this is the 'silent treatment'. You will know just what that is. You may have used it, been on the receiving end of it, or both. Here, you aren't being overtly aggressive (so it's hard to pin anything on you), but you use silence, sulking, leaving a room when the other person walks in, or being deliberately obstructive – you know the routine. Passive-aggressive behaviour can also include the 'poor me' treatment – 'I can see I'll obviously have to write that report myself', 'I'm the only one who does anything around here'. The objective of passive-aggressive behaviour is to get your own way by making the other party or parties feel guilty.

Key skills for assertiveness

When dealing with difficult situations, you can make the mistake of gearing your behaviour to your dominant emotions at the time – rather than to the outcome you wish to achieve. When you behave assertively, you focus on outcomes and results rather than emotions.

Before you can behave assertively, you need to *think* assertively. This is because you need to be able to consider the outcomes and results you want ahead of time. These outcomes and results don't simply include getting what you want; they should also include:

▶ *how you feel about yourself*
▶ *how you feel about the other person*
▶ *how he or she feels about you*
▶ *whether the outcome you have worked for has improved your relationship for the future, enhanced mutual respect, etc. In other words, whether it has left your self-esteem in good shape.*

Thinking assertively is important since it starts off the train of situation–emotions–behaviour–outcome, and is a point at which you can maintain control and get the situation to work in your favour, rather than against you. The work on thought challenging that you have done in earlier chapters is exactly what you need here. For example:

Situation: Debate with your partner over a holiday destination for next year. Your partner is insisting on a venue you have no interest in.

Your thinking: Rather than simply feeling upset at the unfairness of your partner's lack of consideration for your views, say to yourself (something along the lines of) 'My partner isn't failing to consider me. He/she is just so keen to go to this place that he/she is hoping I might get enthusiastic as well. I'll try to understand what they like so much about it, then express my own reservations, and offer some compromises that fit the bill for both of us as nearly as possible.'

Your emotions: Instead of feeling distressed, you feel okay.

Your behaviour: Assertive, listening, acknowledging your partner's enthusiastic preference while focusing on finding a solution to suit you both.

Outcome: Agreement reached, which might be a compromise venue, a decision that each of you chooses in alternate years, etc. Good relationship maintained. Self-esteem intact.

Key point: Thinking assertively is as important as behaving assertively. It allows you to focus on outcomes and results rather than simply running with your emotions and 'seeing what happens'.

Exercise
Think of a situation where you need to use good negotiating skills to achieve the outcome you want. Now jot down what that outcome is and, using the outline above, write a sentence or two under each heading to show how it might go, and what thinking skills you would use to ensure a good outcome.

Behaving assertively

Once you have mastered the skills below, you will be able to:

▶ *confront difficult issues with others*
▶ *stay in control of your emotions while you do this*
▶ *stand your ground when the going gets tough.*

Insight
When we behave assertively we ensure that our own needs are met while also respecting the rights and needs of others. When the Chinese philosopher and political theorist Confucius (551–479 BCE) was asked if there is one word which can serve as a rule of practice for living, he reputedly advised: 'Is not reciprocity such a word? What you do not want done to yourself, do not do to others'.

1. ACKNOWLEDGE THE OTHER PERSON'S POINT OF VIEW

Most people will expect you to 'come at them' with your own arguments and views, so they will be surprised when you first of all reflect an understanding of their problem. Let's say it might be an unrealistic work deadline your boss has imposed on you. An acknowledgement might be, 'The work we are doing now is for our biggest client, and I appreciate your concern that we get this project in on time for them.'

Acknowledging sets the scene for dialogue, rather than confrontation. You are actually indicating that you are on the same side as your boss, and share their goals.

2. STATE YOUR OWN POSITION

Now you have to say where you are in all this. If you really cannot meet the deadline, then you must stand your ground on this point. It is often useful to start this step with a word such as 'However' or 'But' so that you now have, 'I appreciate your concern that we get this project in on time for them. However, even working solely on this project and nothing else, the time scale is unachievable if we are to produce good work.'

3. OFFER A SOLUTION

Sometimes an obvious alternative is not readily available. Nonetheless, remember that this is about results and there has to be a solution – even if it is that the work doesn't get done on time. Your thinking needs to move from 'I can't possibly achieve this' to 'What can we do?' and then state the possibilities.

Using the above steps achieves these vital things:

▶ *It enables mutual understanding of the problems.*
▶ *It gives you the respect of the other person.*
▶ *It prevents you from being forced to accept an unrealistic/ unacceptable/unwanted situation.*

▶ *It encourages a solution to be found that will suit both parties.*
▶ *Your emotions don't get the better of you and cause you to feel upset/angry/disappointed, thus denting your self-esteem.*
▶ *The feel-good factor at the outcome is huge, and excellent for confidence building.*

> **Exercise**
> Now find a situation and practise the above steps. Use all three steps every time. You don't need to wait for a major confrontation; even negotiating over a cup of coffee is a good start, and will get you used to it. You may also wish to practise this with your tape recorder. Think of the possible responses you might get, and work on how to deal with them assertively.

Being assertive with yourself

Learning to be assertive with yourself is as important as learning to be assertive with others. Simply take your assertive thinking skills and apply them to yourself. You have the right to behave however you wish as long as you take responsibility for it. Most of us sometimes find our fridges full of food beyond its 'sell by' date, have messy drawers we never sort out, tell white lies when turning down boring invitations, fail to tidy up the kitchen for days on end until we no longer have a single clean plate, don't ring our mothers enough, or keep the money we found on the pavement, etc. That's fine. It's normal. You are behaving just like everybody else. Constantly recognize and remember not to beat yourself up for what is really very normal, 'everybody does it' behaviour.

> **Insight**
> The learning of assertiveness skills is beneficial to anyone who would like to improve their powers of communication. This also applies to counsellors and therapists whose work is enhanced by a knowledge of the assertiveness principles of clear, direct interaction.

CONDUCT A SURVEY

Write down three issues that consistently lead you into negative thinking. For example, 'I get very nervous speaking in a group', 'My house is always untidy', 'I'm overweight'. Any three examples will do. Now ask at least three friends, family members or work colleagues whether they ever suffer from these problems. What do you conclude from your survey?

HOMEWORK

If you do not already possess assertiveness skills, then you will need to practise a great deal. This in itself may trigger anxiety in you, so here is a strategy for making it much easier.

Get a tape recorder with a good microphone and, considering any difficult situation you may have ahead of you, practise dealing with it on your own, in the comfort of your own home. People often mentally rehearse what they want to say to someone, so how much better to do it so that you can hear how it sounds, and revise it if you need to? Listen to how you sound.

- ▶ *Are you saying too much?*
- ▶ *Are you saying too little?*
- ▶ *Are you sounding too weak?*
- ▶ *Are you sounding too strident?*

Whatever you don't like, note it, and then try again. Eventually, it will become easy and automatic and, even if you still feel nervous, this will not stop you from saying what you want to say, and in the right way.

You may prefer an alternative task of simply visualizing yourself in an upcoming confrontation of some sort or other. Imagine what might be said to you and how you could respond.

You could also recall a situation in the past that you might have handled differently. Replay it, considering what assertiveness techniques you might have used. Do you think that the outcome might have been different? What can you learn from this? How could you incorporate what you have learned next time you find yourself in a similar situation?

SUMMARY

In this chapter you have started to learn how to develop the key skill of thinking and behaving assertively to enhance your life.

▶ *You can assess your own instinctive way of acting and reacting, from passive to aggressive.*
▶ *Assertiveness is by far the best negotiating tool.*
▶ *We have looked at both assertive thinking skills and assertive behaviour, and you have learned the tools to develop working towards a good outcome.*
▶ *Being assertive means considering the outcome that you want, and working towards achieving that in a measured rather than aggressive way. The boost to your own self-confidence as you achieve this will be great.*

FURTHER READING

Dryden, W. and Constantinou, D., *Assertiveness Step by Step* (London: Sheldon Press, 2004).

THINGS TO REMEMBER

▶ There are four basic behaviour types that are commonly identified: passive, aggressive, assertive and passive-aggressive.

▶ While you are likely to be more familiar with what it means to be either passive or aggressive, the term passive-aggressive is generally less understood and refers to a person who tends to behave in covert ways rather than being direct. An example would be if you really don't want to do something that someone has asked you to do and instead of telling them so, you take on the task but deliberately 'go slow' in objection. Passive-aggressive behaviour employs a 'poor me' outlook and the 'silent treatment' tactic.

▶ From the 'What type of person are you?' exercise, you will have a sense of what behaviour type you lean towards (and you are likely to be a mixture, reverting to one or another depending on the circumstances).

▶ Assertive behaviour is about clear, concrete communication, saying what you think and how you feel, even in stressful, potentially upsetting situations, without recourse to ridicule, sarcasm or becoming unduly emotional or aggressive.

▶ Before you can behave assertively you need to think assertively and develop the skills to do so by, once again, making the situation-thoughts-emotions-behaviour link to understand what happens to you in certain situations and what you can do to gain control.

21

Overcoming your anger habit

In this chapter you will learn:

- *to identify your anger triggers*
- *to discriminate between healthy and unhealthy anger*
- *to control your unhealthy anger*
- *to replace your anger with more constructive ways of achieving your aims.*

Anybody can become angry, that is easy; but to be angry with the right person, and to the right degree, and at the right time, and for the right purpose, and in the right way, that is not within everybody's power, that is not easy.

Aristotle, Ancient Greek philosopher (384–22 BCE)

Is anger a problem for you?

One of the hardest emotions to control is anger. For many, no matter how many books they read and seminars they attend on the subject, when push comes to shove, the moment they find themselves riled, emotions take over and they 'lose it'.
This 'anger habit' includes the tendency to experience temper tantrums, feelings of ongoing frustration, resentment and irritability. Of all the emotions, with the exception of passionate love, anger seems to be the hardest to control.

Becoming angry doesn't make you a bad person – but it does mean that there are a great many situations you are unnecessarily on the losing end of. If you find yourself getting angry, quite quickly, a lot of the time, you have a problem and need to deal with it.

Insight

A 'trigger' is an event, person or cognition that sets off an emotional reaction. Trigger recognition is crucial to anger work. The practices of CBT encourage us to become familiar with our personal triggers, and to observe and build an understanding of how we respond to different situations. Possible triggers include: being ignored, criticism, the insensitivity of others, rudeness, having feelings dismissed or ignored by other people, feeling vulnerable, having weaknesses exposed, feeling humiliated, other people's incompetence and frustration.

THE HIGH PENALTIES OF UNCONTROLLED ANGER

High anger can ruin both personal and professional relationships, as well as be detrimental to your health. At its worst, anger can also kill. Road rage is an example. An otherwise rational man or woman becomes so angry at another driver's behaviour that they decide to get their own back by giving chase. An accident results that kills two of the people involved. There may have been many reasons for this crazy, destructive behaviour. Too much to do, setting off late, not allowing enough time to get from A to B, generally feeling that people are inconsiderate – but it was the inability to manage the emotion of high anger that resulted in the tragedy.

ANGER ON THE INCREASE

Many believe that tolerance is decreasing and that rage, expressed both verbally and physically, is increasing. Public areas, including hospital wards, libraries, even post offices, all now have written warnings regarding uncontrolled behaviour leading to possible attacks on staff. What is going on?

Twenty-first century intolerance

People are more concerned than ever with their rights (fuelled, very often, by a compensation culture). They are less philosophical, less inclined to 'put things down to experience'. If their demands are not met now in a way that they have come to expect, they become angry. As you become generally angrier – so do others. This means it takes a lot less to get into a fight with someone, or to be provoked yourself.

Insight

Dogmatic expectations and demands about how others should behave just don't work. Angry self-righteousness dissipates when we respect other people's right to hold different values, belief systems and standards from our own.

Suppressing anger

Expressing anger is becoming less and less acceptable, especially in the workplace. This means that by expressing anger inappropriately you may risk losing your job, or at least some disciplinary action. You might be sued by someone who feels that you have exhibited aggression towards them. You therefore often bottle anger up, instead of dealing with it, and this can be exceedingly harmful to both your emotional and physical well-being.

ME? ANGRY?

People all have different views on what is acceptable and what is not when it comes to anger. What may seem an angry response to person A is a natural way of dealing with situations to person B.

Exercise

Are you aware of your own anger? Do any of the following apply to you? Place a tick next to those that do.

1 *Others comment on my aggressive responses.* ☐
2 *Waiting in queues drives me mad.* ☐
3 *I can't tolerate rudeness.* ☐
4 *I always respond badly to criticism.* ☐

5	*I start arguments easily.*	☐
6	*Driving in traffic causes me huge stress.*	☐
7	*I consider most other drivers on the road to be bad drivers.*	☐
8	*I find most shop assistants and helplines, etc. quite incompetent.*	☐
9	*In difficult discussions with people, I tend to get angry the most quickly.*	☐
10	*I let petty annoyances really work me up.*	☐

Even if you ticked several statements – which suggests you may have a problem managing angry emotions – you can make changes to calm down your anger. Simply accepting the reality that you do get inappropriately angry is half the battle to reducing such responses.

Anger is not always a bad thing

The word 'inappropriate' is important. Anger is not always a bad thing. The key is being able to control your anger, and to use it only when it is appropriate, while containing it when it is not.

What would you say are the differences between healthy, constructive, anger and unhealthy, destructive anger? Let's take a look at some possibilities.

ANGER AT INJUSTICE

You see someone kicking a dog, you hear on the news that innocent people in a far-off country are being brutally treated, you notice someone at work who is always unfairly picked on by the boss: these are situations where injustice prevails, and you need to get angry about these things. World starvation, unnecessary wars, people dying through lack of health care – the only way to get anything done about such situations is for at least some people to feel very angry about them.

ANGER TO GET RESULTS

As a *last* resort, if you really need to get results from recalcitrant staff, motor mechanics, waiters, your children, etc., then reasonable anger can work a treat.

ANGER AS A MOTIVATIONAL TOOL

When you finally hear yourself (or someone else) say, 'Right. That's it. I'm not taking any more of this', you know that either you (or they) are going to blow their top in order to get some action. In a sense, you are bringing some energy to the situation.

ANGER AS A RELEASE

'Letting it all out' has actually been shown to have health benefits, compared to repressed anger that you hold inside and which eats away at you. However, there are ways of letting things out that don't involve you becoming apoplectic, so use this with caution.

Insight

Signs of stress and anxiety may be covering underlying anger which is grumbling away, causing physiological symptoms. Once we know how our anger manifests itself and how it is maintained, we can find alternative, healthy ways of expressing it, and stress and anxiety subside.

ANGER AS AN ALERT SIGNAL

Healthy anger can let you know that something is wrong. You can use this alert to work out what is worrying you, and then do something positive to change it. For example, if you find yourself becoming irritated every time you need to meet with a particular work colleague, ask yourself why they annoy you so. It may be that they are always late for your meetings, always dominate the discussion, regularly cancel at the last minute, etc. Becoming aware of your anger in these circumstances encourages you to change the situation so that it is less stressful.

The point of taking a look at healthy anger is to bring home to you that you do not need to eliminate this emotion from your life. Anger can be a good emotion in appropriate circumstances. Inappropriate anger is a problem.

> **Key point: Don't attempt to eliminate anger from your life – there are many ways in which healthy anger can be a helpful and motivating tool.**

Exercise
To help you discover whether your own anger is healthy or not, think of two or three situations in which you became angry in the last week or two. Now think for a moment about the outcome. Do you feel that, in any of these instances, your anger achieved a good result? If so, what was it? Do you feel that your anger was an intelligent response in these circumstances?

Where anger comes from

Anger is built on your expectations regarding the ideals and behaviours of others. You expect people to treat you fairly and they don't. You expect them to be nice to you and they aren't. You expect them to help you and they walk away.

Each time someone breaks a rule of yours, violates a contract or acts against your wishes, a possible option is to react with anger. You do not absolutely have to – it is your choice.

Unfortunately, people do not always feel that they are in control of this choice – you feel unable to manage your emotions and it is as though it has already been decided for you and you act accordingly.

> **Key point: No one else makes you angry.** You decide whether to respond with anger or not. It is always your choice, and no one else can influence this unless you allow them to.

Earlier in this book (see Chapter 1), we did a lot of work on the thought-emotion connection, and your ability to manage and adjust your emotions by altering your perceptions. You now need to use these skills to help you to manage and reduce your angry thoughts and feelings.

The anger spiral

You are familiar now with the relationship between what you think and how you feel. A situation, such as a rude boss, may be the external trigger and your thought, 'How dare he speak to me like that?' triggers the emotion of anger. It is the thought that drives the emotion – at least initially. However, once in the spiral, the emotion then drives further negative thoughts such as, 'He really is a bully. He shouldn't be allowed to get away with it.' In turn, this makes you even angrier than before – and so on, until the anger gets quite out of control.

Have you recently found yourself in an anger spiral? Think about your emotions at the start of the situation, the middle of the situation and the end of the situation. Did your anger increase in the way described above as your thinking became more negative about the situation? How long did it take for your anger to go down? Were you able to do anything positive to calm yourself?

Using cognitive behavioural therapy skills to manage anger

Let's take a look at someone who gets into an anger spiral and learn from his mistakes. We'll use thought challenging as a tool to see how we can help our guinea pig reduce his angry thoughts and responses.

David is a 35-year-old computer specialist. He works in a high-pressure job, feels stressed most of the time, and is perpetually offended at a myriad of slights and abuses. He is highly competitive and takes absolutely nothing lightly. In his mind, others are just out to annoy him, make his life difficult, and increase his stress – an indifferent shop assistant, a slow driver ahead of him, a leisurely bank clerk – any of these things can trigger his rage.

To help David, we're going to break his pattern of anger down into a series of seven steps. Each step represents a 'choice point'. He can choose to intervene at each step, cool down, and break the pattern – or he can continue along his destructive path.

Exercise
To help you learn how to get out of your own anger spiral, as you read of David's difficulties below, see if you can work out ahead of time what David could do to get out of his anger spiral. What would you be doing if you were him, and what can you learn from what happens?

Step one
As we mentioned earlier, much of your anger is based on the premise that others 'should' think and act the way you do. They 'should' share your values and behave as you believe that they 'should'. So a most important step in getting rid of angry emotions consists of breaking the 'should' rule.

Much of David's life is governed by such rules. He has rules and expectations for his own behaviour, for others' behaviour, and even feels the weight of others' rules on him. He has more rules than a legal tome. The result? Anger, guilt and intense pressure to live up to his standards.

Yet David cannot live up to such unrelenting standards, and neither can others (and neither can you). David demands,

'People should listen to me', 'They should stay out of the way', 'I should have total control over this situation'. But the fact of the matter is that people don't listen, they do get in his way, and he cannot control their behaviour. At this point, David has the choice to accept the circumstances that have arisen or hammer away against reality, demanding that it should not be that way.

It would be strongly preferable if David was listened to and left alone, but he cannot demand it.

A FIRST OPPORTUNITY FOR DAVID TO MANAGE HIS ANGRY THOUGHTS

David now has an option to challenge the 'should' style of thinking that is causing him to get so angry.

What else could David think instead of the thoughts above? Based on the work you have already done on the links between thoughts and emotions (see Chapter 1), write a short script for David. Then check to see if you are thinking along the right lines.

Some anger-reducing thoughts for David:

- ▶ *'The fact of the matter is that people do ignore my wishes and intrude. What, constructively, can I do when that happens?'*
- ▶ *'I can continue to follow my own "rules", to treat others fairly and well, but not insist that they respond to me in the same way. It would be nice if they did, but if they don't, they don't.'*
- ▶ *'I need to stop disturbing myself about something I can do nothing about. In short, I can be part of the solution and not the problem.'*

Key point: Rigid thinking, with lots of 'shoulds' in it will ensure that you lose control of your emotions very quickly when others fail to respond to your rules. Learning to be more flexible in your views of how others behave will reduce anger and stress.

Exercise

This will help you banish your own 'shoulds'. Do you have 'should' rules for how others should behave? Write a few of them down. For example, 'People should not drop litter in the street.' Then rewrite these sentences without using the word 'should'. This may be quite hard to do for some of the rules that you believe in strongly, but it will help you to begin to think more flexibly and reduce the anger you feel when people ignore the rules that are important to you.

Coming to terms with the idea that others might not follow your own ideas about behaviour is a good start.

Step two

Let's look at some other tools to calm these angry situations down. Work out what's really upsetting you. Examine what really hurts when one of your rules is broken. For example, when David is angry and hurt, he can ask himself, 'What really hurts here?' Maybe he thinks, 'People are rude and insensitive', 'I'll be made the victim' or 'I'm powerless to do anything about this'.

What hurts the most is David's inability to change people's behaviour. What could he think instead of the thoughts above? Write a short script for David, then check your suggestions against ours below.

How David might calm himself:

▶ *'There is no evidence that I should be able to control people.'*
▶ *'People are responsible for their own beliefs, behaviours, attitudes and assumptions.'*
▶ *'Perhaps I can see myself not as a victim, but as a person who is able to choose how to react.'*

Step three

The third step is to respond to the hot, anger-driven thoughts with cooler, more level-headed thoughts. In frustrating circumstances David has options:

▶ *David initially thinks, 'How dare he?' but he can replace that thought with, 'He thinks he is trying to help me.'*

▶ *David thinks, 'How stupid can she be?' but he can instead*
  respond, 'She's human.'

Exercise

To help you change your script, think about who or what
annoyed you the most in the last couple of days. Recall how
angry you felt and what you were thinking.

Using any of the three steps we've discussed so far, change the
script. How angry do you think these alternative thoughts would
make you?

Step four
USING RELAXATION SKILLS

The next step is to respond to angry feelings themselves.
David can do this by practising relaxation and deep breathing.
He can relax his muscles and refocus his attention away from
the stressful situation. We discussed these skills in depth in
Chapter 13.

When your emotions take over, your body reacts by increasing
your heart rate in order to move blood very quickly around the
body. This, in turn, causes your breathing to become shallow
and quick. To reduce your anger, your task is to reduce your
heart rate and breathing to a point where your body is able to
relax at will. You can use breathing and muscle relaxation
together for maximum effect. Try both and see if one of them
suits you better than the other or if a combination of the two is
the most ideal.

Step five
PREVENTING STRESS AND ANGER FROM MAKING YOU ACT
SPITEFULLY

As a fifth step to reducing his anger, David needs to look at
how, by his angry thinking, he gives himself permission to
think in a thoroughly spiteful way. These thoughts allow David
to treat others in ways that he himself would not want to be
treated.

- *'He deserved it.'*
- *'I just want her to hurt the way I have been hurt.'*
- *'This is the only way I can get my point across.'*

David can recognize these ideas as con artistry. They con him into throwing aside his morals and engaging in threats, sarcasm and demands. David would do better to remind himself of:

- *the costs of such strategies*
- *the benefits of remaining calm and fair.*

Step six

GAIN CONTROL OF AGGRESSIVE BEHAVIOUR

The sixth step is to look at the aggressive behaviour that comes from angry thinking. David gives himself permission to act aggressively and ignore the rights of other people. Imagine David getting worked up with a sales assistant who is interminably slow. He starts speaking loudly and rudely, and demanding to see the manager. The assistant then gets angry back and a row ensues. What other choices does David have?

- *He could try to understand the cause of the assistant's slowness.*
- *He could put himself in the other person's shoes, imagine what they are thinking and feeling, and attempt to understand their point of view.*
- *He could ask himself how important this delay really is.*

This will help to:

- *decrease David's anger*
- *decrease the other person's anger*
- *increase the likelihood that the other person will hear what David has to say*
- *increase the likelihood of the two of them having a rational and reasonable conversation.*

Step seven

GETTING ANGRY OCCASIONALLY ISN'T FAILING; IT IS LEARNING

The seventh step is to reduce feelings of resentment and guilt about occasionally 'losing it'. David may tend to view angry episodes as a self-perpetuating failure, as a setback. Yet each episode can, in reality, be a success as long as he examines the triggering 'should' statements that promote angering beliefs, the automatic thoughts, the anger arousal, the permission beliefs and the strategies he engages in. If he does this (and if you do too), the episodes can become further and further distant, and less intense.

Learning to own your anger

One of the difficulties of managing anger in difficult situations is the idea that none of this is your fault. If the other person had not done this, that or the other, you would never have reacted in that way. You may be partially right. Someone may have been extremely thoughtless, careless, acted stupidly or whatever, and you may be the victim of their rotten judgement. However, while the other person is responsible for their actions, you are responsible for your response.

- ▶ *You are the owner of your anger.*
- ▶ *You are the decision-maker about when and to what extent you use this emotion.*
- ▶ *No one else decides this for you.*
- ▶ *Of course people sometimes work very hard to provoke you. Nevertheless, managing your anger in an intelligent way is still your responsibility. You control – and therefore decide on – your reactions.*

Reducing angry emotions with humour

Using humour is an excellent tool for defusing anger. It can help you gain a more balanced perspective and see the funny side. For example, if you have spent the entire afternoon putting together a flat-pack bookcase and, as you stand back to admire it, it falls apart, you can either get furious or laugh. Try laughter. This will take a lot of the edge off your fury, and humour can always be relied on to help relax a tense situation.

Exercise

To help you use humour to defuse anger, take an opportunity to use the following technique after you have felt angry about something. Relate the events that have made you angry during the day to a friend or partner. Only this time, you have to tell them as though they are a funny story. Find something amusing about the fact that your scarf caught in the hedge as you were running for a bus, causing you to miss it. Make spilling coffee all over yourself unintentionally at work sound funny. This will get you into the habit of seeing the funny side and you will gradually be able to do this 'in the moment', rather than becoming enraged and only finding humour at a later stage.

Do not discount professional help

If you feel that your anger is really out of control, if it is having an impact on your relationships and on important parts of your life, you might consider professional help to learn how to handle it better. As well as the option of one-to-one therapy, anger management courses are available – learning to manage anger is something many people wish to undertake. Anger is such a strong emotion, and so damaging to the efforts you make in other areas of your life, that if all else fails you should certainly contemplate this course of action. We discuss this option further in Chapter 22.

HOMEWORK

Record a recent situation that caused you to become angry. Now use the example of David, above, to consider the various 'choice points' you may have had to halt the anger spiral. Write down the thoughts that would be helpful to you in achieving this, as well as any behaviours that could have calmed you and given a more positive outcome to the event. Do this several times. To begin with, you will only be able to manage anger by reflecting back 'after the event'. As the emotion is so strong, it can be difficult to stop when it is activated. However, as you practise in this way, developing strength in your alternative options for how to react, you will gradually find that you can introduce these more productive thoughts and behaviours into the anger spiral ahead of time, until they become your default and you can truly manage your anger.

SUMMARY

In this chapter you have learned several ways to manage, reduce and eliminate your angry emotions.

▶ *Of all the emotions you need to learn to manage, anger can be the hardest. It seems to gain a momentum of its own that leaves you feeling you are no longer in control of what is happening. We call this an 'anger spiral'.*

▶ *You can focus on the physical sensations high anger brings with it, and work hard on breathing and relaxing in order to control these. Look as well to your cognitive, thought-challenging skills. Opinions are not facts. They are only points of view.*

▶ *You can constantly challenge your anger-making thoughts. Find different ways to think that stop you getting so wound up. Own your anger. Many people do nothing about managing their anger because they believe it is always caused by somebody else. This is quite untrue.*

▶ *No one else can make you angry. You decide whether to be angry or not.*

▶ *You can become more open-minded and ditch your 'shoulds'. The more rules you have about what others should and should not do, the more likely you are to become angry. While it would be nice if others held the same values and ideas that you have, if they don't, that is fine as well. Your rules are yours to live by if you feel they have value, but it is not for you to decide what others' rules for living should be.*

▶ *You can try to see the funny side. It is hard to both laugh and be angry at the same time.*

FURTHER READING

Bilodeau, L., *The Anger Workbook* (Minnesota: Hazeldon, 1992).

THINGS TO REMEMBER

▶ *A way of assessing if your anger is a real problem for you is by asking yourself questions like: 'Do I often feel angry?', 'Does my anger come on quickly?', 'Does it frequently get out of my control?', 'Is it having a detrimental effect on my relationships with others?'*

▶ *Tackling inappropriate ways of expressing anger begins with owning up to having a problem and taking responsibility. Remember, your anger doesn't make you a bad person.*

▶ *CBT methods teach you how to manage the emotion of extreme anger that can be detrimental to your health (for instance, causing your blood pressure to soar) and damaging to your personal and workplace relationships.*

▶ *Work on your tolerance levels and develop a philosophical perspective. Take a few deep breaths and ask yourself, 'Is this situation really worth getting het up about? What other ways can I look at this?'*

▶ *While high anger levels are generally unhealthy, suppressing anger can be equally emotionally and physically destructive.*

▶ *Anger can be a useful motivational tool, for example, to address an injustice, and the aim is to have the skills to use the appropriate level of constructive anger (that isn't outside of your control) at your disposal when you actually need them.*

▶ *If you believe that your anger is really beyond your control and that it is impacting badly on your relationships and how you generally function, consider the professional help of a therapist or joining an anger management course.*

Part four

Last thoughts

In this part of the book we look at the circumstances in which you might want to consider seeking professional help and at worries you might have about losing the gains you have made. In 'Taking it further' we offer you suggestions for further reading on cognitive behavioural therapy (CBT) generally, as well as organizations you may like to contact if would like to learn more and in greater depth about CBT. We also include sample worksheets in the Appendix for you to copy and use as you work your way through the book.

22

When to consider professional help

In this chapter you will learn:
* **when to consider professional help**
* **how to find professional help**
* **what to expect from professional help**.

None of us has reached where we are solely by pulling ourselves up from our own bootstraps. We got there because somebody bent down and helped us.

Thurgood Marshall, US human rights lawyer (1908–93)

How are you doing?

Having reached this point in the book, you may well be evaluating its help to you. You may have found that the self-help techniques we have taught you are making a real difference. You may be able to see the beginnings of change that you understand and can develop. You may have resolved your difficulties quite quickly once you began to look at them in a more balanced way, or tried out new behaviours that have had good outcomes.

However, you could also feel less certain that self-help techniques are going to be enough. This may be simply because you haven't yet fully understood the techniques or engaged in them, or perhaps you have hoped for good results unrealistically quickly. If it is possible that this is the case, you could benefit from returning to some of the chapters that offer specific help and working through them again so that you understand the principles more fully.

You might reflect on whether you are being over-hopeful about the speed of change you are wishing for. Clients often say to us, 'How long will it take me to get better?' This is a very hard question to answer since it depends on the severity of the problem, the client's willingness and ability to invest a lot of personal time working on making changes, and other factors in the client's life that either enhance or preclude a speedy recovery. Cognitive behavioural therapy (CBT) is regarded as a fast-working therapy – in professional therapeutic terms 6–20 sessions would be regarded as average to achieve a successful client outcome – but this doesn't mean that there is a specific time frame in which you overcome your problems. Your 'marker' should be whether you can see even a small improvement on a week-by-week basis. If you feel that you can, ask yourself whether there is anything further you can do to speed up the rate of improvement.

Insight

Being optimistic while also realistic is the most helpful attitude to adopt when trying to make adjustments in your thinking and behaviour. Don't forget to register movements in these areas, however negligible they may seem.

If you feel that you cannot see improvement, and you know that you have been working hard over a period of time – perhaps a few weeks – this could be the time to consider enlisting the help of a professional. Your emotions will also guide you.

▶ *Where you are suffering from extreme low mood*
▶ *Where you cannot move away from a sense of hopelessness*
▶ *Where your anxiety is extreme and nothing seems to reduce the severity of physical symptoms that are quite debilitating*
▶ *Where your battle with your symptoms is exhausting you*
▶ *Where your emotional life has been changed for the worse to an unacceptable level, for instance, by agoraphobia, or obsessional thinking*

– at this point, professional help becomes a good option.

Where do you start?

While not totally necessary, it is usually a good idea to visit your doctor first. If you are hoping to obtain therapy through the UK National Health Service (NHS), then this must be your first port of call. Even if you decide to seek therapy privately, your doctor will be able to offer a variety of referral options. They will also be able to assess your difficulties, and may wish to discuss medication options with you.

Getting help through the health service

Where it is agreed that CBT will help you, you will have a variety of options. The UK NHS does now offer CBT therapy, but you may find that you have to wait for treatment. Where your symptoms are severe, you may be referred to your Community Mental Health Team and put under the care of a community psychiatric nurse. This is usually fairly immediate, although the extent of the help may be limited, for example, to a set number of sessions.

Private health care options

Where you have private medical insurance, CBT therapy is now covered by most policies. Some do insist that the therapy is only activated after a psychiatric assessment (which your doctor can arrange), but this will depend on the terms of your insurance. Many insurance policies prefer that the CBT is carried out by therapists working in private clinics and hospitals. This is often a good option since, as well as individual therapy, you may have options to join CBT group therapy sessions, which can be very helpful.

FUNDING YOUR OWN THERAPY

Where you decide to seek CBT privately on a self-funding basis, your options are broader. Firstly, you do not need to start by visiting your doctor unless you wish to. Secondly, you can assess the qualifications and personal attributes of different therapists and decide whether you feel they can help you. Thirdly, you can usually start your therapy fairly immediately.

To find a therapist privately, it is worth asking your doctor for a recommended referral. If, however, you feel that you don't want to visit your doctor about these particular difficulties, then the therapist lists of professional associations, such as the British Association for Cognitive and Behavioural Psychotherapies, are a good place to start. We give details of these associations in Taking it further.

However you find a therapist, do ensure that they have relevant CBT training and qualifications. Don't hesitate to ask for the therapist's resumé and practice details. We are still in an era where anyone can call themselves a CBT therapist, and while it is unlikely that they would do this without any training at all, training courses can still consist of a weekend course or a few weeks of distance learning. Ask the therapist how familiar they are with your particular problem. How many clients do they work with who have the same difficulties? How long have they been working with problems such as this?

Some therapists practise other therapy models, such as psychodynamic, person-centred or integrative therapy, and may tell you that they 'incorporate CBT skills'. While this may be helpful, it is not the same as working with a CBT therapist who will have a much greater, in-depth understanding of the complex nature of the therapy, and will be working every day with the various CBT treatment protocols specifically developed for each psychological problem.

Length and structure of treatment

CBT will normally be effective in a short space of time, and we would suggest that you and your therapist work to the following.

▶ *Start with an initial, stand-alone session. This enables both you and the therapist to make an initial assessment of your problems (the formulation/conceptualization) and work out a treatment plan. Your therapist should explain the CBT model to you in session one, and you will mutually decide on the goals of therapy.*

▶ *Where this assessment session has gone well, and you and the therapist have mutually agreed to continue therapy, it would be normal to decide on working together for a number of sessions – say six – with a review at this point. This does not mean that therapy will terminate then, but that you have the opportunity to review progress, possibly reset your goals, and consider how much more therapy might be useful to you.*

▶ *Overall, you will expect CBT to be extremely helpful to you within 6–12 sessions, although sometimes up to 20 sessions can be suggested. It would be rare for CBT to be continued beyond this time scale, although by no means impossible where problems are severe and long-term.*

▶ *It is quite possible for people to find one single session of CBT quite life-changing.*

▶ *Reading this book will help the progress of your therapy because firstly you will already be familiar with the basic skills and concepts and, secondly, you will have a workbook at your side to continue to refer to. It would be sensible to mention to your therapist that you have read this book. In most cases, the therapist will find this positive and may well incorporate its concepts with your treatment plan so that you have an extra reference guide.*

Should you consider medication?

This will depend on both the severity of your symptoms and the type of problem that you have. The most likely sort of medication you will be offered is anti-depressants. Where you are very severely depressed, they do have a place and can help to raise your mood to the point where psychological therapy can be of use to you. In cases of mild depression, anti-depressants will not be effective; while they are unlikely to do you any harm, they are unlikely to help you much either.

Remember that anti-depressants are chemicals and not problem-solvers. Their role is to raise your mood to a level where you can begin to deal with your problems yourself.

The usefulness of medication for specific problems

Specific anti-depressants have proved to be extremely helpful for people suffering from obsessive compulsive disorders (OCD). Often referred to as 'anti-obsessional medication' when used to treat obsessions, research shows that approximately 50–60 per cent of sufferers obtain relief of OCD symptoms purely by taking medication. However, it is not possible to identify who might be the 60 per cent to benefit, and on coming off the medication, the symptoms will usually immediately return. For OCD, it is normal to need quite a high dosage, and for a marked improvement to take about three months. Therefore, we are not especially recommending medication as a treatment option for OCD, but rather wish you to have the chance to consider it as an option if you find your obsessions and rituals an exhausting struggle, even with CBT help.

RELAXANTS

Where you are suffering from an anxiety disorder, it is possible that you may also be offered a relaxant such as diazepam. We would strongly urge you to resist these except as temporary assistance in extreme cases. The reason for this is that CBT encourages you to face your fears and to find that you *can* bear feeling anxious or panic-stricken, that nothing terrible does happen, and that you can overcome these feelings and rid yourself of them. Taking a relaxant will *maintain* your problems, not overcome them. A further reason for avoiding relaxants is their addictive nature. The more you take, the more you need, and the harder it is to come off them.

Anti-depressants, on the other hand, while they may come with temporary side effects such as tiredness, poor concentration and lack of libido (which will diminish quite quickly), are not addictive and you need have no worries about coming off them – although gradual withdrawal is ideal.

THE POWER OF CHEMICALS

When you start a course of anti-depressant medication, you are putting powerful chemicals into your body. For this reason, your doctor (or psychiatrist) will start you on a low dosage so that you body can get used to them, and this dosage will be increased gradually over a period of several weeks. Anti-depressants, therefore, don't offer the instant symptom relief of relaxants but in the longer term they can be extremely effective.

Once you start a course of anti-depressants, you ideally need to continue taking them for at least six months to a year, even when you start to feel better.

HOMEWORK

We would suggest your homework for this chapter depends entirely on what you think about seeking professional help. If you would like to go down that route, your homework could be to find out more about it. Equally, you may wish to include actually making an appointment and attending an assessment session.

If you are undecided, why not make your homework task to use the 'pros and cons' technique to help you come to a decision?

You may also decide that more research would be helpful to you, or perhaps finding someone else who has had CBT that you could talk things over with.

If, on the other hand, you read this chapter purely for informational purposes, you may wish to review whether reading it has had any effect on your views and whether it has added anything to your knowledge base.

SUMMARY

In this chapter we have considered when and whether to consider seeking professional CBT help for your difficulties.

▶ *Consider the circumstances in which you might contemplate professional help, and how your thoughts and emotions can play a part in helping you to decide.*
▶ *There are different therapy options: via the UK NHS; via private insurance – where it might be recommended that you attend a private clinic or hospital that would give you the opportunity of group CBT, either additionally or as an alternative, if you wished it; or self-funding.*
▶ *If you decide to self-fund, look at the choices this gives you and use them wisely.*
▶ *You now know what to expect from a timed therapy structure, and that the course of therapy is regularly assessed and reviewed by you and your therapist together.*
▶ *You can make an informed decision on whether medication might be helpful as a further option.*

THINGS TO REMEMBER

▶ *If you are feeling that the self-help methods presented in this book aren't helping to the extent you hoped, you may benefit from returning to some of the chapters for specific help and working through them again to cement your understanding before you decide that you require the professional help of a therapist.*

▶ *There is a point at which it would be wise to consider the professional help option: for example, when, despite working hard over a period of time with the CBT techniques recommended in this book, you see little or no improvement and your mood continues to be persistently extremely low.*

▶ *You can obtain CBT therapy through the NHS and privately. Either way it is advisable to visit your GP first; they must agree you need it if you are seeking treatment through the NHS and they can provide a variety of referral options if you are seeking treatment privately.*

▶ *Make sure your therapist has training in CBT and follows a model, and structure of treatment, which suits you.*

23

Worries regarding possible setbacks

In this chapter you will learn:
- *cognitive behavioural therapy's excellent record with setbacks*
- *how to deal with a setback if it happens.*

...for the world was built to develop character, and we must learn that the setbacks which we endure help us in our marching forward.

Henry Ford, founder of the Ford Motor Company (1863–1947)

Concerns over maintaining gains

Many people who completely overcome their difficulties by using cognitive behavioural therapy (CBT) still have one remaining concern. What happens if it all goes wrong again? How would you deal with it? Should you be alert to the possibility? Need you take preventative steps now? If so, what are they?

While psychological problems can be resolved successfully using a variety of different methods and treatments, CBT shines out as the treatment of choice for preventing setbacks. Why?

CBT, unlike some other therapies, is an evidence-based educational model. In a sense, the person learning CBT skills, whether in professional therapy or practising on their own, is learning to become their own therapist. Not only are you getting better – but you understand why the emphasis is always on skills and techniques where you (as reader or client) will understand the rationale for the treatment. You will consistently make sense of what you are learning, changing and testing out. The behavioural experiments you try will be devised by yourself, with clear goals set first. You are constantly learning and developing.

In effect, you are retraining your brain to function more effectively and in a more action-orientated way. You are learning to become a problem-solver. None of this is going to suddenly disappear overnight, and these skills will be available for you to use for the rest of your life. How?

You have been encouraged to develop written records as a matter of good practice. It is worth taking the time to ensure that you have at least one set of 'clean' copies of these various worksheets. These become part of your first-aid kit. As you have worked through this book, it has been suggested that you keep notes on what you have found works especially well for you. Reflect on this now. Spend time going back over work that you have done, and evaluate the outcomes again. What have you learned? Which skill or technique had the most impact on you? Which changes led to the most successful outcomes? Keep clear notes of all of these successes and ensure that they are safely kept.

Insight

In Chapter 4, we suggested that you keep your old Thought Records and other worksheets so that you can see how far you have come. At times of relapse, go through the records and you will find evidence of progress and the self-knowledge you have gained, backed by the CBT skills and techniques you have learned.

DO YOU FEEL THE OLD WAYS CREEPING BACK?

CBT does not deny the possibility of setbacks. What it does do is ensure that you have the skills to rectify things. Why might things go wrong again?

▶ *Everyone faces the possibility of unforeseen trauma in their lives. You cannot always be on the alert for such events, and it is not right that you should be. Sometimes, in spite of all your efforts to live positively and resiliently, you can be hit hard by an untoward negative event that knocks you sideways, temporarily.*

▶ *There is the possibility that, although you have done well to master the basic skills that have made you feel better, they may not have become your natural thinking and behavioural bias. In the way that some people, erroneously, stop taking their full course of antibiotics once they start to feel better, it is easy to let the effort of good thinking practice tail off once life seems to be going well again.*

▶ *Where you may have conquered your negative thinking but have possibly not totally identified and replaced negative unhelpful beliefs, some may still linger in the background, and be activated by unexpected events.*

▶ *Sometimes, if you have not developed a resilient attitude, you may find yourself back in the vicious cycle of anxiety. The worries themselves, such as 'I do hope that all these gains last', 'I'm feeling good now, but I don't know how I'll cope if things go wrong again', begin to take their toll and create further anxiety.*

ARE YOU BACK TO SQUARE ONE?

Absolutely not! You may be interested to know that many therapists regard setbacks as a positive, rather than a negative. Why might this be?

▶ *Setbacks give you the opportunity to test out your skills and techniques again, and to discover their consistent effectiveness.*

- Testing your skills and techniques again gives you more confidence and resilience for dealing with future difficulties. Instead of wondering if you will cope, you now know that you can.
- Setbacks may give you the opportunity to develop new coping strategies and cement in others.
- You will gain an opportunity to learn that going backwards does not mean losing all your gains. It does not mean 'going back to square one'; it means that, as in life generally, things can go down as well as up. You will discover this as you work to recover from setbacks (if this happens to you). You will find that you dip less deeply and recover more quickly than you did last time, or than you might have expected this time. This is a further positive learning experience for you.

SNAKES AND LADDERS

We suggest that you think of your self-development as a game of snakes and ladders. Sometimes you are going upwards, sometimes you are simply moving steadily along, and sometimes you are sliding back down a snake. However, you never slide right back down to the first square, and there is always another ladder not too far away for you to climb back up. All the while this is happening, you are inching towards the final square, which will represent the goals you have set yourself, and eventually you will get there.

THERE IS NO SPECIFIED RATE FOR PROGRESS

Progress and recovery is individual. As in a game of snakes and ladders, some people cover the ground very quickly, with a triumphant, 'I've won!', while others are still struggling. You may go down a great many snakes on your way to the final square, and progress is slower. None of this matters. Never put yourself under time pressure. It is all fine.

HOMEWORK

Ensure that you have your first-aid kit of worksheets well organized and put together in a safe place. You may have done this already and, if so, it is a good idea to find time on an occasional basis to review and remind yourself of the skills that have helped you change your life. Never let them slip too far from your mind. Don't simply wait for a crisis before you look at them again. Reminding yourself of them regularly may prevent the crisis itself.

SUMMARY

In this chapter we have looked at an issue that many people worry about – coping with setbacks.

▶ *CBT is highly regarded for its efficacy as a therapy where setbacks are rare. This is because it is an evidence-based teaching model and educates you to become your own therapist, thus giving you instant access to the skills of the model at any time in the future.*

▶ *Developing confidence in your ability to cope with setbacks can in fact be dependent on actually going through a setback – this is regarded as part of therapeutic practice.*

▶ *You now have more understanding of the possible causes of setbacks, some of which you can address yourself ahead of time.*

▶ *You now have the confidence to believe that you will be able to deal with a setback quite effectively if it does happen, and that it will not in any way be 'going back to the beginning again'.*

THINGS TO REMEMBER

▶ The game of snakes and ladders is an easily remembered metaphor for your ongoing self-development in 'the game of life', where you are a winner by your continual perseverance in your goal to make positive changes in your life.

▶ From your own hard work and determination, you are now familiar with a whole host of techniques, strategies and skills that you can draw on at any time.

▶ Occasionally, you may have a setback and, if you do, it might be that a new situation triggers old habits. That is the time to remind yourself of what you have already learned by revisiting the relevant parts of this book as a refresher course.

▶ By doing the exercises throughout this book you have formulated your own evidence to show the progress you have made and how much you have achieved. Look back at this in times of difficulty to help you through.

Taking it further

Useful addresses

If you would like to know more about cognitive behavioural therapy (CBT), either for information, training or to find a practitioner, the following addresses may be of use.

UK

British Association for Behavioural and
Cognitive Psychotherapies
BABCP
Victoria Buildings, 9–13 Silver Street
Bury BL90EU
Tel: 0161 797 4484
Email: babcp@babcp.com
Website: www.babcp.com

British Association for Counselling and Psychotherapy
BACP House, 15 St John's Business Park
Lutterworth, Leicestershire LE17 4HB
Tel: 01455 883300
Email: bacp@bacp.co.uk
Website: www.bacp.co.uk

The British Psychological Society
Division of Clinical Psychology
St Andrew's House, 48 Princess Road East
Leicester LE1 7DR
Tel: 0116 254 9568
Email: mail@bps.org.uk
Website: www.bps.org.uk

Oxford Cognitive Therapy Centre
Warneford Hospital
Oxford OX3 7JX
Tel: 01865 223986
Email: octc@obmh.nhs.uk
Website: www.octc.co.uk

USA

Beck Institute for Cognitive Therapy and Research
One Belmont Avenue, Suite 700
Bala Cynwyd, PA 19004-1610
Tel: 001 610 664 3020
Email: beckinst@gim.net
Website: www.beckinstitute.org

Center for Cognitive Therapy
PO Box 5308
Huntington Beach CA 92615-5308
Tel: 001 714 963 0528
Email: mooney@padesky.com
Website: www.padesky.com

Cognitive Therapy Center of New York
130 West 42nd Street, Suite 501
New York, NY 10036
Tel: 001 212-221-0700
Email: center@schematherapy.com
Website: www.schematherapy.com

Albert Ellis Institute
45 East 65th Street
New York, NY 10065-6508
Tel: 001 212 535 0822
Email: info@albertellis.org
Website: www.albertellisinstitute.org

Further reading

These suggestions are by no means the only possibilities for reading and learning more. They are a broad-based selection of books that we consider might be helpful to you.

Anthony, R., *Beyond Positive Thinking: A No-Nonsense Formula For Getting The Results You Want* (New York: Morgan James Publishing, 2004).

Beck, A., *Cognitive Therapy and the Emotional Disorders* (Michigan: International Universities Press, 1976).

Beck, A., *Cognitive Therapy of Depression* (New York: The Guildford Press, 1979).

Beck, J. S., *Cognitive Therapy: The Basics and Beyond* (New York: The Guildford Press, 1995).

Burns, D. D., *The Feeling Good Handbook* (New York: Penguin Books, 1990).

Clark, D. and Fairburn, C., *Science and Practice of Cognitive Behavioural Therapy* (Oxford: Oxford University Press, 1997).

Covey, S. R. and Hatch, D. K., *Everyday Greatness: Inspiration for a Meaningful Life* (Nashville: Rutledge Hill Press, 2006).

Curwen, B., Palmer, S. and Ruddell, P., *Brief Cognitive Behaviour Therapy* (London: Sage, 2000).

Davis, N., *Resilience: Status of the Research and Research-based Programmes* (US Department of Health, Center for Mental Health Resources, 1999).

Ellis, A., *Rational Emotive Behaviour Therapy* (New York: Allyn & Bacon, 1988).

Leahy, R., *Cognitive Therapy Techniques* (New York: The Guildford Press, 2003).

Neenan, M. and Dryden W., *Essential Cognitive Therapy* (London: Whurr, 2000).

Padesky, C. A. and Greenberger, D., *Mind Over Mood: Change the Way You Feel by Changing the Way You Think. A Cognitive Therapy Treatment Manual for Clients* (New York: The Guildford Press, 1995).

Salkovskis, P. (ed.), *Frontiers of Cognitive Therapy* (New York: The Guildford Press, 1996).

Salkovskis, P. and Kirk, J., 'Obsessive Compulsive Disorder' in Clark, D. and Fairburn, C. (eds.), *The Science and Practice of Cognitive Behavioural Therapy* (Oxford: Oxford University Press, 1997).

Trower, P., Casey, A. and Dryden, W., *Cognitive Behavioural Counselling in Action* (London: Sage, 2006).

Wills, F. and Sanders, D., *Cognitive Therapy: Transforming the Image* (London: Sage, 1997).

Appendix

Simple case formulation/conceptualization

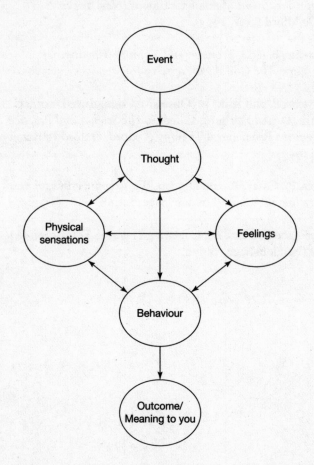

Simple Thought Record

Feelings	Situation	Automatic thoughts
E.g. angry, sad, despairing, anxious. Circle the strongest in your mind.	This may be an actual event, or just an image of these feelings.	What was going through your mind just before you started to feel this way? If you have put down more than one thought, circle the strongest.

Five-column Thought Record worksheet

What happened?	How you felt when this happened	What you thought	Alternative thoughts	How do you feel now?
What were you doing or thinking about?	What did you feel? How bad was it? (%)	What exactly were your thoughts? How far did you believe them? (%)	What more positive alternatives to your negative thoughts can you think of? Try to find as many as you can. How far do you believe each of them? (%)	How far do you now still believe your negative thoughts? (%) Do you feel any better emotionally now, i.e. less downhearted? (%)

Seven-column Thought Record

What happened?	What you thought when this happened (How strongly do you believe this? 1–10)	How you felt (How strongly did you feel this? 1–10)	Evidence to support your negative thought	Alternative thoughts (Generate at least two or three alternatives. Rate your belief in them. 1–10)	Evidence to support your alternative thoughts	How do you feel now? (Rate any possible change now you have looked at things a bit more positively. 1–10)

Thought Record for behavioural experiments

Date and situation	Prediction What do you think will happen? How much do you believe it will? (%) How anxious do you feel? (%)	Experiment What can you do to test out your prediction? (ensure you drop all safety behaviours)	Outcome What actually happened? Was the prediction correct? How anxious do you feel now? (%)	What I have learned Is there a more balanced view? How much do you believe your first prediction will happen in future? (%) How can I build on this?

Case formulation/conceptualization

Early life experiences
Beliefs
Assumptions and 'rules for living'
Trigger events that cause assumptions and rules to be activated
Negative thoughts and behaviours that maintain the problem

Adapted from Beck, 1995

Positive Data Log

Self-critical belief:

How strongly I believe this (%):

Alternative, more helpful belief:

How strongly I believe this (%):

Evidence to support your new belief and weaken your old belief:

1 _____

2 _____

3 _____

4 _____

5 _____

6 _____

7 _____

8 _____

9 _____

10 _____

11 _____

12 _____

Rating for how much I now believe my old belief (%):

And my new belief (%):

Positive Event Log

Date	Positive event	Why this happened

Perfectionism pros and cons

Perfectionist view you hold (1)	
Advantages of holding this view	Disadvantages of holding this view
Could you find a more helpful view now?	
Perfectionist view you hold (2)	
Advantages of holding this view	Disadvantages of holding this view
Could you find a more helpful view now?	
Perfectionist view you hold (3)	
Advantages of holding this view	Disadvantages of holding this view
Could you find a more helpful view now?	

View of friend/colleague (1)	
Advantages of holding this view	Disadvantages of holding this view
Subjective self-esteem rating for friend/colleague (1–10)	

View of friend/colleague (2)	
Advantages of holding this view	Disadvantages of holding this view
Subjective self-esteem rating for friend/colleague (1–10)	

View of friend/colleague (3)	
Advantages of holding this view	Disadvantages of holding this view
Subjective self-esteem rating for friend/colleague (1–10)	

Index

Image credits

Front cover: © Sharon Day – fotolia.com

Back cover: © Jakub Semeniuk/iStockphoto.com, © Royalty-Free/Corbis, © agencyby/iStockphoto.com, © Andy Cook/iStockphoto.com, © Christopher Ewing/iStockphoto.com, © zebicho – Fotolia.com, © Geoffrey Holman/iStockphoto.com, © Photodisc/Getty Images, © James C. Pruitt/iStockphoto.com, © Mohamed Saber – Fotolia.com